The Early Kabbalah

EDITED AND INTRODUCED BY
JOSEPH DAN

TEXTS TRANSLATED BY
RONALD C. KIENER

PREFACE BY
MOSHE IDEL

PAULIST PRESS
NEW YORK • MAHWAH • TORONTO

Cover Art:
One of Israel's best known painters, MORDECAI ARDON was born in 1896 in Tuchov, Poland. He studied at the Bauhaus from 1920–25 under Klee, Kandinsky and Feininger. He emigrated to Israel in 1933 and has received the Unesco Prize, the Israel Prize, and honorary doctorates from the Hebrew University, the Weizman Institute and Tel Aviv University. The artist created these beautiful stained glass windows at the Jewish National and University Library of the University of Jerusalem.

Library of Congress Cataloging-in-Publication Data

The Early Kabbalah.

    (The Classics of Western spirituality)
    Bibliography: p.
    Includes indexes.
    1. Cabala—Collected works—Translations into
English. 2. Mysticism—Judaism—Collected works—Translations into English. I. Dan, Joseph, 1935–
II. Kiener, Ronald C., 1954–   .   III. Series.
BM525.A2E18   1986   296.1'6   86-5116

ISBN: 0-8091-2769-5 (paper)
      0-8091-0373-7 (cloth)

Published by Paulist Press
997 Macarthur Boulevard
Mahwah, New Jersey 07430

Printed and bound in the United States of America

Contents

Editor and Introducer of this Volume

JOSEPH DAN, Gershom Scholem Professor of Kabbalah at the Hebrew University in Jerusalem, Israel, was born in Bratislava, Czechoslovakia, in 1935. He is a graduate of the Hebrew University and earned his Ph.D. there in 1963. An editor of the journals *Tarbiz* and *Jerusalem Studies in Jewish Thought*, he has published fourteen books in Hebrew and numerous articles. Among his English titles are *Hasidic Teachings* (1982), *Gershom Scholem and the Mystical Dimension in Jewish History* (forthcoming), and *Jewish Mysticism and Jewish Ethics* (forthcoming).

Translator of this Volume

RONALD C. KIENER, Assistant Professor of Religion at Trinity College, Hartford, Connecticut, was born in Minneapolis, Minnesota, in 1954. He is a graduate of the University of Minnesota and received his Ph.D. from the University of Pennsylvania in 1984. His published studies have focused on the relationship between Jewish and Islamic mysticism.

Author of the Preface

MOSHE IDEL, Associate Professor of Jewish Thought at the Hebrew University in Jerusalem, Israel, was born in Rumania in 1947. He is a graduate of the Hebrew University, where he also received his Ph.D. An editor of *Jerusalem Studies in Jewish Thought*, he is the author of numerous articles on the history of Kabbalah and Jewish Renaissance thought.

Foreword

The texts presented in the following pages span nearly a century and represent the variety of Jewish mystical currents alive in Europe during the thirteenth century. What is unique about the Jewish mysticisms of this century—whether mixed with Neoplatonism, or Gnosticism, or ethics, or some combination of these—is the myriad of spiritual possibilities put forward. The thirteenth century proved to be a time of explosive creativity, as the pioneering and masterful studies of Gershom Scholem have established. No static dogma or interpretive traditions predetermined how a Jewish mystic might resonate with his tradition. For later generations of Jewish mystics, the *Sefer ha-Zohar* (Book of Splendor) set the parameters for theosophical speculation, but for the mystics of the thirteenth century, nearly all possibilities were open.

Some of the texts appearing in this volume have never appeared in print before, either in translation or in their Hebrew original. The obscurity of the documents—their provenance, their language, and their mystical content—proved to be extremely vexing, but we trust not insurmountable. In every instance we sought to present texts that were representative, historically significant, and translatable. Taken with the other volumes devoted to Jewish mysticism in The Classics of Western Spirituality series, our volume supplies a crucial link between the Hellenistic Judaism of Philo and the authoritative theosophy of the *Zohar*. In fact, the reader will discover that many

FOREWORD

of the mystical trends present in the Early Kabbalah ultimately found an authoritative venue in the *Zohar*. Thus, as a reader in the history of Jewish mysticism, the texts presented herein are essential for a proper diachronic understanding of Kabbalah. And though our work provides important historical material, the volume was also intended to be a reader in Jewish spiritual inventiveness and dynamism.

In pursuing this twofold purpose, we did not shy away from dense or ramified texts, and in many instances we offer an interpretation or translation that will quite probably give rise to debate. We are well aware of the difficulties present in these texts, but this awareness did not deter us from our task of providing a useful and accurate rendition of often perplexing material. It is our hope that the notes and introductions will orient the reader and provide even the uninitiated with the proper tools to study the Early Kabbalah.

Our thanks go out to the people and institutions that contributed to our collaborative effort. First and foremost, we thank our colleague Arthur Green for bringing us together on this project. For their care and assistance, we thank Richard Payne, originator, and John Farina, editor, of this series. Our home institutions, the Hebrew University in Jerusalem and Trinity College, have provided generous support for researching, typing, and editing the manuscript.

It has been six years since our project began. Though this is certainly not a ringing endorsement of long-distance, overseas collaborative efforts, each of us has benefited from the strengths and talents of the other. Our work is all the better for it.

Preface

No area of Kabbalah has enjoyed such an abundance of research as the period of its development in Provence (or Languedoc) and Catalonia. Since the second half of the nineteenth century, scholars like M. Landauer, H. Graetz, A. Jellinek, and D. Neumark—to name only a few—have been fascinated by what were considered to be the first Kabbalistic documents; these were published, analyzed, or translated time and time again. Far and above all others, the late Gershom G. Scholem provided several comprehensive versions of his numerous researches on this period, the last and longest being the monumental *Ursprung und Anfänge der Kabbala*, completed in 1963. These findings focus on two major developments that contributed to the emergence of the Kabbalah in Southern France: (1) the appearance of the *Book Bahir* in Europe; according to Scholem, this work came to Languedoc from Germany; (2) the rise of circles of Jewish mystics in Languedoc, including such figures as R. Abraham ben David of Posquieres and R. Jacob ben Shaul ha-Nazir of Lunel. Due to their mystical inclinations and experiences, these and other teachers innovated mystical interpretations and techniques of prayer using as material, again according to Scholem, Gnostic elements that were present in the traditions of the *Book Bahir*. Roughly speaking, these views have been accepted as a framework for further research into Kabbalah by Scholem's followers. The present book is situated in this line of research, both in the introduction, by J. Dan, and in the choice of texts.

Of course, difficult choices had to be made in selecting the materials for such an anthology, and not all the important sources could be included. Moses ben Naḥman (Naḥmanides), a towering figure among the Kabbalists of the mid-thirteenth century, is notably absent, although, of course, some of his works are available elsewhere in English. Here, for the first time, an English-speaking reader will be able to encounter not only a scholarly *interpretation* of early Kabbalah *apud* Scholem, but also a significant segment of literature written during the first hundred years of the existence of Kabbalah as a historical phenomenon.

As we all know, translation is also interpretation, and therefore the reader will enjoy relatively "clear" texts, due to their rendering into English. In the Hebrew original, these texts are only rarely so transparent as are their English versions; sometimes their obscurity can but tantalize even the scholar who struggles to comprehend them. An example of such difficulties is the commentary on Midrash Konen, attributed to R. Isaac Saggi-Nėhor (the Blind), translated in this volume.

The importance and novelty of the present endeavor lies, therefore, in the struggle the editor and translator had to wage, with the rendering not only of specific phrases, or even short passages, but also with rather comprehensive Kabbalistic texts; the obscurities that remain in our understanding of the material bear evidence as to the real nature of the early Kabbalistic literature, substantial parts of which, even after hundreds of years of scholarly research, remain highly problematic.

Any perusal of early Kabbalistic texts, whether in Hebrew or English, will undoubtedly perplex the reader who sees their complexity and opacity, in comparison with the relatively clear expositions of Kabbalah by contemporary scholars. This plight is partly due to the inceptive stage of the scholarly study of Kabbalah: significant parts of Kabbalistic literature, including important texts written in the first century of the emergence of Kabbalah, are still in manuscript form; their authors, *viri obscuri;* some of their basic concepts, ignored. For the time being, the fact that great segments of Kabbalistic literature remain beyond the scope of academic research prevents more profound analysis of the texts in print.

This plight is partly the result of the overemphasis academic research had placed on the historical and philological approaches at the expense of phenomenological analysis, on the one hand, and com-

PREFACE

parative studies on the other. Mainly focused on names, dates, places, bibliography, and literary sources of the Kabbalah, academic research has rather systematically evaded the psychological and phenomenological facets of this branch of mystical literature. Scholars of Kabbalah have made only rare and scant efforts toward such kinds of analysis. Given the complexities inherent in the Hebrew texts, scholars of other areas of mysticism have only rarely referred to Kabbalistic sources in their comparative studies. This volume does not constitute an intentional departure from the main avenue of Kabbalistic research; it will, however, contribute—as I hope—to improving the acquaintance of scholars of mysticism with Kabbalistic texts, helping the integration of Kabbalah into the general study of mysticism, and thereby enriching our perception of mysticism as a whole. Likewise, students of Renaissance thought will profit from this relatively comprehensive collection of texts, parts of which represent modes of thought that served as a starting point of a bizarre branch of Christian theology—the Christian Kabbalah. The general reader will encounter a significant literature that constitutes a turning point in Jewish spirituality.

Introduction

1. THE EMERGENCE OF KABBALAH

The texts presented in the following pages provide an overview of Jewish mystical speculation during the first hundred years of the movement known by the Hebrew term *Kabbalah* (literally, "Tradition"). The beginnings of this movement are usually set in the last decade or two of the twelfth century C.E., and this period of Kabbalistic incubation is generally thought to end with the composition of the masterful *Sefer ha-Zohar* (The Book of Splendor).[1] Thus, "early Kabbalah" is the period of Jewish mystical creativity in Kabbalistic form bracketed by two literary creations of mystical theosophy: the *Sefer ha-Bahir* (The Book of Brilliance) marks the beginning of this stage and the *Zohar*, written by the Spaniard Kabbalist Moses de Leon (c. 1240–1305), marks the end.

Scholarship in the last century has brought to light a wealth of material concerning this first century of Kabbalistic speculation. The efforts of the pioneering historian Gershom Scholem, who devoted many of his studies to this period,[2] have been followed by complementary studies by both Israeli and diaspora scholars.[3] We are now in the possession of a detailed picture of the main trends and the most important works of many of the mystics belonging to this period. Yet a myriad of unanswered questions remains. In the following pages of this introduction, we will provide a brief overview and characterization of this crucial period in the history of Jewish mys-

1

ticism. To accomplish this characterization, we will first need to place Kabbalah in the wider context of Jewish mysticism; then we shall describe briefly the essential differences that delineate the Kabbalah from previous or contemporaneous Jewish mystical trends.

A millennium of Jewish mystical creativity preceded the Kabbalah. The first evidence of Jewish mystical trends dates to the period of the Tannaim (the Sages cited in the Mishnah), in second century C.E. Palestine.[4] These first mystics contemplated a visionary experience devoted to the divine *heikhalot* (palaces) and the *merkavah* (the divine chariot). Though this movement can be traced to the circle of Rabbi Aqiba in the first half of the second century C.E., the *heikhalot* and *merkavah* texts that have reached us were written much later. Therefore, it is a formidable task to describe in any accurate sense the historical sequence and the interrelationship of the various trends within Jewish mysticism of Late Antiquity. It is quite clear, however, that for at least five centuries there was an active mystical tendency within Rabbinic Judaism of Late Antiquity that produced several works having an important impact on the subsequent development of Jewish mysticism in the Middle Ages.

The principal works of these early Jewish mystics describe experiences in terms of an ascent (and often in terms of a descent!) to the divine chariot[5] and a vision of the supreme palaces, one above the other, which in their totality comprise the divine realm. An early work of this mystical school, *Heikhalot Zutartey* (The Smaller Book of Celestial Palaces), deals with the ascension of Rabbi Aqiba to the seventh palace, and is structured around the famous and enigmatic Talmudic account of the four Sages who entered *pardes*.[6]

The most detailed work of this genre, *Heikhalot Rabbati* (The Greater Book of Celestial Palaces), describes a similar experience by Aqiba's contemporary Rabbi Ishmael. Here Rabbi Ishmael is portrayed as the most junior scholar in the mystical school of Rabbi Nehunia ben ha-Qanah, a relatively obscure *tanna* whose name became prominent only in the later history of the Kabbalah.[7] Similarly, *Heikhalot Rabbati* is constructed around another famous Talmudic legend, this time the martyrological account of the torture and execution of Rabbi Ishmael, Rabbi Aqiba, and eight others by the Roman authorities.[8]

These early mystical works reflect in part a continuation of a literary and ideological trend first present in the Enoch literature of the Pseudepigrapha. They also build on an esoteric interpretive tradition of the first chapter of the book of Ezekiel and its description of the divine chariot. But these new mystics were not only preserving earlier traditions; it seems that a major new element was introduced early in the second century c.e. that was destined to have an enormous impact on all subsequent Jewish mystical thought. This new element centered around a novel interpretation of the biblical Song of Songs.

The central document expressing this new attitude to the Song of Songs is entitled *Shi'ur Qomah* (The Measurement of the Divine Height).[9] The work is based on the physical description of the divine lover in the Song of Songs. The book contains a detailed description of the limbs of the Creator in what seems to be an extreme indulgence in anthropomorphic imagery. Each divine limb is given a magical name, usually concocted from a nonsensical and unpronounceable combination of disjointed Hebrew letters. Each limb is also measured in millions of parasangs. With magnitudes such as these, it is not surprising that the basic unit of measure is nothing less than the divine little finger, extending from one end of the earth to the other.

It is possible that the work is not really the anthropomorphic travesty it first appears to be. When compared with the lover/God of the Song of Songs, the *Shi'ur Qomah* seems to insist that the description of the Creator's limbs should not be taken literally, but rather in an esoteric, interior, and ultimately mystical sense. Clearly, the magnitudes serve to evoke the awesome and ineffable object of mystical meditation. Similarly, the concatenation of meaningless names for the divine limbs border on magical incantations.

The works of this early period gave later Jewish mystics two basic elements that served as a foundation for their formulations down through history: the *heikhalot* books provided a hierarchic description of the divine realm, one stratum above the other; they also provided for the possibility of ascending in mystical experience through these layered strata. The *Shi'ur Qomah* approach to the Song of Songs combined this element with an interior and mystical investigation into the nature of God. Thus, a theological element was added to the earlier visionary theme of the *heikhalot*. Medieval Kabbalah, though different in many respects from *heikhalot* and *merkavah* mysticism, preserved and developed these two complementary elements.

Another contribution of this early Jewish mysticism to the Kabbalah of the Middle Ages is the perception of the Tannaitic age as the apex of Jewish mystical activity and authority. Both the *Bahir* and the *Zohar* are ascribed to Tannaitic masters: the *Bahir* to Rabbi Nehunia ben ha-Qanah and the *Zohar* to Rabbi Simeon bar Yohai, student of the great Rabbi Aqiba. This was not just an external ascription, for these books were purposely written in the literary forms prevalent in the Tannaitic period. Thus, both the *Bahir* and the *Zohar* were written in midrashic (running commentary of Scripture) form, couched whenever possible in the language and expression of second-century Hebrew and Aramaic. Since literary form cannot but have an impact on content, the affinities between ancient and medieval Jewish mystical schools were preserved in the strongest possible way, even though enormous differences reflected the transition from the late Roman Empire to Christian Europe in the High Middle Ages.

While it is possible to compare textually and ideologically ancient Jewish mysticism with the Kabbalah and thereby discover the terminology and ideas that passed from the former to the latter, it is much more difficult to describe the history of Jewish mysticism during the intervening centuries. The basic problem of the emergence of the Kabbalah is the difficulty in discovering a continuous line of development from Palestine and Babylonia in Late Antiquity to southern Europe in the twelfth century. This key question in the history of Jewish mysticism is still quite obscure.

When the first Kabbalistic circles began to appear in Provence and Spain in the Middle Ages, their symbols and terminology, as well as their concept of the divine world, seemed to be completely novel. Though we do not have a clear understanding of the roots of the Kabbalah in the generations immediately preceding its appearance, we do have some evidence that what is characteristic of the concepts of the first Kabbalists was not known to scholars living only a short time before them.

Early in the twelfth century there lived in Spain a Rabbi Judah ben Barzillai of Barcelona, a great rabbinic authority who was in possession of a wealth of ancient speculative theological material. He developed a keen interest in Jewish esoteric traditions and collected everything he could find. His library included many sources that were later lost. He presented the material he had collected in a detailed and extensive commentary to the unusual *Sefer Yeṣirah* (Book of Creation; to be described below).[10] This commentary tells us much about the status of medieval European Jewish theology, for it

4

is revealing in what it contains as much as what is absent. Careful examination of this work fails to reveal any trace of specific symbols, ideas, or formulae characteristic of the Kabbalah.[11] It is difficult to assume that Rabbi Judah ben Barzillai deliberately obscured these ideas, for they are no different in their degree of esotericism from many others that he explicitly details.

In a similar vein, we have many volumes of esoteric and mystical works from the medieval German Pietist schools in the late twelfth and first half of the thirteenth centuries (this movement is described below, section 3). In all the detailed discussions in these Pietist tracts of topics that were to play a central part in later Kabbalistic theories, we do not find any evidence of the unique Kabbalistic approach.[12] Though an argument from silence should always be regarded with great caution, it still is a fact that the eruption of Kabbalistic symbolism in the late twelfth century seems to be a revolutionary rather than an evolutionary process.

This issue becomes even more complicated once we introduce another key element into it: the Gnostic tendencies in the early Kabbalah. *Heikhalot* and *merkavah* literature has been described by scholars as belonging—at least to some extent—to the great and variegated family of Gnostic phenomena.[13] G. Scholem once characterized this "palace room" and "chariot" literature as expressing a specifically Jewish/Gnostic world view.[14] This thesis has been severely criticized in recent years, due largely to parallel investigations into contemporary Christian Gnosticism.[15] Furthermore, much of the later Jewish esoteric systems lack most of what is regarded as classical and characteristic Gnostic symbolism. But early Kabbalah (and, somewhat surprisingly, sixteenth-century Kabbalah) abounds in Gnostic ideas and symbols.

In fact, the appearance of the Kabbalah in the twelfth century might best be regarded as an eruption of Gnostic attitudes in the heart of Rabbinic Judaism of southern Europe. Where did these Gnostic symbols come from? How did they suddenly appear in the late twelfth century after languishing for more than a millennium in the labyrinths of obscure and largely ignored *heikhalot* and *merkavah* texts?

One tempting answer to these questions rests in proposing a connection between the early Kabbalah and contemporary Christian movements containing Gnostic elements. Such Gnostic movements as the Cathars and Albigensians dominated the theological horizon of southern France, in close proximity to the Provençal rabbinic centers where the Kabbalah first appeared. If such a connection could be proven, a singularly perplexing question in the history of Jewish mysticism would be solved. However, sixty years of scholarship have failed to establish even one close textual, terminological, or ideological parallel between these Christian heresies and the teachings of the *Sefer ha-Bahir* and the early Kabbalists of Provence.[16] Moreover, Scholem's detailed study of the *Bahir* indicates a reliance on eastern—and not European—traditions and sources. If Gnosticism had an impact on the seminal *Bahir*, it was a Gnosticism of the Oriental world, centuries before the Catharic and Albigensian movements developed.

It is a difficult task to properly delineate between terms, symbols, and ideas that could not originate without being influenced by previous schools that employed them and those terms, symbols, and ideas that were invented and reinvented time and again throughout the history of religious ideas. In the case of the Gnostic element in the Kabbalah it is an even more formidable task, due to a surprising historic phenomenon. For while the Kabbalah in general certainly ought to be classified as belonging to the category of Gnostic phenomena, it is nevertheless a fact that the Gnostic characteristics of the Kabbalah become most pronounced as it develops furthest removed from any likely ancient Gnostic source. For instance, early Kabbalah did not possess the concept of an independent evil power governing the world until the second half of the thirteenth century, as in the *Zohar*. Lurianic Kabbalah of the sixteenth century strengthened further the Gnostic, dualistic, and mythological symbols with regard to the notion of divine evil, and later permutations of Kabbalistic doctrine reveal even stronger Gnostic components.[17] It is indeed very difficult to assume that the *Zohar* was subject to Gnostic influence, and it is even more far-fetched to assume that Isaac Luria of sixteenth-century Palestine suddenly discovered new Manichean sources that shaped his mythology of evil. To be sure, during the history of the Kabbalah some Gnostic-type symbols and attitudes were reborn within the internal Jewish mystical schools. But if so, one may ask, why not assume the same set of developments in early Kabbalah, especially in the *Bahir?* Can we really be certain that the early Kabbalists were in contact with ancient Oriental Gnostic sources, while the more extreme and radical trends of the later Kabbalah were solely the result of internal developments?

INTRODUCTION

We cannot be sure, were it not for indications provided by the philological clues provided by the *Bahir*, which seem to indicate that Gnostic sources of some sort did reach the author or editor of the work. The content of these sources and their precise path of transmission is still a mystery. The question of why this injection of Gnosticism did occur at precisely the end of the twelfth century is presently unanswerable, and thus a full account of the emergence of the early Kabbalah is far from complete. However, some important facts concerning the circumstances of this emergence can be understood when we survey the mystical background to this emergence, especially while remaining cognizant of the cultural and historical factors that coalesced just before the appearance of the Kabbalah. Before we can embark on this task, however, some definition of the Kabbalah and its symbolism is required.

2. THE NATURE OF EARLY KABBALAH

The Kabbalah is only one of many forms of Jewish mysticism during its nearly two millennia of development. Since the thirteenth century it has emerged as the most important current, and in subsequent centuries all Jewish mystical expressions were made, with few exceptions, through the symbolism provided by the Kabbalah. In the period of the development of the early Kabbalah it was not the only Jewish mystical system; it achieved this status only after the *Zohar* became the authoritative text of Jewish mysticism. It is necessary now to explain briefly the dividing lines between Kabbalah and other Jewish attempts at mystical expression.

The most characteristic and recognizable symbol of the Kabbalah is that of the ten *sefirot* (singular: *sefirah*). This strange and untranslatable term first appears in the *Sefer Yesirah* (Book of Creation), a short cosmological and cosmogonical work probably written during the fourth century c.e.[18] Some of the terms used in this work are closely related to the *heikhalot* and *merkavah* literature, but its cosmology and terminology have no prior source in Hebrew literature. All later theologians undoubtedly drew the term *sefirah*, as well as many other terms that became central to Jewish philosophical and mystical speculation in the Middle Ages, from this short tract.

The *sefirot* in the *Book of Creation* probably denote the concept of "numeral" and are ten in number.[19] As cosmological symbols these ten *sefirot* express ten extremities or polarities in a three-dimensional world: up, down, east, west, north, south (the dimensions of space); beginning and end (the dimension of time); and good and evil (the moral dimension).

In the Kabbalah, the *sefirot* are a series of divine emanations, spreading forth from the Godhead[20] and comprising the divine world, which separates the created worlds—the world of angels, celestial bodies, and earth—from the hidden Godhead. This hidden Godhead does not take part in any change or activity, thus resembling to some extent the Aristotelian concept of the Prime Mover or First Cause, or the Plotinian One.

As described by the early Kabbalists, the *sefirot* contain many elements derived directly from Neoplatonic theologies and cosmologies. For example, the metaphor of radiating light emanating from a blinding Godhead is often employed by Kabbalists. The Godhead itself is beyond all symbolic description and can therefore be described only by negative statements. The most frequently used negative appellation for the Godhead is *Eyn Sof* (No End), but this term does not contain any specific meaning that renders it superior to any other negative term such as "no beginning" or "no color." Symbolism begins with the first *sefirah*, containing an element of specific characterization that can be hinted at by a symbol (most often by "Thought" or "Supreme Thought" or "Will").

The system of the ten *sefirot* can be, therefore, nothing more than a philosophico-cosmological attempt at explaining the world, both earthly and divine—not very different in most respects from similar ones put forth in the eleventh and twelfth centuries by Muslim, Christian, and Jewish philosophers influenced by ancient Neoplatonic world views. What differentiates the Kabbalah from other systems that use emanation as the metaphor for the unfolding of Being is twofold: first, the unique symbolic values, and second, the dynamic qualities of the *sefirot*.

When a philosopher states that there are ten divine emanations, each playing a part in the creation of the physical world as we know it, he is usually stating what he believes to be an accurate description of things as they are, and he tries to prove his statement by logical and verifiable arguments. His statement is subject to challenge on these grounds, and he will do his best to show that objections do not place in doubt the factual correctness of his statement. The Kabbalistic attitude toward the *sefirot*, though sometimes expressed in terms that seem to be very close to those of such philosophers, is completely different. The source from which this insight is derived is neither logical nor experimental, but divine revelation through mystical interpretation of the biblical text or other sacred texts. It cannot be challenged on any grounds, for it is both divine revelation and mystical intuition, and not the conclusion of human minds. It even cannot be challenged on religious or theological grounds, as at least one opponent of the Kabbalah tried to do in the thirteenth century when he described the sefirotic system as grossly polytheistic, a belief in ten gods instead of the One God.[21] The Kabbalist's answer to such a claim will be: The *sefirot* are symbols and so is their number; symbolism should not be confused with sensual or logical truth. A symbolic expression rather hints at a truth that is very different from its symbolical referent.

The Kabbalistic symbol may be described as the one-ninth of an iceberg that floats above the surface of the water, while the full import of the symbol is the hidden iceberg below. There is a deep, inherent connection between the protruding tip and the whole; the texture is the same, as are the temperature and color. But the shape, the size, and the meaning are completely different. On the one hand, the tip is undoubtedly a part of the iceberg; but on the other hand, it cannot be said that the tip *is* the iceberg. Anyone who takes the symbol, the tip, to be the whole truth is making a great mistake.

In this way the Kabbalists are completely immune to any theological, philosophical, or logical criticism. If attacked, they can always answer that their symbols have been taken literally; when confronting mystical truth itself, these attacks will carry no weight whatsoever. Thus they achieve the mystical freedom that allows them to present to the Jewish society of the thirteenth century—an intellectual environment ruled by a Maimonidean philosophy emphasizing monotheism in more strict and absolute terms than any other—ten divine powers and at the same time avoid being immediately condemned as heretics. Considering the revolutionary nature of Kabbalistic symbolism, it is really astonishing to note that few Jewish thinkers ideologically attacked the Kabbalists throughout the Middle Ages and early modern times.[22]

The symbol as used in Kabbalah does not stand instead of some other human concept, and therefore it cannot be explained or interpreted in human language. It is the maximum approximation that can be achieved by language of a hidden, mystical truth that is beyond logic and expression. The symbol is the only means by which

INTRODUCTION

truth can be communicated, with the proviso that its users remain cognizant of the limitations of such contact and do not take the symbol literally. The concept of the ten *sefirot*, therefore, does not denote ten divine powers; rather, it suggests that the human word "ten" is the closest approximation to something beyond comprehension. The human distinction between "one" and "ten" does not hold when both terms do not represent their arithmetical, literal significations but are instead symbols of a hidden truth, where they might be united in a fashion completely alien to human epistemology and logic.

In the same way, the various terms for the philosophical concept of *emanation*—terms used by theistic Neoplatonists to explain a certain divine process—are only the closest words in language that symbolize a mystical process that is utterly hidden and only marginally similar to the philosophical concept. The Kabbalah is unique in Jewish mysticism in its ability to develop a vast system of symbols that were used generation after generation. This recurring use of the same symbols sometimes created the false impression that the Kabbalists really formed a theosophical school that developed along the same lines as every other school of thought, developing the same key concepts. This impression ignores the symbolic aspects of these terms. Two Kabbalists may employ the same symbols, but analysis will often show that they perceive in them completely different world views and basic attitudes. The adherence to a system of symbols reflects the Kabbalah's external conservatism as it conceals an internally free and revolutionary character.

According to this conception of symbolism, creation of symbols becomes nearly impossible. If a symbol is the maximum approximation possible by human language to a truth that is completely beyond language, a mystic must be sure that the term he uses is unique and cannot be replaced by any other word. The Kabbalists overcame this difficulty by their use of the divinely revealed Jewish holy books. These books—first and foremost the Hebrew Bible—were directly from or mediated by God; therefore, they were thought to contain the complete, mystical truth. Yet the language of the Torah is comprised of nothing more than everyday human language, which cannot possibly convey the totality of the hidden truth. Therefore the Kabbalists had no doubt whatsoever that the Torah and other authoritative works were written in a symbolic language that was misunderstood by the non-mystics as representing ordinary human speech.

INTRODUCTION

The Kabbalists saw in Scripture an enormous library of mystical symbols that express the true function and interrelationship of the ten *sefirot*. Every biblical noun became a symbol for one of the *sefirot* and every verb helped to describe the dynamic interplay of the sefirotic organism. Thus Kabbalah acquired an extensive symbolic vocabulary thought to be of divine origin, derived from the fount of Torah. This attitude toward Scripture necessitated a revolutionary reinterpretation of Torah, uncovering new, esoteric, and mystical strata in every verse. Therefore, much of Kabbalistic literature throughout the ages is nothing more than extended commentaries and exegetical homilies on the Bible. By extension, the great rabbinic continuations of Scripture—the Talmud and Midrash—were also regarded as repositories of profound symbols.

Scripture in the widest sense served as the main source for Kabbalistic symbolism, but it was not the only source. God created the earth and everything on it to reflect His hidden truth; therefore, every worldly phenomenon, if interpreted in proper mystical fashion, can reveal a symbolic nature. This divine truth, by which the physical and metaphysical world was created, is hidden within creation. God created man in His own image: Man also contains this hidden symbolic dimension. That man was created with a left hand and a right hand cannot be explained simply according to functional needs. This would render creation completely meaningless, for meaning can be derived from truth alone, and truth is completely independent of earthly, sensual needs. Man's hands reflect a parallel divine essence, expressed through the "tip of the iceberg" limbs of flesh and blood. Man was created with two hands because of that unique aspect of the divine realm which cannot be expressed in earthly symbols but by these two hands. At the same time the Kabbalist may speak of God's left and right hands, thereby resurrecting the anthropomorphic terminology of the *Shi'ur Qomah* in an entirely new context of the sefirotic symbol.

In this way all existence underwent a complete transformation in Kabbalistic literature, where literal meaning was supplanted by a wealth of mystical symbolism. Every part of nature, society, and history received a novel, symbolic transvaluation that did not contradict the mundane, everyday meaning attached to these elements. On the contrary, they were all imbued with a new depth.

This was especially important with regard to the *mitzvot*, the commandments and ritual norms that direct every moment of a traditional Jew's life. The issue known as "the reasons for the commandments" troubled many Jewish thinkers in the eleventh and twelfth centuries. Some commandments, such as the prohibition against murder, were easily explained; others, like the puzzling law of the red heifer (see Numbers 19), remained baffling. Within the Kabbalistic system all *mitzvot* easily took on a symbolic and profound meaning. The commandments reflect essences and processes within the divine world, and by their observance the mystic is able to take a part in these processes. That some *mitzvot* did not have logical explanations did not in any way diminish their attraction as symbols—on the contrary, the symbol became more powerful because of its mysterious nature on the literal level. Since the last decades of the thirteenth century, many works or portions of works were given over to a detailed exposition of the symbolic nature of the *mitzvot*. In this way the Kabbalah completely transformed the everyday lives of its believers on the spiritual level, without changing anything on the practical level.

Kabbalistic symbolism imparted to everyday religious, ritualistic, and ethical deeds a new, profound level of meaning and importance, and thus strengthened the normative demand for performance of the *mitzvot*. In this area the dual nature of the Kabbalah as both a radically revolutionary and a conservatively orthodox force is clear: the Kabbalah gave the medieval Jew a new and revolutionary impetus to uphold and preserve his ancient tradition without change. It is clear that a rationalistic explanation for the reasons of the *mitzvot* might make the commandments subject to change as circumstances change; whereas a mystical interpretation on the symbolic level—claiming that the real reasons are completely hidden and beyond human comprehension and that the symbol dimly denotes something concerning an esoteric meaning—cannot be used to bring negation or change. The Kabbalah thus became a conservative force in Jewish religious practice and behavior. It is no wonder that the most orthodox communities in contemporary Judaism are those led by adherents, in one way or another, of Kabbalistic thought.

The symbolic interpretation of the *mitzvot* in Kabbalah serves to illustrate the second major characteristic of the Kabbalistic attitude toward the emanated *sefirot*—namely, the dynamic activity of the *sefirot*. When Neoplatonist philosophers describe an emanated system of divine essences they usually regard it as static and fixed since the beginning of the world: for them, emanation is a mechanical process. According to them, the impact of these emanated powers is constant and unchanging. The Kabbalistic *sefirot* are completely dynamic (the *sefirot* are not really dynamic and changing; the human terms for dynamism and change are the closest approximation to their true, though inexpressible and hidden, character), constantly moving in a rhythm of change. This is the Gnostic, and to a large degree mythical, element that the Kabbalah most probably received from Eastern sources and that first found expression in the *Sefer ha-Bahir*, spreading to all later Kabbalistic works in the Middle Ages and early modern times.

The dynamism of the *sefirot* reflects the constant change in divine providence and the relationship between God and His creation. The *sefirot* contain elements of divine justice and mercy, each insufficient to rule the world separately. Only when God uses both these symbolic "hands" (justice to the left and mercy to the right) in the correct proportion can creation exist at a given moment. The organic structure of the *sefirot* is often described symbolically as a family composed of a Father, a Mother, a Son, and a Daughter, Bride and Bridegroom, Husband and Wife. These mythical symbols, which often invoke sexual metaphors, express the dynamic quality of the divine structure: lovers draw away from each other and then come close again; husband and wife separate and are once again united. When harmony and love prevail in the divine world—in the realm of the *sefirot*—tranquillity and happiness are to be found on earth. When strife tears the divine powers from each other, chaos reigns in the created world.

According to most Kabbalistic systems, the force that decides the fate of the divine powers is manifest in the individual Jew's observance of the *mitzvot*. Divine light emanates in abundance from the Godhead and fills the *sefirot* with pleasure and harmony when the people of Israel pray the proper prayers and observe the commandments in the most minute detail. Darkness flows from the Godhead when Israel does not obey the rule of Torah, and sin stands as a barrier between the Godhead and the *sefirot*, which are sustained by the divine light. In a purely symbolic, though obviously mythic, manner, every deed of every Jew at every moment has an impact on the stature of the whole divine realm. While the *sefirot* rule creation and determine its fate, the actions of the individual Jew decide the fate of the *sefirot* themselves. Thus, the source of change in the divine world is to an extent brought about by the constant fluctuations of

human propensities toward frailty and sin on the one hand and obe-
dience and faithfulness on the other. These vicissitudes of human
behavior cause dynamic movement in the realm of the divine powers
and thereby result in change in the lower world ruled by them. From
all this there clearly is an enormous and complex synergism of cause
and effect in which the expression of human free will in the realm of
religious and ethical behavior becomes the decisive element in a
grand cosmic scheme. Thus Kabbalah is one of the most profound
celebrations of human free will and religious autonomy among medieval theologies, even though its own conception of "commandment" is completely heteronomous, denying the possibility that
human logic can understand the reasons for God's demands.

This dynamic conception of the *sefirot* is one of the most important theological revolutions brought about by medieval Kabbalists. There is not a hint of this concept in the *Sefer Yesirah*, the ancient
source from which the doctrinal foundations for the sefirotic concept
first appear. When the medieval Kabbalists began to use the term
sefirah for their symbol of the dynamic emanations, they followed a
long tradition of transvaluating the terms and phraseology of the *Sefer
Yesirah* through commentary on the text. The unavoidable fact, however, is that in this ancient work, and in the commentaries written
on it in the centuries before the Kabbalah first appeared, the *sefirot*
were described as fixed and static elements of cosmogony and cosmology, lacking in any mythical or dynamic element. These latter
components were introduced by the Kabbalists only in the twelfth
century.

This system of ten divine emanations symbolically represents
the divine world. Their dynamic, mythical quality is the most important characteristic differentiating the Kabbalah from other prior
or contemporaneous Jewish mystical movements and trends. Before
we describe in greater detail the historical development of the early
Kabbalah and its distinctive theology, it will be necessary to briefly
survey the spiritual atmosphere that prevailed when the Kabbalah
first made its appearance.

3. JEWISH PHILOSOPHY AND ASHKENAZI HASIDISM

The first Kabbalistic circles in Europe appeared and developed
within a Jewish culture that was absorbing the newly translated ideas

of Jewish philosophy. Although the development of Jewish philosophy in the Middle Ages began in the tenth century in Babylonia and achieved great stature in eleventh-century Muslim Spain, it was only in the twelfth century that it became a preeminent cultural force capable of shaping the basic attitudes of the Jewish intelligentsia. During the second half of the twelfth century Moses Maimonides (1135–1204) wrote his monumental *Guide for the Perplexed*,[23] which became the classic work of Jewish philosophy, expressing the profound conviction that Jewish tradition could be integrated with the sophisticated and compelling insights of Greek and Arabic science and philosophy.

In our context, it is worth reiterating that medieval Jewish philosophy developed primarily in Islamicate lands, and the major compositions of Jewish philosophy were thus written in Judaeo-Arabic (and only later translated into Hebrew). The Kabbalah, however, developed in Christian or newly reconquered Christian lands at the hands of Jewish scholars completely illiterate in Arabic. In part, then, the timing and scope of the development of the Kabbalah is related to the appearance of these various theological treatises in a Hebrew idiom.

The impact of medieval philosophical thought on Judaism created an awareness of problems never before paramount in Jewish thought. Such questions as the nature of God, His relationship to creation, His demands of man, and the meaning of religious worship and ethical behavior received a new importance and urgency. Jews were ruled by peoples of widely different beliefs and in every instance Jews—for either external or internal reasons—were called upon to justify their uniqueness and right to religious autonomy in terms acceptable to medieval intellectuals. As a result, the most cosmopolitan thinkers of the Jewish people became well versed in the philosophical legacy of the ancient Greeks as mediated by the Arabs.

The strong belief of Jewish philosophers that the Torah contained the ultimate in religious and intellectual truth had to be demonstrated not only to non-Jews but to the Jewish community itself, if only to preserve a sense of intellectual self-respect and self-confidence. In this way, Platonic, Aristotelian, and Neoplatonic concepts became extremely relevant to everyday Jewish life and thought, especially in those circles that functioned in constant contact with non-Jewish society and culture.

As a result of the continuous attempts to harmonize the Torah with philosophy and science, Judaism faced crucial challenges of a basic and religious nature. The Aristotelian conception of God as professed by medievals did not allow for the possibility of change in the Godhead. The supreme divine power was conceived as the Unmoved Mover, the First Cause, infinitely removed from any interaction with subordinate powers or entities. How could such a God be the moving power in history, punishing the wicked and sustaining the righteous, listening to prayer and acting on it? The eleventh-century philosopher Judah Halevi put the following brutal words into the mouth of an Aristotelian representative: "[God] does not know thee, much less thy intentions and actions, nor does He listen to thy prayers or see thy movements."[24] A personally concerned God seemed to be completely denied by the philosophers, leaving the believer facing a totally transcendent God with whom he cannot communicate. Jewish religious tradition, which was based more on the performance in practice of the religious, ritualistic, and ethical *mitzvot*, seemed to be facing a crisis; contemporary theology was drawing away from the traditional way of life.

This gulf undoubtedly contributed to the emergence of a mystical attitude, but it would be erroneous to suppose that Jewish mysticism emerged as the result of the spiritual crisis created by the impact of Greek philosophy. Indeed, two generations ago one of the foremost historians of Jewish medieval thought offered such an explanation for the appearance of the Kabbalah. According to David Neumark, the Kabbalah was based almost exclusively on philosophical concepts that were turned around by the mystics to reestablish the personal God within Jewish thought.[25] While it is undeniable that certain ideas and formulations in thirteenth-century Kabbalah arose out of the context of philosophical thought, it is not the case that philosophy was the formal cause of Kabbalah. The book *Bahir*, for instance, does not use philosophical terminology in an attempt to create an antiphilosophical system; it is permeated with mythical Gnostic symbolism that bears little relevance, if any, to the central ideological problems that troubled thinkers of the twelfth century. The Kabbalah is by far too large and complicated a body of images, myths, and symbols to be explained away as an alternative to Maimonidean theology. To be sure, some segments in Kabbalistic theology do seem to reflect a direct answer to conflicts raised by the injection of Aristotelianism into Judaism (as, for instance, some mystical theories on the nature of prayer), but as a whole the Kabbalah seems to stand independently from the immediate stimulae of its cultural surroundings. Were it not for the challenge of Aristotelianism the Kabbalah would have indeed been different, but not much different from the system that evolved in the twelfth and thirteenth centuries.

Another point that should be stressed in this context is that the first teachers of the Kabbalah in Provence and northern Spain were not the people most affected by the onslaught of philosophical ideas. The first Kabbalistic circles that are known to us were rooted in the great rabbinic academies in the Midi and Catalonia, and the first identifiable expositors of Kabbalah were the great rabbis of these academies. These scholars were aware of the new philosophical ideas, but their deep roots in Jewish law and tradition were not threatened by the new ideas.

Throughout the thirteenth century, Provence was the scene of a vitriolic controversy between Maimonidean supporters and detractors, and it is interesting to note that Kabbalists were among the leaders of the opposition to the Maimonideans.[26] But it would be a leap of logic and historical reasoning to suppose that these first Kabbalists developed their symbolism in order to offer an alternative to Aristotelian philosophy. It is possible that a new emphasis on ethical teachings within the academies was motivated by the wish to offer an alternative to "dry" philosophy. But such ethical teachings emphasized the old, traditional values of *halakhah* and *aggadah* and shunned the new, Gnostic symbols.

In a general survey of mystical trends in the thirteenth century, we would be remiss were we to pass over the currents that developed out of a mystical rereading of Maimonides' *Guide*. In Egypt, Maimonides' son Abraham (d. 1237) constructed a defense of his father's strict rationalism out of a Ṣufi (Islamic mysticism) mold.[27] A string of pseudo-Maimonidean writings, stressing an interiorized Neoplatonism, surfaced in the thirteenth century.[28] Finally, there was Abraham Abulafia (d. after 1290; see below), the Spanish peripatetic mystic who wrote three progressively longer commentaries to the *Guide* and built a highly unitive mysticism around Maimonides' Aristotelianism.[29] It should come as no surprise that none of these three "Maimonidean options"—except perhaps Abulafia—proved to have any lasting impact on the emerging Kabbalah.

How deep-rooted the forces that gave birth to the Kabbalah were can be discerned when we survey other contemporary major trends in Jewish spirituality. The predominant movement in southern Europe was Jewish philosophy, but in northern and central Europe, and particularly along the Rhine, another movement was having an enormous impact on Jewish thought and was in the process of creating a series of new theological postures and symbols that would persist in Judaism for centuries to come.

Ashkenazi Ḥasidism—also known as German Pietism—is remembered in Jewish history primarily as a pietistic movement that helped shape Jewish spiritual and ethical trends throughout the Middle Ages.[30] The central document of the movement, the *Sefer Ḥasidim* (Book of the Pious), was written by Rabbi Judah the Pious of Regensburg (d. 1217) and was intended as a pietist guidebook for a new sectarian Jewish community, based on strict and well-defined ethical principles.[31] But aside from the behavioral/ethical demands of the movement, there arose a vast body of theological literature of an esoteric quality, sharing with the nascent Kabbalah a similar set of mystical impulses and doctrinal approaches.[32]

Three basic characteristics seem to be common to the early Kabbalah and the esoteric theology of the German Pietists. First, both movements claimed to rely on ancient and unique sources of Jewish wisdom, transmitted through the back channels of Jewish history.[33] Second, both movements evidence an unmistakable reliance on the small amount of Jewish philosophy of the twelfth century that was available in Hebrew. Here we recall such Spaniards as Rabbi Abraham bar Ḥiyya and Rabbi Abraham Ibn Ezra, two of the few theologians of twelfth-century Spain who shunned Arabic for the Holy Tongue. We also note the dissemination among Germans and southerners of a strange, lyrical, almost quasi-mystical Hebrew paraphrase of what was originally a dry, scholastic philosophical treatise by the venerated scholar Saadia Gaon (882–942; Iraq).[34] Third, both movements relied heavily on the *heikhalot* and *merkavah* literature of Talmudic and Geonic times. Much of Pietist esoterica is nothing more than paraphrases of and commentaries on the ancient visionary texts, which provided the central terms and basic symbols of Pietist theology.

The two subjects around which most of Ashkenazi Ḥasidic esoteric thought revolved were divine revelation and the meaning of the prayers. While the second question is dealt with mainly in the form of commentaries to the liturgy, the first—revelation—is the main theme of the more theologically inclined works of this movement. The basic question confronted in these works is one that could not have been posed before the advent of Jewish philosophical inquiry: How could the supreme Godhead have been revealed in physical form to the prophets?

The philosophers usually interpreted biblical and Talmudic descriptions of physical revelation as an allegory or a metaphor. But the Ḥasidim, relying to some extent on terminology derived from the Saadianic Paraphrase, developed a theory claiming that there is a special revelatory agency at the command of God called the *kavod* (Divine Glory), an extension of the rabbinic conception of the immanent *shekhinah* (Divine Presence).[35] Saadia claimed that the *kavod* was a created angel whose function was to represent God before the prophets, and he explained the figure portrayed in the *Shi'ur Qomah* literature as a "*kavod* above the *kavod*," thus implying a series of such intermediaries. This concept was used by Abraham Ibn Ezra (1089–1164) in his commentary to the Mosaic revelation contained in Exodus 33. According to Ibn Ezra, this *kavod* was indeed the agent of revelation, not a created angel but a semi-divine power whose interface with the Godhead is as divine and transcendental as the Godhead itself. Rabbi Judah the Pious wrote a supercommentary to Ibn Ezra's exposition in which the concept of a divine, revelatory, and emanated *kavod* was further elaborated. Once such a notion began to develop, it could not remain confined to explaining biblical anthropomorphisms as they relate to revelation. The *kavod* in Ashkenazi Ḥasidic thought assumed more and more functions in the working of divine providence.

The Pietist theology of the *kavod* can be described as containing a hierarchy of divine emanated powers much like the Kabbalistic *sefirot*. There is, however, a basic difference between the Kabbalistic *sefirot* and the Ashkenazi Ḥasidic *kavod* system, even when it is specifically stated that there are ten *kavod*s.[36] When analyzing Ḥasidic esoteric theology one can discern—though often with some difficulty—the process of reasoning and the homiletic and hermeneutic reasons that gave birth to certain ideas or symbols. But when analyzing the Kabbalistic system it seems as if the hierarchy of divine powers existed first, and only then came the commentators and theologians to give expression to their existence. The process of creation of symbols is relatively clear in Ashkenazi Ḥasidism, whereas Kabbalistic literature seems to be an attempt to justify a system received from earlier sources, which then has to be explained as an answer to contemporary problems.

The Ashkenazi Hasidic *kavod* theory was fused with the wealth of material that the Hasidim inherited from *heikhalot* and *merkavah* literature. All the ancient descriptions of the divine throne, the seven heavens, the seven palaces, and the many powers connected with the divine chariot were now combined into one picture of a divine, complex world surrounding the *kavod* or *shekhinah*. The Hasidim saw themselves as guardians of the ancient traditions, and they copied these works (most of this material in our possession today comes from Pietist manuscripts), commented on them, and absorbed them into their works. The Hasidim thus bequeathed upon esoterically inclined Jewish thinkers of the Middle Ages a picture of a colorful, rich, and variegated divine world containing myriads of angels and secondary powers. One of the questions we cannot answer today is whether the Hasidim used all this material only passively, transmitting and commenting on it, or whether they tried to follow in the footsteps of the ancient descenders into the *merkavah* and actively participate in similar visionary experiences. A few scattered sentences in Pietist literature would suggest a personal experience of this sort, but the interpretation of these sentences is subject to dispute.

The problems of the prayers were connected by the Ashkenazi Hasidim to those of revelation in their claim that prayers should be directed toward the *kavod* (this claim appeared only in their esoteric works; in their popular works they insisted that prayers belong to the Godhead alone). But in the context of the interpretation of the prayers they developed a new world view that carried some clear mystical undertones.

Though the Jewish prayer book is attributed to scholars of the Mishnaic period, and not directly to divine revelation, the Hasidim insisted that it was divinely inspired and reflected the divine system in creation and providence of the world. Their attitude was based on a conception of language that followed in the footsteps of the *Sefer Yesirah*, according to which the creative power of God is expressed through the twenty-two letters of the Hebrew alphabet. Each letter has its own distinctive power, which is expressed in a numerologic symbol, for each Hebrew letter in sequence stands simultaneously for a number: the first letter, *alef*, can be read as "one"; the second, *bet*, as "two"; the eleventh, *kaf*, as "twenty" and so on. The idea that the world was created by the powers of the letters is an ancient one, probably as old as the Mishnaic tradition concerning "the ten utterances *(ma'amarot)* by which the world was created" *(Pirqey Avot* 5:1), where the "utterances" are composed of the twenty-two letters of the alphabet. The Ashkenazi Hasidim, claiming to be the recipients of this tradition via the mysterious Aaron ben Samuel of Baghdad, developed these concepts in a new way.

The dual character of every letter and word in Hebrew—containing at the same time both a meaning component and a numerical component—is always considered together. And since the sacred texts—the Bible, Talmud, and the prayers—are divinely inspired, both components reflect the divine harmony governing the world. The Ashkenazi Hasidim, in a manner hardly equaled by any other Jewish group, believed in divine providence and guidance of even the most minute details of the world. There is one divine master plan, which is revealed in everything that happens, and the blueprints of this divine plan are to be found in the letters of the sacred texts. It is no accident, for instance, that a certain hymn in the Book of Psalms contains 213 words, which corresponds to the number of words in a section of the prayers, which in turn may correspond to some biblical name or historical event. It is again no accident that a certain benediction contains only twenty-one letters, of which one is "missing" *(ne'elam* is the term used by the Hasidim); the import of this missing letter clarifies the real divine intention of the prayer. The Hasidim sought out *gematrias*—numerological computations—of whole biblical passages, uncovering corresponding equivalences in other sacred texts, events, or occurrences. A complex and indisputable chain of associations and interrelations was thereby established. There could be no doubt that there was an underlying mystical harmony combining all ostensibly scattered phenomena of religion, history, and man into a unified whole governed by the divine plan for the world.

This attitude of the Ashkenazi Hasidim gave the movement an extreme character. If everything in the divine plan of the world is intertwined, predestined, and determined, one should follow the sacred books to the most minute detail, for the slightest divergence destroys the underlying harmony on which creation and divine providence rest. A man cannot judge divine intentions and then adapt them to his situation as he understands it; he cannot understand the full scale of the divine plan and where he fits into it. All he can do is follow every word and letter of the divinely inspired Scriptures and carry out their meaning as traditionally interpreted.

The Ashkenazi Ḥasidic world view is probably the most deeply pessimistic ever developed in Jewish theology. According to the Pietists, the world was created for one purpose only: to differentiate between the righteous and the wicked. God Himself is the supreme goodness, but He did not create the world to reflect this goodness. On the contrary, the laws that govern creation are as bad as they can be, because the earthly abode is where people are being tried and the pious separated from the sinners. Such trial and separation cannot be achieved in a "good" world, where temptation is minimal and circumstances drive men to do good. God created this world in its present configuration as a compromise. Originally He intended to create a completely evil world, in which no element of good would be present. He could not do that, for He saw that not even one righteous person would emerge from such a world. In the present creation He introduced an element of goodness—just enough to have, from time to time, a righteous person who would justify the divine endeavor of creation. The laws governing nature, human society, human history, and the structure of the human soul were planned in such a way that they allowed only the most devoted Pietists to stand up to the difficulties and trials that existence puts before them and overcome them. In this, God is first and foremost the power that sets these trials in motion; only then does He become the benevolent divinity that assists the tested.

This principle is reflected also in the Ashkenazi Ḥasidic understanding of the *mitzvot*. For the Pietists, the *mitzvot* were not given in order to assist man, give him pleasure, or facilitate his existence. God designed His laws in a way that they will clash with natural human desires and thereby create as deep and severe a conflict as possible: This is the main trial that the righteous have to withstand and overcome. The pious devotee does not follow the precepts because he wishes to do so, but in spite of his desires and inclinations he follows God's commands. The Ashkenazi Ḥasidim were suspicious of everything that might give a man pleasure in this world: if satisfaction is present, sin must be nearby. Their system of repentance included elements of self-inflicted suffering: the penitent should pay with pain for the pleasure he derived from sinning. Sin is usually connected with pleasure and righteousness, that is, with suffering. The Ḥasidim did not invoke a dualistic theology (imputing evil to Satan, for example) in support of this pessimistic attitude. Everything is derived directly from the divine plan, and all the pain that is characteristic of human existence was designed by God Himself to test the elect.

The Ashkenazi Ḥasidic theology is understandable when the historical circumstances in which it developed are taken into account. Since 1096 the Jews in northern France and Germany lived under the constant threat of mortal danger at the hands of the Crusaders who passed through their communities. In 1096 many of the Jewish centers were destroyed and thousands were martyred at the hands of the Crusaders, and the massacres were repeated several times well into the thirteenth century. Rabbi Eleazar of Worms himself was wounded in one of these onslaughts, his son and daughters killed before his eyes.[37] The Pietists came to regard these persecutions, which occurred regularly in every generation, as a part of the natural laws governing the world in which they lived, and they incorporated these trials into their religious thought.

Martyrdom is the supreme sacrifice of all human effort, a submission to the divine Will. If this is the supreme religious commandment, than other commandments have to reflect the same disregard toward the human body and its desires, and their negation must be the purpose of religious behavior. The challenge of *qiddush ha-shem* (the sanctification of God's name in martyrdom) should direct man's behavior throughout his life. In every deed he must see himself sanctifying the holy Name to some degree by subjugating his humanity to the divine Word. Thus evolved the Ashkenazi Ḥasidic system of ethical behavior, the most strict and extreme of all Jewish systems.

Ashkenazi Ḥasidic esoteric theology, which developed just before and simultaneous with the early Kabbalah, proves that medieval Judaism was developing new theological and mystical approaches to confront medieval challenges of both a physical and an intellectual nature. During the thirteenth century the Kabbalah became the most important Jewish mystical school, and after that it became the dominant one. But when the Kabbalah first appeared it was but one example within Judaism of a search for new ideas, terms, and symbols with which to give expression to a powerful religious impulse.

4. EARLY MYSTICAL SCHOOLS

The receptivity of Jewry to mystical ideas at the turn of the thirteenth century is evident in several different circles of esoteric theologians, none of which are directly connected with either the Kabbalah or Ashkenazi Hasidism. One of the most interesting is the circle of thinkers who attributed their works to a tradition received from a legendary figure, Rabbi Joseph ben Uziel, portrayed as the grandson of Ben Sira (Ecclesiasticus), who in turn was said to be the son of the prophet Jeremiah. [38] The theologians behind these works are designated as the circle of the "special cherub" (ha-keruv ha-me-yuhhad), after a symbolic figure that is central to their theology. The works stemming from this circle were often lumped together with Ashkenazi Hasidic esoteric literature, but in truth these works possess a distinct theological profile and they differ from Pietist works in many respects, such as the use of pseudepigraphy as their means of publication. [39]

The works of this circle reflect a development of texts, commentaries, and supercommentaries that took at least a few decades to evolve, yet at present we know the name of only one author from this group—Rabbi Avigdor ha-Sarfati ("the Frenchman"), who probably flourished in the second half of the twelfth century. The focal point of the circle's esoteric curriculum was the *Sefer Yesirah*, to which was appended a pseudepigraphical addendum entitled "The *beraita* of Joseph ben Uziel." This short addendum puts forward the basic ideas of the *Book of Creation* as interpreted by this circle, and much of what we have from this circle is comprised of commentaries in prose and verse to this *beraita*. The most prominent texts that survived from this circle are a commentary to the *Book of Creation* attributed incorrectly to none other than Saadia Gaon, and the compositions of a later scholar, Rabbi Elhanan ben Yaqar of London, who preserves the theology of the circle through commentaries on the *beraita*. [40]

The esoteric works of this circle seem to be the earliest among Jewish mystics to explicitly use both the concept and the term emanation (ha'asalah) in describing the process of creation. They adopted the Ashkenazi Hasidic conception of the divine Glory (kavod), but proceeded to expand on this image by positing a separate divine power whose task it is to be revealed to the prophets—the "special cherub," emanated from the divine Glory. It seems that once the *kavod* was described by the Pietists as the power receiving human prayers, it could no longer serve as the revelatory power, for that would mean that man was praying to a power that has a form and can be seen. Thus, the process of the evolution of a system of emanated powers below the Godhead went one step further, coming closer to the sefirotic system of the Kabbalah. The writers of this circle devoted much of their speculation to detailed descriptions of the throne of Glory on which this special cherub resides, surrounded by all the angels and heavenly powers from the *heikhalot* and *merkavah* literature. It seems that these theologians did not have any contacts with the schools of Rabbi Judah the Pious and Rabbi Eleazar of Worms, but they shared some common sources and religious needs.

A somewhat similar religious phenomenon is attested to by another book written at the turn of the thirteenth century entitled *Sefer ha-Ḥayyim* (The Book of Life). Despite having been ascribed to Rabbi Abraham Ibn Ezra, it remains an anonymous composition.[41] Like the "special cherub" texts, this work was also thought to be connected to the German Pietists, but every detailed examination of its ideas indicates that the differences far outweigh any similarities.

The author of the *Sefer ha-Ḥayyim* was more scientifically inclined than most other Jewish theologians in the central Europe of his time. He makes full use of Jewish scientific sources, including first the *Sefer Yeṣirah*, and then a bevy of astronomical, astrological, and medical treatises that medieval Jewry received from more ancient times. Furthermore, the author seems to be aware of, if not well versed in, many medieval scientific concepts not found in Jewish sources. He attempted to present his theology in a systematic manner, though the result is still somewhat removed from what would be regarded by Spanish rationalists as "systematic." He deals with the problems of the Godhead, of the secondary divine powers, especially the *kavod* (and he seems to suggest that there are several such powers, or even ten), of the heavenly and angelic worlds, and of earthly natural phenomena. However, most of the work is dedicated to an investigation of the human soul and its relationship to the divine powers, its ascension and contact with pure spirituality, and problems connected with revelation and God's presence in creation.

It is often difficult to distinguish between scientific and mystical motives in the statements of the *Sefer ha-Ḥayyim*. Its language is completely impersonal, and it presents a world view in factual, and not experiential, terms. Still, this work reflects an original attempt to grapple with basic religious problems such as the relationship between man and God, and a quest for new terminology and new images that would describe this relationship. Many of the doctrines of the *Sefer ha-Ḥayyim* are to be found in later mystical writings, though this fact alone does not necessarily prove any direct influence; sometimes common problems and solutions can explain the similarity. The *Sefer ha-Ḥayyim* is one more example of the readiness of the Judaism in that period to embark on the development and adoption of a new set of symbols.

The last example of this type of mystical experimentation—and the first to be represented in the texts published in this volume—is the *'Iyyun* circle of Jewish mystics, so called because of its most famous work, the brief treatise *Sefer ha-'Iyyun* (Book of Contemplation). In the works of Gershom Scholem dealing with early Kabbalah, this circle is described as an early group of Kabbalists who flourished in southern Europe, possibly in southern France, in the early thirteenth century.[42] Scholem prepared a detailed list of thirty-two brief tractates that he believed for philological reasons to be the literature of this circle.[43] Most of these texts are found only in manuscripts and scholarly research into their nature is just beginning. Yet it is already manifestly evident that there is a basic problem concerning the history of Jewish mysticism that revolves around the doctrines expressed in these lost and hidden texts.

Most of the tractates enumerated by Scholem in his list of 'Iyyun works describe in detail the system of the ten *sefirot* as we know it from the *Sefer ha-Bahir* and the works of the early Kabbalists of Provence. But a small number of the texts, including the *Sefer ha-'Iyyun*, contain not a single reference to the Kabbalistic *sefirot*. They certainly discuss a series of divine emanated powers, but their number is now thirteen and not ten, and the symbols attached to these powers are completely different from those used by the Kabbalists. It is not that the symbols of the Kabbalistic *sefirot* are absent in these works; the term *sefirah* appears, but only in the limited, non-Kabbalistic sense derived from the ancient *Sefer Yeṣirah*.

In fact, if Kabbalistic symbols were to appear in these texts they would be both superfluous and out of place. These mystical works can—and perhaps should—be read as comprising a Jewish mysticism completely free of the symbols and theories of the Kabbalah. These texts share neither the sources nor the symbolic theosophy of the Kabbalah. Instead, they develop an independent brand of mystical symbolism based on the terms of the *heikhalot* and *merkavah* in an ambience of faltering Neoplatonism. Only later would a series of authors compose some two dozen tracts in which these unique theories would be conjoined (and confused) with Kabbalistic symbolism. This later fusion should not be projected back into the founding of the school (as some have done), just as the blending of Pietist and Kabbalist theories in late thirteenth-century texts must not be seen as evidence of an initial commingling of these two movements at an earlier period.

The works of this early phase of the 'Iyyun circle can be regarded as the first corpus of medieval Jewish mystical literature. The authors were deeply influenced by Neoplatonic ideas and terminology, which may derive from ultimately Latin sources. The Neoplatonism was adopted and fused together with the symbols of the *merkavah*, just as the 'Iyyun works were pseudepigraphically attributed to the rabbinic masters of the *merkavah*.

In the three 'Iyyun works translated in the following pages— the *Sefer ha-'Iyyun* itself, the *Ma'ayan ha-Ḥokhmah* (Fountain of Wisdom) and the *Interpretation of the Four-lettered Holy Name*—we do not find the symbolism of the ten Kabbalistic *sefirot*. Furthermore, the *Sefer Yeṣirah* is utilized in a remarkably unusual way, here as a blueprint for the creation of a homunculus, a *golem*. This story in the *Interpretation of the Four-lettered Holy Name* is based on a tale found in a twelfth-century commentary to the *Sefer Yeṣirah* by Rabbi Judah ben Barzillai of Barcelona. In later years it would become a classic tale of Jewish magic and folklore.[44]

The 'Iyyun texts abound with long lists of divine powers and processes, usually arranged in chains, one linked to the other and each deriving from its counterpart, reflecting a theological system that cannot be deciphered because the key terms are often obscure and incomprehensible. It is as if the 'Iyyun mystics were struggling with the anemic Hebrew vocabulary of the Middle Ages, trying to give expression to ideas and experiences defying not only Hebrew, but all human language.

Some trends, however, are apparent. There is a special emphasis on fire and color symbolism, combined with well-known *merkavah* images. The series of powers are usually described in rhythmic prose, reflecting enthusiastic, experiential expression. It seems that unlike most Kabbalistic texts, the works of the 'Iyyun circle did not undergo a stage of theologization and systemization, so that the enthusiastic elements connected with firsthand mystical experience are not completely erased. Still the pseudepigraphic literary expression succeeded in hiding from us the personalities of the authors, leaving them anonymous, and it is impossible to trace the exact historical and social circumstances in which this literature evolved.

5. THE BOOK BAHIR

One of the earliest and most important discoveries of Gershom Scholem, the great and pioneering scholar of the field of Jewish mysticism, was the identification of the *Sefer ha-Bahir* (Book of Brilliance) as the earliest disseminated text of Kabbalistic thought, the first to utilize the symbolism of the dynamic and emanated *sefirot*. Previous scholarship had given priority to a variety of other and much later Kabbalistic works, but thanks to Scholem we are now reasonably able to establish the sequence of the Kabbalistic texts of the thirteenth century and to systematically develop a history of Kabbalah.

But while the basic problem of sequence has been solved, a myriad of questions remains; and the *Bahir*, despite its name, is far from being clear to us. As explained above, no satisfactory explanation has yet to be proposed for the appearance or even the sources of the Gnostic symbols in the *Bahir*. Furthermore, the literary structure of the book is both a hodgepodge and a mystery: one scholar has even suggested that at some early point in the transmission of the text individual pages of the *Bahir* were scattered in the wind and reassembled in an incorrect order.

Still, some of the sources of the *Bahir* can be identified. The *Sefer Yesirah* and the traditions of the *heikhalot* and *merkavah* literature were undoubtedly the main sources from which the unknown author lifted terminology and imagery. But medieval sources also had some impact. The author's use of the terms *tohu* and *bohu* (the "unformed" and "void" of Genesis 1:2) to denote Aristotelian matter and form is derived from a twelfth-century philosophical treatise by Rabbi Abraham bar Ḥiyya.[45] It is possible that the author of the *Bahir* knew of Rabbi Abraham Ibn Ezra's theory of the *kavod* as described in the latter's commentary to Exodus 33.[46] If this latter supposition is correct, the *Bahir* must have received its final form only a short time before its appearance in the academies of Provence. There are some connections between the *Bahir* and the esoteric literature used by the Ashkenazi Ḥasidim. An ancient book entitled *The Great Secret (Raza'*

Rabbah) captured the imagination of some of the German Pietists as well as the author of the *Bahir*.[47] Both the Pietists and the *Bahir* were indebted to a collection of obscure commentaries to the Holy Divine Names.[48] These shared sources may help to clarify the origins of the *Bahir*, but it should be noted that none of these sources contain anything even remotely similar to the sefirotic or Gnostic doctrines characteristic of the *Bahir*.

The work was written in a form that mirrors that of ancient midrashic style. The book is comprised of brief homiletical paragraphs, each beginning with the name of a speaker or speakers, and each interpreting a biblical verse or pericope with the aid of other scattered verses, following the classical form of the Hebrew homily. The book is traditionally attributed to a master of the *Heikhalot Rabbati*, Rabbi Neḥunia ben ha-Qanah, because the opening homily of the work (and no other) is reported in his name. Other speakers include some of the most famous Tannaim (such as Rabbi Aqiba), and many sections are attributed to apocryphal rabbis bearing fictional names (such as Rabbi Amora). The language is mostly Hebrew with an occasional Aramaicism, which underlies the conscious attempt by the author to create a Tannaitic-type text. One literary element employed for this purpose is the frequent use of parables, especially parables centered on an earthly king of flesh and blood and his royal family, his loyal and disloyal subjects, and his majestic palace (now, of course, lofty symbols for the teeming world of the *sefirot*).

This literary device is essential for correctly understanding one of the most important among the many new concepts introduced by the *Bahir*: the conception that the divine world includes both masculine and feminine elements. In many passages the *Bahir* describes the figure of the Queen, the Bride, the Sister, the Wife, the Daughter, and the Matron who stands at the side of the masculine divine power, usually the King. She is sometimes portrayed in terms very reminiscent of Gnostic terminology: "the daughter of light" who came "from a far away country."[49]

There is little doubt that this feminine power is usually identified with the *shekhinah*. This grammatically feminine term was used for nearly a thousand years before the advent of the *Bahir*, but only as a designation of God in His immanent facet and never as a hypostatized feminine power. The *Bahir* is the first Jewish mystical work to introduce the idea that sexual and familial symbolism is appropriate for the description of the essence of the divine realm. This sexual motif was to become one of the most central and distinctive themes of the Kabbalah.

Another basic symbol of the *Bahir*, employed frequently in parables but often independently of them, is the portrayal of the emanated powers as a living tree. The divine world is portrayed as an enormous phalanx of intertwined limbs, roots, trunks, appendages, leaves, buds, and sprouts. Once again, it appears that this symbol reached the *Bahir* from a Gnostic source. It is even possible that the biblical term *male'* (fullness), so prominently invoked in the *Bahir* in describing the divine powers, is nothing more than a translation of the Gnostic *pleroma* into Hebrew.[50]

Many sections of the *Bahir* are dedicated to an investigation of the evil element in the upper and lower worlds. This kind of emphasis is unusual when compared with the traditional stress given to such considerations in rabbinic literature, and the metaphors for portraying the workings of evil are often quite new. Philosophical notions can be detected in the *Bahir*'s linkage between matter and evil. In most passages it seems that the evil elements in the universe are no more than divine emissaries: obedient messengers of the divine command. In such a case evil is not an independent force; the messengers are not evil in essence, nor is there an independent divine source of evil in the *pleroma*. In other sections of the text such an interpretation would run into difficulty, for in these passages it is implied that there are indeed two separate realms, one wholly good and the other entirely evil. Though hints of such a Gnostic and dualist picture are indeed present, the early Kabbalists who studied and commented on the *Bahir* did not use it to develop a dualistic system. To be sure, Gnostic, dualist theologies do appear in thirteenth-century Kabbalah (see below), but the dualist theosophists do not follow the symbolism of the *Bahir*.

The most important new element in the *Bahir* is the system of ten divine powers, arranged in a specified sequence and studied in great detail. The main discussion of these powers begins in the latter half of the work with the question: "What are these ten utterances [with which the world was created]?" (see Genesis 1 and Mishnah *Pirqey Avot* 5:1). Then begins a list, some powers passed over quickly, others the object of intense speculation. A wealth of new symbols are laid forth, to be used by Kabbalists in all subsequent generations. The system described through these symbols provides a glimpse into the divine dynamism, and rules every aspect of the earthly realm. There are important and puzzling differences in the order, symbolism, and function of the *sefirot* as presented in the *Bahir* and among other thirteenth-century Kabbalists, but there is not a single Kabbalist who does not reflect—at least to some extent—the basic symbolism of the *Bahir*.

6. RABBI ISAAC THE BLIND

Rabbi Isaac "the Blind" (Aramaic: Saggi-Nehor; literally "full of light") is the first Jewish scholar whom we know by name that dedicated all his creative powers to the field of Kabbalah. His predecessors in Provence who founded the Kabbalistic school were first and foremost halakhists who eschewed Kabbalistic compositions while concentrating on works in Jewish law. Their Kabbalistic views are known to us only from sayings and quotations included in the works of their later disciples. Rabbi Isaac wrote a Kabbalistic treatise as a commentary on the *Sefer Yesirah*.[51] With this commentary the history of Kabbalistic literature by medieval authors who can be historically identified begins.

Rabbi Isaac the Blind was the son of Rabbi Abraham ben David of Posquieres (the RaBaD; c. 1120–1198),[52] a great Jewish legalist of the Middle Ages and the spiritual leader of Provençal Jewry. RaBaD's commentaries to Talmudic tractates had an enormous impact on subsequent study of the Talmud. One of his most publicized works is his *hassagot* (critical glosses) to Maimonides' code of Jewish law, the *Mishneh Torah*. RaBaD's many works do not contain any clear mystical expression, though some polemical remarks against Aristotelian philosophy can be found in them.[53] Still, his life was undoubtedly dedicated to the study of the Talmud, and he cannot be described as a Kabbalist first. His disciples in the next two generations quote his sayings on several basic problems of the Kabbalah, revealing his deep interest in esoteric and mystical material, but they are so brief and cryptic that it is difficult to construct around them a specific mystical system. It is even difficult to pinpoint the influence of the *Bahir* in the terminology and symbolism of these sayings. It is clear, however, that RaBaD was a leader of a group of esotericists, and that he was not the first to lead such a group in Provence: the Kabbalists describe a chain of tradition in the rabbinic academies of Provence, expressed sometimes as a series of revelations from the prophet Elijah, of which RaBaD and his son are later links. To some extent our knowledge supports these traditions, and it seems that there was an undercurrent of mystical speculation in the rabbinic circles of Provence at least from the middle of the twelfth century.[54]

These traditions were combined with the symbolism of the *Bahir* by Rabbi Isaac the Blind into a profound mystical system that included most of the basic Kabbalistic ideas that would serve this movement for centuries to follow. Rabbi Isaac was the first to present (in brief sayings that were preserved by his disciples) a Kabbalistic attitude toward communion with God *(devequt)*, toward prayers and other Jewish rituals; but mainly he contributed to the crystallization of the Kabbalistic interpretation of biblical verses as a concatenation of symbols. His commentary to the *Sefer Yesirah* includes a panoramic mysticotheological presentation of creation and of divine providence over the world. It is written in a concise—and sometimes cryptic—style that enabled later Kabbalists to interpret his teachings to suit new ideas.

In the Kabbalah of Rabbi Isaac the Blind we find for the first time the Kabbalistic system of symbols for the ten *sefirot* in the manner adopted by most later Kabbalists. The main symbols of the seven lower *sefirot* were based on one biblical verse in I Chronicles 29:11,[55] a verse not cited in the *Bahir*. This fact, combined with other similar differences, raises the question whether the concept of the ten *sefirot* reached Rabbi Isaac only by way of the *Bahir*, or perhaps through another traditional source that Rabbi Isaac combined to create his own synthesis. There are some indications that tend to prove that there were mystical symbol-systems in Provence that were not derived from the *Bahir*, but the evidence is far from conclusive, and it is possible to assume that all the symbols found in Rabbi Isaac's Kabbalah that are not taken from the *Bahir* were created by him, by his teachers, and by his circle.

A large part of Rabbi Isaac's teachings revolves around the first chapter of the Book of Genesis. Concerning this chapter there is a vast division between the Kabbalists who read the story as a theosophy and the rabbinic traditionalists who read this chapter as a literary history of the creation of heaven and earth. For Rabbi Isaac, the creation of the physical world is a later stage in the process of creation, for the emanation of the *sefirot* must have preceded the appearance of a physical heaven and a physical earth. Therefore, this chapter in the Bible should include first a description of the relationship between the eternal Godhead and the first beginning of a thought to create something outside the Godhead; then, the intervening steps leading from the eternal unity of the Godhead to the lower divine powers; and lastly the *sefirot* themselves must be emanated, and their nature described. The Kabbalists in general did not accept the literal meaning of the Bible as sufficient, but concerning this specific chapter symbolical reading was imperative, for otherwise the Bible could not be described as containing the whole mystical truth; this truth must begin with divine processes, and not with material creation.

Rabbi Isaac dealt with this problem in his commentary to the first chapter of Genesis and several of his sayings preserved by later Kabbalists refer to interpretations of verses connected with creation. It seems, however, that his disciples concentrated his teachings about this chapter into a short, concise treatise that was circulated among the early Kabbalists. The two earliest versions of this treatise were preserved as self-contained works: one by Rabbi Asher ben David, a disciple of Rabbi Isaac who was sent early in the thirteenth century from Provence to Gerona to bring to the Kabbalists there Rabbi Isaac's teachings; and the other as a work by Rabbi Joseph ben Samuel. This second version was appended to the polemical work *Meshiv Devarim Nekhohim* (Response of Correct Answers) by a prominent Kabbalist of Gerona, Rabbi Jacob ben Sheshet (see below).[56]

There are some differences between these two versions, and they both differ from other versions offered by Rabbi Ezra ben Solomon of Gerona (see below) and Rabbi Isaac ben Solomon of Acre (first half fourteenth century), but it is still obvious that the text is one and the same, written neither by Rabbi Asher nor by Rabbi Joseph but a summary of Rabbi Isaac the Blind's views concerning the symbolical meaning of the first chapter of Genesis.

Kabbalistic tradition holds that Rabbi Isaac was born blind. That is strange indeed, for his mystical expressions abound with color imagery. The Kabbalists further claim that Rabbi Isaac, though blind, could perceive the nature and history of the soul of every person he encountered. With the true and legendary biography of Rabbi Isaac there emerges a long chain of charismatic Jewish leaders who dealt in Kabbalah and the Kabbalah enhanced their impact on the spiritual life of the Jews. Rabbi Isaac's teachings were transmitted to a new Kabbalistic circle in Gerona, near Barcelona, where a new leader and a new Kabbalistic circle emerged and strengthened the hold the Kabbalah was beginning to achieve in the very center of Jewish spirituality in the Middle Ages.

7. THE GERONA CIRCLE

The largest body of Kabbalistic works from the pre-Zoharic period derives from a circle of Kabbalists writing in Gerona,[57] a small town in Catalonia near Barcelona. The dominance of this circle of early Kabbalists is reflected in the selections presented in this volume—these works constitute the largest group of translations.

The center of the Kabbalah in Gerona was established by the disciples of Rabbi Isaac the Blind, especially two great writers: the elder Rabbi Ezra ben Solomon and his younger colleague Rabbi Azriel. In later generations these two pioneering Spanish mystics were often confused with each other (no doubt because of the similarity of their names) or with their compatriots, but thanks to the studies of Scholem and I. Tishby we are now able to establish their unique tendencies and theological perspectives. For example, Ezra's commentary to the Song of Songs has for years been attributed to the great Geronese Bible commentator and fellow Kabbalist Rabbi Moses ben Nahman (Nahmanides, 1195–1270)—a recent edition of Nahmanides' corpus still includes this commentary—but both stylistic and theological features bear the unmistakable mark of Azriel's Kabbalah.

These two mystics and their later Geronese disciples laid the foundation for all future Kabbalistic speculation. Much of the terminology and basic ideas that prevailed in the Kabbalah during the next seven centuries was formulated in Gerona, and despite enormous metamorphoses in Kabbalistic thought, the legacy of Gerona survived intact. In their own way, the mystics of Gerona turned the heretofore cloistered and peripheral Kabbalah into an active spiritual and intellectual force within medieval Jewish culture.

That these Gerona mystics, particularly Rabbis Ezra and Azriel, wrote Kabbalistic books was not universally regarded as a positive development among other Kabbalistic esotericists. Rabbi Isaac the Blind sent an angry missive to Gerona, demanding that Kabbalistic theories be kept secret and protected from the public forum. He forbade the dissemination of exoteric compositions of Kabbalah because, as he wrote, "a book which is written cannot be hidden in a cupboard." The dean of the Provençal Kabbalists declined an invitation to visit Gerona, sending instead his nephew, Rabbi Asher ben David, in order to instruct the circle in Gerona as to the proper modes of mystical speculation.[58]

This admonition concerning the nature of Kabbalistic creativity had important consequences for the younger generation of budding Geronese Kabbalists. It seems that after receiving Rabbi Isaac's letter, the Spanish Kabbalists decided not to write Kabbalistic works any more and to hide—at least to some extent—the full meaning of their mystical world view. Some of them, like Rabbi Jonah Gerondi, composed ethical works based on Talmudic and Midrashic homilies, totally lacking in Kabbalistic symbolism. Naḥmanides inserted into his non-Kabbalistic Bible commentary a number of esoteric passages, "according to the true path" ('al pi derekh ha-emet), which contained veiled and guarded Kabbalistic allusions that are not obvious in the least. Again, Rabbi Jacob ben Sheshet, one of the important leaders of this circle, wrote an ethical treatise entitled *Sefer ha-Emunah ve-ha-Bittaḥon* (Faith and Trust) and an anti-Maimonidean critique entitled *Meshiv Devarim Nekhoḥim* (Reply of Correct Statements): In neither work does Kabbalah or Kabbalistic symbolism loom prominently.[59]

But the most important Kabbalistic works of this circle were written by Rabbi Azriel, probably before Rabbi Isaac's letter ever reached Gerona. (In fact, it may well be that Rabbi Azriel's prodigious literary output was the cause of Rabbi Isaac's admonition.) Rabbi Azriel's works represent an important step in the systematization of Kabbalistic symbolism and its application to various aspects of Jewish religious life. Rabbi Azriel, like other Gerona Kabbalists, was well educated in philosophy, and it is due to his mastery of that subject that many philosophical terms were incorporated into the Kabbalah. These often scholastic and unemotional terms became powerful and cherished symbols of an inner spiritual quest, laden with new layers of mystical significance. Some of the most profound and penetrating expressions of pre-Zoharic Kabbalah are to be found in Rabbi Azriel's harmonious blend of philosophy and mysticism as found in his commentary to Talmudic legends and his shorter thematic treatises.[60]

The selections offered in this book from the works of the Gerona mystics are centered around Rabbi Azriel, the systematic mystic with philosophical leanings; and Rabbi Jacob ben Sheshet, the ethicist and Maimonidean critic with Kabbalistic tendencies. These two writers in particular had a lasting impact on the development of Kabbalistic thought for generations to come.

8. THE KOHEN BROTHERS OF CASTILE

The last phase in the development of early Kabbalah immediately preceding the "Zohar generation" (second half of the thirteenth century) was witness to a new phenomenon in the development of Kabbalistic circles: a group of writers who, not belonging to any school of general Jewish learning such as *halakhah* or homiletics, dedicated themselves only to Kabbalah. At the center of the new circle representing this trend were Rabbis Jacob and Isaac, the Kohen brothers, sons of Rabbi Jacob ha-Kohen. This circle was one of the most important of the thirteenth century, for the insights of the Kohen brothers had a profound and lasting impact on the author of the *Zohar*, Rabbi Moses de Leon.

Gershom Scholem, who first uncovered the writings of the Kohen brothers, referred to them as "the Gnostics from Castile," and indeed in their works, especially in those of Rabbi Isaac, we find a surprising reawakening of ancient Gnostic forms of mythic descriptions of evil intertwined with daring Kabbalistic symbolism.[61]

This group of mystics created a radical new form of pseudepigraphy, first claiming to have in their possession ancient mystical traditions and treatises and then inventing elaborate stories designed to convince the reader of the authenticity of these newly discovered texts. In most cases it seems that any such claim to authenticity is completely without merit, and the citations appearing in their works are in fact their own compositions. It is as if Rabbi Isaac were aware of the radical nature of his new symbols, and tried to minimize his own responsibility by inventing nonexistent sources. However, the Gnostics were not functioning in a vacuum—they were influenced by other schools, among which are the German Pietists.

Rabbi Jacob ha-Kohen's commentary to the letters of the alphabet was one of the most popular works on this intriguing subject in the Kabbalistic library. It is a typical example of the way in which thirteenth-century mystics used their newfound symbolism of the ten *sefirot* to unite all the elements, external as well as material, visual as well as aural, of the traditional sacred sources, and use them to present a mythical world view. The commentary to the Hebrew letters does not contain revolutionary ideas concerning the divine realm, but rather reflects the accepted attitudes of the Kabbalists of the period.

On the other hand, Rabbi Isaac's *Treatise on the Left Emanation* is one of the most important and revolutionary books in the history of the Kabbalah. This work introduced a full-blown Gnostic dualism into Kabbalistic symbolism. While earlier Kabbalists treated the problem of evil in a manner very similar to that of the philosophers, Rabbi Isaac created a demonological parallel structure of evil emanatory powers ruled by Asmodeus, Satan, Lilith, and their hosts, deriving from the left side of the sefirotic tree. And in fine mythic form, these various demons are seething with lusts and desires, jealousies and hatreds, flailing about madly in their demon world, waiting to pounce on the hapless humans below.[62]

Together with the dualistic concept Rabbi Isaac introduced in this treatise the first Kabbalistic myth of the apocalyptic and messianic end-time. The struggle between the forces of good and the forces of evil will be decided in the final struggle between the Messiah and Satan. The Messiah will finally be victorious and will deliver not only the Jewish people but also the divine forces that were threatened by the devil and his servants. Earlier Kabbalists did not deal with the problem of the future redemption, concentrating their mystical efforts in achieving individual salvation through the approach to the divine emanations. Rabbi Isaac was the first Jewish mystic in the Middle Ages to present a mystical mythology in the form of an eschatology. His views and symbols were accepted and used by the author of the *Zohar*, and their inclusion in that classic and monumental work made them an integral part of Kabbalistic speculation for centuries to come.

With the Kohen brothers the first hundred years of the development of Kabbalah came to an end. A detailed, sophisticated system of symbols and concepts was created by the author of the *Bahir*, the Kabbalists of Provence, the 'Iyyun circle, and the mystics of Provence and Castile. The stage was set for the great Kabbalists of the late thirteenth century, the "Zohar generation": Abraham Abulafia, Rabbi Joseph Gikatilla, and Rabbi Moses de Leon. To be sure, each of these great men was a pioneer in his own right; equally certain is their indebtedness to these first Kabbalists who appear in the following pages.

INTRODUCTION

Notes

1. The term "early Kabbalah" is sometimes used to denote the pre-Lurianic Kabbalah, or the Kabbalah as it developed until the radically new mysticism of Rabbi Isaac Luria of the sixteenth century. In this book however, the term is used consistently to denote the first century of Kabbalistic creativity, until the generation of the author of the *Zohar*. For a comprehensive introduction to the *Zohar*, see G. Scholem, *Major Trends in Jewish Mysticism* (henceforth *MTJM*) (New York, 1954), pp. 156–243; and the new partial translation by Daniel Matt, *Zohar: The Book of Enlightenment* (New York, 1983).
2. See his soon-to-be translated *Ursprung und Anfänge der Kabbala* (Berlin, 1962); and his earlier *Re'shit ha-Qabbalah* (Jerusalem, 1948).
3. An extensive bibliography of scholarship on the Kabbalah in the thirteenth century would include Isaiah Tishby, Ephraim Gottlieb, Joseph Dan, and Moshe Idel among the Israelis, and Georges Vajda and Alexander Altmann amongst diaspora scholars.
4. The *heikhalot* mystical texts reached us only by way of medieval manuscripts. Linguistic and philological considerations seem to prove that they were composed mainly between the third and sixth (possibly seventh) centuries C.E. The mystics themselves may have begun their efforts somewhat earlier than the period established for the composition of the extant texts. See I. Chernus, *Mysticism in Rabbinic Judaism* (Berlin, 1982).
5. They called themselves *Yordey ha-Merkavah*, "the Descenders into the Chariot."
6. This work was recently published as a critical edition by R. Elior, *Jerusalem Studies in Jewish Thought*, Supplement I, 1982. The manuscripts of all these texts were published in P. Shäfer's *Synopse zur Hekhalot Literatur* (Tübingen, 1981).
7. The *Sefer ha-Bahir*, the first work of Kabbalah, was attributed to Rabbi Nehunia; other Kabbalistic works in later times were similarly attached to his name because of his prominence in the early *merkavah* texts.
8. The story of the ten martyrs was disseminated during the Middle Ages as both prose and poetry, eventually finding its way into the liturgy for the holiest day of the Jewish calendar, the Day of Atonement. The source for this martyrology, however, seems to have been the *Heikhalot Rabbati*.
9. On this work see J. Dan, "The Concept of Knowledge in Shiur Komah," in *Studies in Jewish Mysticism and Intellectual History Presented to Alexander Altmann* (Birmingham, 1979), pp. 67–73; and M. Cohen, *The Shi'ur Qomah: Liturgy and Theurgy in Pre-Kabbalistic Jewish Mysticism* (Lanham, 1983), which also contains a translation.
10. *Commentar zum Sepher Jezira*, ed. Halberstam (Berlin, 1885).
11. See Scholem, *Ursprung und Anfänge*, pp. 40–42.
12. On the relationship between Ashkenazi Hasidic mysticism and the early beginnings of the Kabbalah, see J. Dan, *The Esoteric Theology of Ashkenazi Hasidism* (Hebrew) (Jerusalem, 1968), pp. 116–128.
13. H. Graetz, *Gnosticismus und Judenthum* (Krotoschin, 1846).
14. See *MTJM*, pp. 40–78, and *Jewish Gnosticism, Merkabah Mysticism and Talmudic Tradition*, 2nd ed. (New York, 1965).

15. See, among others, I. Gruenwald, "Knowledge and Vision," in *Israel Oriental Studies* 3 (1973): 88ff. Gruenwald, D. Flusser, and H. Jonas seem to have missed Scholem's insistence that his thesis was based more on phenomenology than history.

16. See Scholem, *Ursprung und Anfänge*, pp. 11–13, 168–171, 206–210 *et passim;* and S. Shahar, "Catharism and the Beginnings of the Kabbalah in Languedoc" (Hebrew), in *Tarbiz* 40 (1971): 483–507.

17. See Scholem, "Kabbalah and Myth," in *On the Kabbalah and Its Symbolism* (New York, 1965), pp. 87–116; and I. Tishby, "Gnostic Doctrines in Sixteenth-Century Jewish Mysticism," in *Journal of Jewish Studies* 6 (1955): 146–152.

18. On this early work see G. Scholem, *Kabbalah* (Jerusalem, 1974), 21–30.

19. The first part of this work was translated into English and studied by I. Gruenwald, "Some Critical Notes on the First Part of *Sēfer Yezīrā*," *Revue des Études Juives* 132 (1973): 475–512.

20. It should be emphasized that no connection whatsoever exists between the term *sefirah* and the Greek *spheres*, the celestial wheels in which the stars are fixed. The word is rather related to the Hebrew *mispar*, "number."

21. Meir ben Simeon of Narbonne, in a letter published by Scholem in "A New Document for the History of the Beginning of the Kabbalah" (Hebrew), in *Sefer Bialik*, ed. Fichman, (Tel Aviv, 1934), pp. 148–150.

22. Only in post-Renaissance Italy do we find serious activity among Jewish intellectuals in condemnation of the Kabbalah. The most important work is Rabbi Judah Aryeh of Modena's *Ari Noḥem* (A Lion's Roar), published in 1648.

23. The English translation by S. Pines (Chicago, 1963) is recommended.

24. *Sefer ha-Kuzari*, I:1.

25. *Geschichte der judischen Philosophie des Mittelalters*, Band I (Berlin, 1907), 179–236.

26. A recent summary of this controversy is included in B. Septimus, *Hispano-Jewish Culture in Transition* (Cambridge, 1981).

27. *The High Ways to Perfection of Abraham Maimonides*, ed. Rosenblatt, vol. I (New York, 1927); vol. II (Baltimore, 1938). See S. Goitein, "Abraham Maimonides and his Pietist Circle," in *Jewish Medieval and Renaissance Studies*, ed. Altmann (Cambridge, 1967), pp. 145–164.

28. See, for example, *Peraqim be-Haslaḥah*, ed. Davidowitz (Jerusalem, 1939).

29. For a general introduction, see Scholem, *MTJM*, pp. 119–155.

30. A survey of Ashkenazi Hasidic ethics can be found in J. Dan, *Ethical and Homiletical Literature* (Hebrew) (Jerusalem, 1975).

31. See most recently I. Marcus, *Piety and Society* (Leiden, 1981).

32. See Dan's *The Esoteric Theology of Ashkenazi Hasidism* (Hebrew) (Jerusalem, 1968).

33. The historical details of this transmission were studied by A. Grossman, "The Migration of the Kalonymus Family from Italy to Germany" (Hebrew), *Zion* 40 (1975): 154–186.

34. Scholem, *MTJM*, p. 86, and Dan, *Esoteric Theology*, pp. 47–8.

35. See ms. Vatican 266, folio 41b.

36. In the *Sefer ha-Ḥayyim*, a mystical and ethical work written in Germany

around the year 1200, there appears a succession of such "glories" similar to the chain of emanated powers described by the Kabbalists.

37. The poem that contains an account of this tragic event was published by A. M. Haberman in his anthology of Jewish accounts of the Crusader massacres, *Sefer Gezerot Ashkenaz ve-Sarfat* (Jerusalem, 1946), pp. 161–167.
38. See J. Dan, "The 'Special Cherub' Circle in Ashkenazi Hasidism" (Hebrew), in *Tarbiz* 35 (1966): 349–372; idem, *Hugey ha-Mequbbalim ha-Ri'shonim* (Jerusalem, 1972).
39. The story is derived from the ninth- or tenth-century Eastern collection of stories known as *The Alphabet of Ben Sira*. See J. Dan, *The Hebrew Story in the Middle Ages* (Hebrew) (Jerusalem, 1974).
40. One of Ben Yaqar's commentaries to the *Sefer Yesirah* was published by G. Vajda in *Kovetz Al Yad* 16 (1966); his *Sod ha-Sodot* (Secret of Secrets) and a second commentary to the *Sefer Yesirah* were published in *Ashkenazi Hasidic Theological Texts* (Hebrew), ed. J. Dan (Jerusalem, 1978).
41. See the new edition of Moses Taku's *Ketav Tammim*, ed. J. Dan (Jerusalem, 1984).
42. See Scholem, *Ursprung und Anfänge*, pp. 273–291.
43. *Re'shit ha-Qabbalah*, pp. 255–262.
44. Scholem, "The Idea of the Golem," in *On the Kabbalah and Its Symbolism* (New York, 1965), pp. 158–204.
45. *Sefer Hegyon ha-Nefesh*, ed. G. Wigoder (Jerusalem, 1969).
46. Sections 128–129 of the *Sefer ha-Bahir* display awareness of Ibn Ezra's terminology. This section of the *Bahir* is translated in our collection.
47. Scholem published the German Pietist text that includes the quotations from the *Raza' Rabbah* in an appendix to his *Re'shit ha-Qabbalah*, pp. 195–238.
48. See J. Dan, *The Esoteric Theology*, pp. 74–76 *et passim*.
49. Translated below, pp. 59–69.
50. See Scholem, *Ursprung und Anfänge*, pp. 59–62.
51. At the end of Scholem's *ha-Qabbalah be-Provans* (Jerusalem, 1963).
52. See I. Twersky, *Rabad of Posquières* (Cambridge, 1962).
53. Ibid., pp. 258–300; and Scholem, *Ursprung und Anfänge*, pp. 180–200.
54. Scholem, *Ursprung und Anfänge*, pp. 175–179, 201–218.
55. "Thine, O Lord, is the Greatness, and the Strength, and the Beauty, and the Victory, and the Majesty . . ."
56. For Asher ben David's version, see Y. Dan, ed., *The Kabbalah of Rabbi Asher ben David* (Hebrew) (Jerusalem, 1979), pp. 52–56. For Jacob ben Shehshet's version, see G. Vajda, ed., *Sefer Meshiv Devarim Nekhohim* (Jerusalem, 1968), pp. 193–196.
57. On the Gerona circle, see G. Scholem, *Ursprung und Anfänge*, pp. 324–407; and his *Kabbalah*, pp. 48–52. Finally, see his Hebrew book on the subject, *ha-Qabbalah be-Geronah*, ed. J. Ben-Shlomo (Jerusalem, 1964).
58. Rabbi Isaac the Blind's epistle was published by Scholem in *Sefer Bialik* (Tel Aviv, 1934), pp. 141–162.
59. The relationship between mysticism and ethics in the works of the Gerona Kabbalists is presented in detail by J. Dan, *Jewish Mysticism and Jewish Ethics*, forthcoming.

60. Rabbi Azriel's *Perush ha-Aggadot* was edited by I. Tishby and published in 1943 (reprint 1983).
61. See Scholem, *Kabbalah*, pp. 55–56. The works of this circle were published by Scholem in *Mada'ey ha-Yahadut* 2 (1927): 165–293, and in a series of articles scattered throughout the journal *Tarbiz*, vols. 2–4 (1931–1934).
62. On this problem, see J. Dan, "Samael, Lilith and the Concept of Evil in the Early Kabbalah," *AJSreview* 5 (1980): 17–40.

The 'Iyyun Circle

INTRODUCTION

Few texts of the 'Iyyun circle have been published, and what has been published is full of errors and not really useful. Adolph Jellinek published a version of the *Sefer ha-'Iyyun* in 1853, and another version was edited by Hassida in *Ha-Segullah*, volume 2 (1934) from the Musajoff collection in Jerusalem. It has since become apparent, thanks to the work of M. Verman, that there are a variety of different recensions of the *Sefer ha-'Iyyun*. A version of the *Ma'ayan Ḥokhmah* was published twice in Warsaw (1863 and 1866) and once in *Ozar Midrashim* (ed. Y. Eisenstadt, New York, 1915: 307–311).

The three texts partially translated below are based on manuscript witnesses edited in the 1940s by Scholem and reedited by the translators. Our text of the *Sefer ha-'Iyyun* follows a recension found in ms. Munich 408, which largely agrees with ms. Musajoff 64. Our text of the *Sefer Ma'ayan Ḥokhmah* follows ms. Hebrew U. 8 330; and our *Perush Shem shel Arba' Otiyyot* follows ms. Florence 2:41. For further bibliographical details, see Scholem, *Re'shit ha-Qabbalah* (Jerusalem, 1948): pp. 255–262; and Verman, *Sifrei ha-Iyyun* (Ph.D. diss., Harvard University, 1984).

The Book of Speculation
(SEFER HA-ʿIYYUN)

This is the *Book of Speculation* of the great Rabbi Ḥamai,[1] foremost expositor of the Innermost.[2] In it he revealed the essence of the entire reality of the revealed Glory, whose source of existence and quintessence no living being can accurately fathom, for He is in a state of balanced unity. In His perfection the upper and lower worlds unite one to another, and He is the foundation of all, both hidden and revealed. From Him pours forth all that is emanated from the wondrousness of the Unity. Rabbi Ḥamai has explained all these matters by way of the Chariot and interpreted the prophecy of Ezekiel, peace be upon him.[3] Here begins the book in the proper order.

Blessed and exalted is God, glorious in power. He is one, united in all His powers as the flame is united in its colors. The powers which emanate from His unicity are like the light of the eye which springs forth from the pupil.[4] [These powers] are emanated one from the other, as a fragrance from a fragrance or a candle from a candle. One emanates from the other, and from that another. The power of each resides in that which is emanated from it, yet the emanator lacks for nothing. Thus, before creating any entity, the Holy One, blessed be He, was one and eternal, beyond examination and boundary, without compound or distinction, without change or movement, concealed through existence itself.

When the thought arose in His mind to bring objects into being, His glory became visible. Then were His Glory and Splendor revealed together.

Knowledge of Him is made explicit through five means: restoration *(tiqqun)*, utterance *(ma'amar)*, combination *(serruf)*, grouping *(mikhlal)*, and calculation *(heshbon)*.[5] Knowledge of these five matters is unique in the branches of the root of change and it increases in the course of the thirteen sorts of transformation *(temurah)*.

What is restoration? [One] removes a thing from utterance, and utterance from the thing; grouping from calculation, and calculation from grouping; so that [one] causes all things to resemble a flaming fount. The flame is unfathomably and immeasurably within the fount. Infinite light lies hidden within the mysterious darkness. To truly know oneness is to know this blackness.

The meaning of all this is clarified by what Rabbi Ishmael ben Elisha,[6] High Priest in the Chamber of Hewn Stone, explained. For it is taught: Rabbi Ishmael said, "On that very day, we—I and Rabbi Aqiba—were before Rabbi Nehunia ben ha-Qanah, and Rabbi Hanina ben Tradiyon was also present. I requested from Rabbi Nehunia ben ha-Qanah the following: 'Rabbi, show me the Glory of the Sovereign of the world so that His knowledge will be as clear to me as all His other effects.' He said to me, 'Prideful one, go and let us examine the great ring which is inscribed with the heavens and whose name is *aR'aRiTa'*,[7] and [then] the ring of the earth, which is *'HW*,[8] and I will show all to you.' I went into the inner chamber of the Outer Holy Palace and I removed from there a book of Rabbi Nehunia ben ha-Qanah entitled *The Book of Palaces*, and thus did I find written in the beginning of the book: 'Mighty in chambers and grandeur is He who sits above His Chariot's wheels, sealed with "I am that I am" (Exodus 3:14), and with the great ring on which is inscribed the heavens, whose name is *aR'aRiTa'*, which is His name.' It is an abbreviation for "One is His foremost Unity, His first Unicity; His permutation is One."[9] He is One, Alone, Unique. The ring of the earth has the name *'HW*, an abbreviation for "He is and will be One."[10] Mediating between these two rings is YHVH. This is a "word spoken on its revolutions" (Proverbs 25:11).' "

Know that the Holy One, blessed be He, existed before the world's creation, exists in this world, and will exist in the World to Come. The indication of this is [provided by the verbal tenses applied to God in the Bible]: "He did . . . He does . . . He will do."

Another indication are [the terms of kingship applied to God in the Bible]: "God is King" (Psalms 99:1)—that is, God is; "God ruled" (Psalms 10:16)—that is, God was; and "God will rule" (Exodus 15:18)—that is, God will be. He rules in this world, He ruled before this world, and he will rule in the World to Come.

In this order are all the forms of the divine Name in the Book of Creation to be explained. These are revealed counsels of the highest hidden mystery called "Artisan" *(oman)*,[11] which means the source of faith *(emunah)*, for faith emerges by His power. He, may He be blessed, is united in His powers, yet He remains completely beyond and transcendent to them, elevated endlessly. These are the thirteen powers with which He is united, and each has its own name, each one higher than the former. The first is called "primeval wisdom"; the second, "wonderful light"; the third, "electrum"; the fourth, "mist"; the fifth, "throne of light"; the sixth, "the wheel of greatness," also called *ḥazḥazit*—meaning the place of vision for visionaries *(ḥezyon ha-ḥozim)*. The seventh is called "cherub"; the eighth, "wheels of the Chariot"; the ninth, "the surrounding ether"; the tenth, "the curtain"; the eleventh, "the Throne of Glory"; the twelfth, the dwelling of the souls called "the chambers of splendor"; and the thirteenth, the secret of the supernal structure, called "the outer palace of holiness."

These thirteen powers are revealed as one from the highest hidden mystery called "Artisan"—the source of faith—from which faith emerges. And before He, may He be blessed, created anything whatsoever, He was called *El*—strong—for His power was not known. When He began to bring His deeds into existence He created the two products of mystery and faith, while maintaining unicity and essence. For no one may grasp knowledge of the world's Creator.[12]

Notes

1. A pseudepigraphic attribution to a legendary rabbi.
2. The rather surprising appearance of the term *sefirot penimiyyot* (inner *sefirot*), which Scholem preferred, occurs only in the Munich manuscript, and may represent a later interpolation of Kabbalistic terminology. All other versions of the text have *penimiyyut* (innermost), with no reference to *sefirot*.
3. Much of the terminology used to designate the emanations is taken from the visions of Ezekiel.
4. An image earlier employed by Solomon Ibn Gabirol (c. 1021–1058), the

great Hebrew poet of Spain, to describe the act of creation. See G. Scholem, " 'Iqvotav shel Gabirol be-Qabbalah" in *Me'assef Sofrey Eres Yisra'el* (Tel Aviv, 1940): pp. 160–178. Here the emergence of light from dark parallels the movement from hiding to revelation.

5. Kabbalistic operations by which mystics performed quasi-magical transformations of nature, also mentioned in the *Fountain of Wisdom*. Other recensions of the *Sefer ha-'Iyyun* make no mention of these operations.

6. All figures mentioned in this episode are Talmudic Rabbis of second-century C.E. Palestine.

7. An abbreviation.

8. An entire text stemming from the 'Iyyun circle is devoted to this particular divine name. The name *'HW[Y]* is regarded as the true, primeval tetragrammaton, divided into two different biblical names—*YHVH* and *'HYH*—at the moment of the revelation of the Torah at Sinai.

9. *Ehad R'osh Ahduto R'eshit Yihudo Temurato Ehad.*

10. *Ehad Hayah Ve-yihyeh.*

11. See Isaiah 25:1. In other circles, this term designated the first and most concealed *sefirah, keter* or Crown.

12. Mystical knowledge and insight penetrate deeper than "scientific" investigation.

The Fountain of Wisdom

. . . And now behold and direct your heart to the first attribute, long and true and straight like a scepter. Regarding these matters, each of the attributes is called a flame. Now these flames are scepters, and the scepters are eyes, and each of the eyes themselves divide into five matters. Now these matters divide into sources, the sources into a structure, and the structure congeals. This congealment becomes a glowing ember, and it is to the ember that the five matters cling. For this reason the flame is linked to the ember.[1] From the flame the ether springs forth, and the ether is the principle which informs structure, action, restoration, mechanics, calculation, utterance, and grouping: These together are the essentials of all being.

Now we must think and understand, contemplate and examine in the hidden depths of our heart and thoughts, in our logic and our vision, in our spiritual vicissitudes and in the whisper of our tongues and the utterances of our mouths until we achieve clarity and certainty and comprehension in all these subjects. We will begin with the first matter, since it is foremost among all firsts, the restoring of all restorations. It will lead us along the true path.

Know that the Holy One, blessed be He, is the First Existent. He is called "Existent" for no other reason than that He brought Himself into existence. And since He brought Himself into existence, it is incumbent for us to understand and contemplate an examination of His reality, and how He began creation, and in what

49

way did He step and stand. In which path did [He emanate]? Was it one path or many paths? Did they divide into parts or extended entities? Or should one say "road" or "path" or "channel"? For "channels" are narrow and short while "paths" are excessive and "roads" are wide. Also, channels are like children while paths are akin to mothers, and roads are engraved with the archetypes of male and female.

Regarding this issue, wonders abound and are clarified. The wonders become more wonderful, and from them [come] the flames, and from the flames the thread extends outwards, and the threads thicken, and in this thickened state they grow stronger until they become scepters. This, then, is the point: Everything is again and again dissolved and then returns to the ether as it once was, and the ether is the essential element.

For before the celestial world—known as the 377 compartments of the Holy One, blessed be He[2]—was revealed; and before mist, electrum, curtain, throne, angel, seraph, wheel, animal, star, constellation, and firmament—the rectangle from which water springs—were made; and before the water, springs, lakes, rivers, and streams were created; and before the creation of animals, beasts, fowl, fish, creeping things, insects, reptiles, man, demons, specters, night demons, spirits, and all kinds of ethers—before all these things there was an ether, an essence from which sprang a primordial light refined from myriads of luminaries; a light, which, since it is the essence, is also called the Holy Spirit.

Know and comprehend that before all the above-mentioned entities there was nothing but this ether. And this ether darkened because of two things, each having different sources. The first issued an infinite, inexhaustible and immeasurable light. The gushing forth was sudden, not unlike the sparks which fly and burst forth when the craftsman forges with a hammer.[3]

After [the first light] another fountain was drawn out from which flows darkness. Now this darkness is itself a combination of three hues. The first is a darkness like that of dawn, a kind of green. The second was combined from green and light blue, and the third is a white darkness, composed of green, light blue, and red. And this is the primeval darkness which springs out of the ether. Do not try to perceive or examine it or investigate it scientifically for even Moses our teacher, peace be upon him, was unable to ask about it. If he was unable to inquire, then how much more so would be our investigation!

Everything that Moses stated[4] was said so that his knowledge of the image of the Holy One, blessed be He, would be unchanged in his heart, and that the knowledge regarding Him would be true and unified. That is to say, at the moment when the matter became clear to [Moses], knowing the true knowledge, he intended in his mind—even though there was no need—to examine and gaze and inquire into the higher levels. When he apprehended His secret thoroughly and the image of his understanding of the Holy One, Blessed be He, remained unchanging within his heart, he rejoiced and asked his intended question.

At this point [Moses] requested, "Show me now your ways" (Exodus 33:13). The Holy One, blessed be He, responded to this request, saying, "You cannot see My face" (Exodus 33:20). That is to say: This darkness, about which you have requested knowledge, is all from Me alone and is My own source, and you cannot comprehend it with any studious clarity. Therefore God said, "You shall see My back, but My face shall not be seen." This means that that which preceded the existence of the universe you cannot apprehend, so you will not be unable to say that I [i.e., God] am like all other entities, having a particular origin or place. Therefore you cannot apprehend knowledge of this darkness which was parallel to My existence. But from that point on you may know all: everything from and below the darkness, even My essence, the power of My Name, and My Glory.

At that moment Moses began to observe the primeval light, the root of all. And he found it to be a darkness composed of two entities stemming from two sources, one flowing with light, the second with darkness. Now this flow extends and gushes forth by way of channels, and the flow again becomes weak like a stream, and the stream again becomes minute, turning into a thread. And in this exiguity it extends and is directed until it becomes small, tiny droplets. These droplets grow and become fragmented entities, and the fragments continue to grow until they burst forth in great strength, mingling and interacting one with another, expanding and conjoining until a sap pours forth from them. Now this sap flows and extends and is congealed; and through this coagulation they are polished, purified, and clarified such that the original fragments that we mentioned are utterly disintegrated. From them come forth a kind of foam which floats on the water, and it transforms everything into a juice, and from this juice comes forth a wind, that is, the Holy Spirit. Therefore it is written hintingly, "And the Spirit of God hovered upon the water" (Genesis 1:2). This means that the Spirit grew stronger in holiness and transformed into many blades, each blade transforming into a branch, and each branch transforming into a root from which came forth a myriad of powers, entities, and objects.

And now you have a clear image so that you will know and understand that the Holy Spirit is a wind which emerges from the sap which comes forth from the fluxes, one flowing with light, the second with darkness. The remaining foam is white resembling red, for red is set in white and white in red. They confound the eyes, uniting one to the other imperceptibly. Then they once again become fine and minute like the sources from which the streams flow. This is the one matter which stems from the primeval light and points towards form, creation and change of form. Creation is separate and distinct from the image of the others, for it is like the example of a pillar which is bent. It is central, surrounding and occupying the head, absorbing the powers of all the others, reckoned with all the others, and they all emerge and extend forth from it—there is neither image nor differentiation except for the vision of whiteness and redness. Therefore it turns into sections. From the sections evolve the sources, and from one source flows light, which in turn is divided into the two hues that we have mentioned—whiteness and redness. From the second source flows the darkness composed of three colors—green, blue, and white—to the changing sources, and as they go forth their colors change. For when they are subject to the power of the primeval darkness they are not other than two colors like other darkness. But as they are drawn out, their colors change into many hues included in the five colors that we have already mentioned. These five colors are akin to a flame extending from ether, refracting as they change. For we have already said that the two flows are really one matter coming from the primeval darkness, alluding form. When this form is altered, it paints itself through its courses and the hues of its colors into ten, and each separate hue contains the number ten, arriving at a total of one hundred. The hundred returns again and again into utterance, calculation, and the grouping of entities; calculation in calculation, utterance in utterance, until they return to the sum of one, and one is the essence.

THE 'IYYUN CIRCLE

Notes

1. See *Sefer Yesirah* 1:7.
2. The numerical value of "heavens" *(SHaMaYiM)* is 390, minus the thirteen attributes.
3. A similar motif of emanations as a result of hammer blows can be found in the *Zohar* I:15a.
4. Exodus 33:12–23.

Explanation of the Four-Lettered Name

We have found in the *Book of Reliance* composed by Rabbi Judah ben Beteirah that the prophet Jeremiah—peace be upon him—was studying the *Sefer Yesirah* on his own. A heavenly voice came forth and declared: "Find yourself a companion!"

He went to Sira his son and they together submerged themselves in the *Sefer Yesirah* for three years, to uphold that which is written: "Then they that feared the Lord spoke one with another . . ." (Malachi 3:16).

At the end of three years, when they set about combining the alphabets by means of combination, grouping, and word formation, a man was created for them on whose forehead was written: *YHVH elohim emet.*[1] But there was a knife in the hand of this created being, and he erased the *alef* of *emet*, leaving only *met.*[2] Jeremiah rent his garments and said, "Why have you erased the *alef* from *emet?*"

He replied, "I shall tell you a parable. To what may this be compared? An architect built many houses, cities, and courts, and no one could copy his style and no one understood his knowledge nor possessed his skill. Then two men forced themselves upon him. He taught them the secret of his trade, and they knew every aspect of the craft. When they had learned his trade and his secret and his skills, they began to argue with him until they broke away from him and became independent architects, charging a lower price for the same services. When people noticed this, they ceased to honor the craftsman and instead came to the newcomers and honored them and gave the commissions when they required to have something built.

"So too has God made you in His image, shape, and form. But now that you have created a man like Him, people will say: 'There is no God in the world other than these two!' "

Then Jeremiah said, "What solution is there?"

He answered, "Write the alphabets with intense concentration backwards on the earth you have strewn. Only do not meditate with the intention of honor and restoration, but rather the complete opposite."

So they did, and the being turned to dust and ashes before them. Then Jeremiah—peace be upon him—said, "Truly, one should study these matters only to know the power and omnipotence of the Creator of the universe, but not to practice them, for it is written: 'You shall not learn to do' (Deuteronomy 18:9)."

Sira said to him, "My lord, know and understand that I have examined these esoteric subjects; and that God, may He be blessed, is united in the branches of the principle of sound which emerge from the lips of man and extend and strengthen into thirteen sorts of transformations, especially restoration. And so we find in *The Book of the Fountain of Wisdom*:[3] 'What is this restoration? [One] removes a word from an utterance, and an utterance from a word until all things are established like a fountain of unlimited and infinite size to the light hidden by the addition of mysterious darkness included in the 42 letters between the *bet* of *bere'shit* [the first letter of Genesis 1:1] to the *bet* of *u-bohu* ["and void" of Genesis 1:2].' Contained therein is a great matter of the unity of God, in their totality, their letters and their vowels—as the Sages, may their memories be blessed, said: 'The forty-two-lettered Name, holy and sanctified, is entrusted only to one who is middle-aged, pious, free from ill temper, a teetotaler and he who shuns the taking of revenge. And one who knows [the Name] and guards it and is heedful thereof and makes use of it in holiness and purity is beloved above and dear below. His teachings endure, his fear lies upon all, he inherits two worlds—this world and the world to come.' "[4]

And the Sage said: "I say that these letters—which are forty-two in all—are not one separate word nor one separate name; rather they are gathered letters which indicate the divinity of God, that He is One."[5]

Notes

1. Literally: "The Lord God is Truth."
2. Literally: "death." Now the statement on the forehead reads "The Lord God is dead."
3. This passage partly appears in the *Sefer ha-'Iyyun*.
4. BT Qiddushin 71a. The order of this quote varies slightly with the printed edition of the Talmud.
5. The exact source for this statement is unknown. However, it seems most probable that the unidentified "Sage" is none other than Rabbi Hai Gaon (939–1038), whose responsa contain discussions of the forty-two lettered name of God. Eventually, a variety of pseudo-Hai texts concerning the divine Names were produced that were spread among the German Pietists and early Kabbalists, particularly within the 'Iyyun circle. See Scholem, "Le-Heqer Qabbalat R. Yishaq ben Ya'aqov ha-Kohen," *Tarbiz* 4 (1932/33): 54–61 and 5 (1933/34): 51–58.

The Book Bahir

INTRODUCTION

The 15 sections translated below (chosen from the 200 that make up the Bahir) comprise one of the few sustained passages in the *Sefer ha-Bahir* about which it is possible to assume the existence of a continuous homily. This passage is doubly valuable in that to some extent it explains the mystical symbols used throughout the Bahir. This is a clear example of the fusion of old midrashic, homiletical, and hermeneutical styles used by the Kabbalists to present their new, Gnostic symbols.

The main Gnostic symbols in this unit are those of the "root of the tree" and the "daughter from the side of the light." Kabbalistic and Ashkenazi Ḥasidic symbols such as the "special and united" divine power, the three patriarchs as the three central divine emanations, and the ten cosmic dimensions that constitute the divine world are presented in the framework of a homily based on two numbers—three and ten—and two central parts of the daily prayers—the priest's benediction and the Trisagion (Isaiah 6:3: "HOLY, HOLY, HOLY is the Lord of hosts; the whole world is full of His Glory") used in the daily prayers.

All references to sections of the Bahir follow the divisions of Reuven Margoliot in his Jerusalem, 1951, edition.

Text and Commentary

SECTION 124[1]

And what is the reason for the raising of the hands and blessing them with a benediction? This is because there are ten fingers on the hands, a hint to the ten *sefirot*[2] by which the sky and the earth were sealed.[3] And those ten correspond to the ten commandments, and within these ten all 613 *mitzvot* are included.[4] If you count the number of letters of the ten commandments you will find that there are 613 letters, comprising all 22 letters of the alphabet, except for the letter *tet*, which is absent. What is the reason for that? To teach you that the *tet* represents the *beTen* (stomach, abdomen), and not the *sefirot*.[5]

Notes

1. This section continues the homily in the previous section on the verse in Leviticus 9:22, concerning the priest's benediction: "And Aaron raised his hand and blessed the people." This verse is connected with Numbers 6:24–26, which constitute the actual text of the benediction, part of the daily liturgy.
2. The *sefirot* here refer to the listing of the ten dimensions of the cosmos found in the *Sefer Yesirah* (Book of Creation), a mystical-cosmological work of the Talmudic period. These dimensions, or directions, are: up, down, east, west, north, south, beginning, end, good, and evil.
3. The term "sealed" is used both in *Sefer Yesirah* and in ancient Jewish mystical literature to denote God's actions in the universe using His holy name or attributes.

59

4. In the Hebrew text of the Decalogue there are 613 letters. The number 613 (*TaRYaG* in numerology) is the classic representation of the sum total of Jewish commandments, composed of 248 negative and 365 positive commandments.
5. The ninth letter, *tet*, is absent from the text of the Decalogue. The reason given by the Bahir is unclear. Is it because it denotes an unclean part of the body?
   And compare the Bahir section 84.

SECTION 125

And why are they called *sefirot?* Because it is written: "The heavens declare *(mesaprim)* the Glory *(kavod)* of God"[1] (Psalms 19:2).[2]

Notes
1. Another version of the Bahir quotes a different verse: "The heavens are my throne and the earth my footstool" (Isaiah 61:1). The verse from the Psalms is probably the correct version.
2. The mystical homilist uses the threefold connection, based on the *Sefer Yesirah*, between *sefirot* and *misparim* (numbers), to which he now adds "declare" *(mesaprim)*, to express the new idea that the heavens express the Glory of God by the ten *sefirot*.

SECTION 126

And what are they [i.e., the *sefirot*]? They are three,[1] and they include three armies and three realms.[2] The first realm is light, and the living light of water. The second realm is the holy beasts and the *ofanim* and the wheels of the chariot.[3] And all the hosts of God bless and praise and glorify and magnify and sanctify the King who is extolled in sanctity and praised in the innermost great sanctity, a terrible and terrifying King, and they crown him with "three holy's."[4]

Notes
1. The mystic author presents an intentional paradox: The ten *sefirot* are indeed three, and they represent three celestial forces. Thus he moves from the framework of ten, which governed the previous sections, to the number three, which is the basis of the revelations to come.
2. Only two realms are explained here. The first is most obscure, probably

based on the system of the emanation of the *sefirot* in the *Sefer Yesirah*. The first is *ruah Elohim hayyim* (Spirit of the living God), which is hinted here by the substitution of "light" for "spirit," and the third there is the water, which comes from the spirit.
3. The second realm is that of the divine chariot described by Ezekiel in the first chapter of his book. The description here follows the terminology current in *hekhalot* mysticism.
4. The transition to the number three is emphasized by the conclusion, which relates the homily to Isaiah 6:3 (when the homily began with the three elements of the priest's benediction). The Trisagion is the subject of the next sections, which are actually a mystical homily on the third benediction of the daily *'amidah* (standing) prayer, the *qedushah* (Sanctification).

SECTION 127

And why are there "three holy's" and not four? This is because celestial sanctity is always expressed in threes,[1] as it is written: "God is King, God was King, God will be King forever and ever."[2] And it is written: "God will bless you . . . He will give you light . . . He will raise His face" (Numbers 6:24–26).[3] And it is written: "God, God" (Exodus 34:6) and the rest of the *middot*. And the third is which? It is "God is a merciful God"—the thirteen *middot*.[4]

Notes
1. The homilist dedicates this section to the explanation of why "holy" appears three times in the Trisagion. It is because this is the number that governs all celestial powers, and he goes on to give three examples.
2. The first example is a nonexistent verse, but a formula that was accepted into the prayers: God's kingdom in the past, present, and future. This formula was used to explain the meaning of the vocalization of the name YHVH in the Bible, understood to mean "God will be, He is, and He will be."
3. The second example is the priest's benediction itself, which is comprised of three elements in three subsequent verses.
4. The third example is the names of God in the verse in Exodus, which was understood in rabbinic tradition to denote the thirteen divine attributes of mercy. This verse includes God's name three times.

SECTION 128

And what are HOLY, HOLY, HOLY and then "the Lord of hosts whose Glory fills the earth" (Isaiah 6:3)?[1] They are HOLY—

the Supreme Crown;[2] HOLY—the root of the tree;[3] HOLY—
united and special in all of them:[4] THE GOD OF HOSTS
WHOSE GLORY FILLS THE EARTH.

Notes

1. In this section the full force of the mystical symbolism of the Bahir is revealed, when the divine world is divided into the three categories corresponding to the triad of "holy's" in the *qedushah*.
2. The highest part is the Supreme Crown, which in subsequent Kabbalah was regarded as the first and highest of the divine emanations. This is an original Bahiric symbol (as far as we know) and in the list of the ten divine powers in the Bahir, section 141, it also appears as first.
3. The second is based on the Bahiric symbolism (probably based on Gnostic sources) that pictures the divine powers as an enormous divine tree, whose roots come from above and whose branches reach downwards. The root, therefore is the highest part of this divine tree.
4. The third, which is the most important one for the interpretation of the *qedushah*, is described by two conflicting terms (see below, section 133). It is both united with the others and separate from them. The terminology is derived from Rabbi Abraham Ibn Ezra's commentary on Exodus 33, and from the Ashkenazi Hasidic symbol of the "special cherub," the divine power revealed to the prophets that sits on the Throne of Glory.

SECTION 129

And what is that HOLY which is united and special?[1] This can be explained by a parable: A king had sons, and to his sons—grandsons. When the grandsons fulfill his wishes he enters among them and makes everything exist and provides them with food and pours goodness upon them, so that both the fathers and the sons will be satisfied. But when the grandsons do not fulfill his wishes he provides for no more than the needs of the fathers.[2]

Notes

1. This section is intended to explain the paradox of "united" and "special" (meaning here: separated). How can He be both simultaneously?
2. The parable, based on the theurgic element in Bahiric mysticism, explains that when the people of Israel (the "grandsons") fulfill God's wishes, the celestial powers and the people on earth are amply provided for by God and He is "united" with them. But if they do not, God gives the celestial powers

(the "sons") the minimum they need, and the earthly people are punished by God's being "special," remote and separated.

SECTION 130

And what is THE WHOLE EARTH IS FULL OF HIS GLORY? It is all that land which was created in the first day, which is above, corresponding to the Land of Israel, full of the divine Glory.[1] And what is it? Wisdom, as it is written: "Honor (*kavod*, Glory) of the wise will inherit" (Proverbs 3:35),[2] and it is said: "Blessed be the Glory of God from Its place" (Ezekiel 3:12).[3]

Notes
1. The author interprets the verse in Genesis 1:1 as referring to a previous, celestial creation of the heavenly Land of Israel.
2. According to the verse from Proverbs, the "Glory" is the lot of the wise (using the double meaning of the Hebrew *kavod*: both honor and Glory, therefore the essence of the Glory is wisdom, and it fills up the celestial Land of Israel.
3. The author introduces here the verse from Ezekiel, which is part of the *qedushah*, probably to denote that the remote place of the Glory ("from Its place") is the celestial Land of Israel. The same verse is the subject of the next sections.

SECTION 131

And what is this divine Glory? This can be explained by a parable: A king had a great lady in his room.[1] She was loved by all his knights, and she had sons.[2] They all came every day to see the face of the king, and they blessed him. They asked him: "Our mother, where is she?" He said to them: "You cannot see her now." They said: "Blessed is she wherever she is."[3]

Notes
1. The *matronita'*, "great lady," is the divine Glory. It is doubtful whether this parable can be understood to hint at the feminine nature of the *kavod*. The description of a lady is part of the parable, and does not necessarily reflect accurate symbolism.
2. The distinction between knights and sons refers to the belief that the *qedushah*

is said both by angels (as attested by Isaiah) and by the praying Jews. The first are the knights, while the sons are the people praying in the synagogue.

3. This parable explains the traditional interpretation of the verse from Ezekiel (found also in BT Ḥagigah 14b). The angels and the people do not know the place of the Glory, and they praise it wherever it is. The next section, however, gives a completely different meaning to this verse.

SECTION 132

What is the meaning of that which is written FROM ITS PLACE?[1] Because no one knows Its place. This is like a king's daughter who came from afar, and nobody knew where she came from. When they saw that she was a fine lady, beautiful and just in all that she did,[2] they said: "She undoubtedly was taken from the side of the light, for her deeds give light to the world."[3] They then asked her: "Where are you from?" She answered: "From my place." They said: "If so, the people of your place must be great! Blessed are you and blessed is your place!"

Notes

1. The meaning of "from Its place" in this parable is exactly the opposite of that in the previous one (131). Here the Glory itself is known and present among the people (unlike the hiding *matronita'* in 131), only her place of origin is hidden. They bless the princess in her presence, and they refer to her origin by "wherever she comes from."

2. While the feminine description of the *kavod* in the previous section does not necessarily denote a specific symbol, here it seems that the use of a princess instead of a prince (especially as she is not described as a mother) seems to convey a notion of the feminine nature of the *kavod/shekhinah*.

3. The Gnostic character of the Bahiric symbolism is apparent here more than in almost all other sections of the book. The picture of the "daughter of light," in exile in the material world, representing her hidden, unknowable place of origin "on the side of the light" is a stark Gnostic one.

SECTION 133

But is not this divine Glory one of God's hosts? Why is it the subject of a special blessing?[1] This can be explained by a parable: A man had a beautiful garden, and outside the garden but very near to it there was a beautiful piece of land, a field. He planted a garden there. When he watered his garden, the water flowed over the whole garden but did not reach that piece of land, which is not united, even though it is all one.[2] Therefore he opened a place for it, and watered it separately.[3]

Notes
1. The question here is: Why do we include in the prayers Ezekiel's verse, and thus give a separate blessing to, the Glory? Is the Glory not united with God, and does not the blessing to God (of Isaiah 6:3) include the Glory as well? After the question the text includes two words (*lo' gara'*, "nothing is missing"), which is not clear and was therefore left out of the translation.
2. The parable seems to return to the terminology of "united and special" in 128–129. The garden is the fullness of the divine powers, symbolized by the Supreme Crown and the root of the Tree, while the third part is united, but outside, this framework, and therefore needs the separate blessing of Ezekiel 3:12.
3. The term "from Its place" receives here its third explanation: From the special place God opened to provide for the Glory independently from the other powers in the garden.

SECTION 134

Rabbi Reḥumai said: "*Glory* and *Heart* are one,[1] but the Glory is called by a name corresponding to a celestial action, while heart is called by a name corresponding to a lower one. But they are one and the same—the Glory of God is the same as the heart of heaven.[2]

Notes
1. The numerical value of the Hebrew letters by which these two words, *kavod* (K-B-V-D) and *lev* (L-B; "heart"), are written is the same: 32. This denotes that they must represent the same secret.
2. The Glory is, therefore, the celestial counterpart of the "heart" in the lower realms of creation. It seems that the author refers to the opening paragraph of the *Sefer Yeṣirah*, which describes the creation by 32 "paths," often called *lev*.

SECTION 135

Rabbi Yoḥanan said: "What is the meaning of that which is written: 'When Moses lifted his hand Israel was victorious, and when he dropped it Amalek became more powerful' (Exodus 17:11)?[1] This is to teach that the world exists because of the lifting of the hands in prayer, in the priest's benediction. Why? Because of that power which was given to our patriarch Jacob, whose name is Israel."[2]

Abraham, Isaac, and Jacob were given powers, one to each one of them, and it was given to each of them according to the character of his ways. Abraham performed acts of Lovingkindness to the whole world, for he used to invite all the people of the world and all the passers-by on the roads, provide them with food and run to welcome them, as is written: "And he ran toward them" (Genesis 18:2), and it is written: "and he bowed down to the earth" (ibid.). This was a perfect act of Lovingkindness, and God bestowed upon him according to his measure and gave him the measure of Lovingkindness, as it is written: "You shall give Truth to Jacob and Lovingkindness to Abraham which you swore to our forefathers in ancient days" (Micah 7:20).

What is the meaning of IN ANCIENT DAYS? This is to teach that if Abraham had not performed acts of Lovingkindness and not merited the measure (middah)[3] of Lovingkindness, Jacob would not have merited the measure of Truth,[4] for it is because Abraham was worthy of the measure of Lovingkindness that Isaac merited the measure of Fear, as it is written: "And Jacob swore in the fear of his father Isaac" (Genesis 31:53).[5] Is there a man who will swear in this way in the faith of his father's fear? But at that point Jacob did not yet receive his own power, so he swore by the power which was given to his father, as it is said: AND HE SWORE IN THE FEAR OF HIS FATHER ISAAC.

And what is [Isaac's fear]? This is the tohu[6] from which the evil which confuses (ha-mathe') people proceeds. And what is it? It is that about which is written: "And fire fell and burnt the sacrifice and the wood and the stones and the earth and the water which were in the canal it touched" (1 Kings 18:38), and it is written: "For your God is a consuming fire, a jealous God" (Deuteronomy 4:24).[7]

Notes
1. The homilist returns here, after dedicating a detailed discussion to the qed-ushah, to his original theme—the priest's benediction, and deals with the historical episode in which the power of prayer and the raising of hands were most clearly demonstrated.

2. The term "Israel" here is clearly symbolical, referring to a divine force that was awarded to Jacob when his name was changed.
3. The author uses here the term *middah*, which has many meanings. It is an ethical characteristic, but it is also a measurement, and also a divine attribute. In Kabbalistic literature the term is sometimes used for the divine emanations more often than the term *sefirot*.
4. The author emphasizes the correspondence between what Abraham did and what he received. Abraham, like Isaac and Jacob, is treated here as both the ancient father with his specific personal characteristics, and as a manifestation of divine attributes that were given to him and that he comes to represent, following the Bahir, throughout Jewish mystical literature. Abraham, Isaac, and Jacob are consistently described in Kabbalistic literature as the symbols of the three divine emanations, the fourth—Lovingkindness; the fifth—Justice or Fear; and the sixth—Truth or Mercy.
5. According to the author, Abraham did not only win the *middah* for himself, but because of his righteous deeds Isaac and Jacob became worthy to receive theirs.
6. The term *tohu* is explained in the Bahir consistently as the material realm from which evil emerges. In section 11 it is evil, the opposite of peace, and it is repeated in section 12. In section 2 it is described as that which is nothing, probably referring to the Aristotelian description of the relationship between form and matter, when matter does not exist by its own right, only in combination with specific form. It is probable that the Bahir derived this homiletical interpretation of Genesis 1:2 from Rabbi Abraham Bar Hiyya, a twelfth-century philosopher and scientist in Spain.
7. The verses quoted explain "fear" as "fire," which is both the essence of God and the terrifying tool He uses to burn his enemies in the world.

SECTION 136

And what is Lovingkindness? It is the Torah, as it is written: "All who are thirsty go to the water" (Isaiah 55:1).[1] And to him who does not have money, it is money, as it is written: "Go and take and eat, go and take it without money and without price, wine and milk" (ibid.). He will feed you and teach you Torah for you already have become worthy of it because of the merit of Abraham who used to do charitable deeds, and used to feed without pay and give drinks of *wine* and *milk* free of charge.[2]

Notes

1. After explaining the essence of Isaac's fear, the mystical homilist identifies Abraham's charity with the Torah.

2. In this section it may seem that the subject is actual food, but the next section explains the symbolic meaning of the terms used here.

SECTION 137

What are wine and milk? And what is the connection between them? This is to teach us that the wine is Fear, and the milk is Lovingkindness. Why did he mention wine first? Because it is nearer to us.[1] Do you really think they are wine and milk? But it is the image of wine and milk. And because of the worthiness of Abraham who won the measure of Lovingkindness, Isaac won the measure of Fear. And because Isaac was worthy of the measure of Fear, Jacob won the measure of Truth, which is the measure of Peace.[2]

And God gave Jacob a measure which is his own measure, as it is written (Genesis 25:27), "And Jacob was innocent and dwelt in tents." "Innocent" means Peace, as it is written (Deuteronomy 18:13): "You should be innocent with your God." This verse is translated as: "You should be in Peace." "Innocent" means the Torah, as it is written (Malachi 2:6): "Torah of Truth was in his mouth." And what is written after that? "In peace and justice he went with me," and "justice" is really peace, as it is written: "Innocence and Justice" (Psalms 28:21).

This is why: "When Moses raised his hand Israel was victorious." It teaches us that the measure called Israel includes in it *the Torah of Truth*.[3]

Notes
1. In the usual order of the divine emanations in the Kabbalah, Lovingkindness, which is the fourth emanation, comes before Fear, which is the fifth. Since the order is reversed in the verse the homilist comments on, he has to explain the changing of the order.
2. The interrelationship between the patriarchs is presented here, symbolically, as the process of emanation from the fourth down to the sixth divine manifestation. The symbols of Torah, Truth, Peace, and Justice are the basic ones in the Bahir and in later Kabbalah for the sixth and central divine power (called *tif'eret*, "Beauty," by the Kabbalists in Provence and Spain). Jacob and Israel are its biblical names in this tradition.
3. In the conclusion of this section the author joins together the homily on the patriarchs with the central theme of this part of the Bahir—the power of the priest's benediction and the raising of hands. The connection is that "Israel"

is understood to represent the divine power, which, when addressed by Moses' raising of his hands (when Moses represents the Torah), is strengthened and causes victory.

SECTION 138

And what is *the Torah of Truth?*[1] This is that power which represents the truth of the worlds, and He operates by Thought.[2] And He gives existence to ten Utterances by which the world exists, and He is one of them.[3] And He created in man ten fingers on the hands to correspond to the ten Utterances, and when Moses raised his hands with the minimum[4] of his heart's intention to that measure which is called Israel in which there is the true Torah, and points out to Him his ten fingers to signify that he makes the ten exist, and if He will not assist the people of Israel the ten Utterances will not exist every day—this is why Israel was victorious. And when Moses let his hand down Amalek would win. Did Moses cause Amalek to win, as it is written "When he let his hands down Amalek would be victorious" (Exodus 13:11)? But it is forbidden for a person to stay for three hours with his hands turned toward heaven.[5]

Notes

1. This section concludes the homily and combines its central elements, especially those of the three (elements of prayers, patriarchs) and those of ten (fingers, utterances).
2. The true Torah, probably still referring to the sixth *sefirah*, is in the center of existence and governs all the divine powers, using the force of Thought, which is the supreme divine emanation.
3. The theme of the ten Utterances was originally presented in Rabbinic literature as the ten occurrences in Genesis 1:1 in which God created by speech ("Let there be light", etc.), and by these ten the whole world was created. See Mishnah Pirqey Avot 5:1. In the Bahir, as in later Kabbalah, these Utterances were identified with the ten divine emanations.
4. The word *mi'ut* (minimum) is difficult in this context.
5. The source of this dictum of the Bahir, which forbids prayer with outstretched hands for more than three hours, is unclear.

Rabbi Isaac the Blind of Provence

INTRODUCTION

The following two texts are ultimately derived from the school of Rabbi Isaac the Blind, though the second text has been attributed to a variety of real and fictional authors.

"The Mystical Torah—Kabbalistic Creation," presented as an interpretation of Midrash Konen, has never been published, and is translated from a manuscript found in the Jewish Theological Seminary, Enelow Collection no. 699.

"The Process of Emanation," cast as a running commentary to the first chapter of the book of Genesis, was published by J. Dan in *Qabbalat R. Asher ben David* (Jerusalem, 1979): 52–55.

The Mystical Torah—Kabbalistic Creation

LEGEND: It is written, "God by wisdom founded the earth" (Proverbs 3:19). Wisdom *(ḥokhmah)* is nothing other than Torah. It is called Torah due to the number of its commandments.[1] Also, its name was Amon before the world was created, as it is written, "I was by him, as an architect *(amon)*" (Proverbs 8:30). And if you were to say that the Torah was [written] on something or other: on a tree?—it had not yet been created; or parchment?—it had not yet been created; or silver or gold?—they had not yet been created. If this be the case, then on what was the Torah [inscribed]? The Sages, may their memory be blessed, said: The world was created in the right side of the Holy One, blessed be He, as it says, "But He is unchangeable, and who can turn Him?" (Job 23:13). What did He do? He took the Torah and drew from it a single name, and drew therefrom three droplets of water . . . and due to [His] abundant love for Israel, He gave them the Torah.

*   *   *

Up to this point is the text of the legend that I found, and what follows is its commentary written next to it.

IN THE RIGHT SIDE OF THE HOLY ONE, BLESSED BE HE, was engraved all the inscriptions which were destined to change from potentiality to actuality, due to the emanation of all the crowns which are inscribed, pressed, and formed in the degree of Lovingkindness (ḥesed).[2] Its image is inward and esoteric, beyond all scrutiny. Thus it is called the beginning of the thought of the Torah, and it includes the Torah of Lovingkindness. In general, all the engravings which are inscribed on it are of two types. The image of the first engraving is the Written Torah and the other image is the Oral Torah. The image of the Written Torah is of the colors of a white-hot fire, while the image of the Oral Torah is the color of a kind of black fire. And all the engravings and even the very Torah which encompasses them all existed in potentia and were not visible, neither spiritually nor sensibly visible. But then the Will arrived which awakened Thought (maḥshavah)[3] into actuality by means of primordial Wisdom and hidden Knowledge (daʿat).

Prior to any action there existed [this] Torah—which is the right arm [of God]—encompassing all the impressed inscriptions hidden therein. This is what he meant to say: The Holy One, blessed be He, TOOK the primordial TORAH, which is derived from the quarry of repentance[4] and from the source of Wisdom. He emanated by spiritual activity this encompassing Torah to render permanent the foundations of the world from this very inscription, which is the beginning of the emanation of the Holy One, blessed be He. When [this encompassing Torah] was actualized, HE DREW FROM IT A SINGLE NAME. He hewed from it one name whose essence and name are from one quarry and one essence and He called it by one spiritual name, [and that name is] Lovingkindness.

Afterward, HE DREW FROM IT A SINGLE NAME. This means that the Holy One, blessed be He, emanated from the quarry of the primordial Torah a different name, an emanation divided into three [further] emanations. Put another way, He brought forth from the degree of Lovingkindness one power which divides into three forces, a single emanation which expands and transforms itself into three names by the power of '-M-SH and M-SH-'.[5] By means of the image of permutation these were called THREE DROPLETS OF WATER which trickle from the source of Lovingkindness. And these [three] are: Ḥasdiʾel transformed to Saḥdiʾel transformed to Dashiʾel.[6]

Every occurrence of the term "drawing forth" (N-Ṭ-L) with regard to this matter is a term of emanation and lifting, like the meaning in "And he took them and lifted them" (Isaiah 63:9). And when, at the beginning of the legend, it says, "He is One who sits on His throne," it is a hint to Wisdom, which resembles the image of a king sitting upon his throne. Afterward the proof text "But He is One" (Job 23:13) is cited in order to teach about Understanding *(binah)*, which is brought forth from the emanation of the two utterly inner grades of Thought and Wisdom. This is the statement BUT HE IS ONE.[7]

I will resume interpreting the legend. He brought forth a second name—this is a second grade which is the mammoth inferno called the attribute Strength *(gevurah)*.[8] He drew from it three droplets of fire—this means he brought forth from Strength three powers similar to three flames of fire. It is the image of one force dividing into two forces: Shalhavi'el transformed to Halshavi'el.[9] From one force was created the Holy Hosts, whose sweat is fire. And from the second force the fire of Gehenna came forth. And from the third force— [a force] that was not as strongly burning as the first two for blended in it was the power of the element of water—from this [third force] was created the heavens composed of fire and water so that the world not be engulfed in flames.[10]

He drew forth a third name, called the image of the Written Torah, and it is the hue of a white fire. He brought forth from it three droplets of one light which divided and transformed itself into three powers of light: Urpani'el changed to Pani'uri'el changed to Re'upani'el.[11] From the first light the throne of Glory was created. This throne itself is a throne to the upper Throne and in it is encompassed all the crowns which are below the upper Throne of Glory, established on the basis of Lovingkindness, Strength, and Mercy *(rahamim)*. From the second light the world to come was created, a world of Severity *(din)* and Mercy, these being the qualities of Kingdom *(malkhut)*, where punishment and reward are found. From the third light this world was created.[12]

This first light is a light which glitters and explodes into the last throne of Glory, which contains three types of luminaries—or say three crowns—the Foundation *(yesod)* of the world, Endurance *(nesah)*, and Majesty *(hod)*. Now this light is a light which comes and goes, glittering from the crown of Mercy, at times revealed and at times concealed.

The World to Come, which we have already stated is the world of Severity—either as punishment or as reward, is the crown of Kingdom, the Oral Torah. It is the hue of a black fire on white fire, which is the Written Torah. Now the forms of the letters are not vowelized nor are they shaped except through the power of black, which is like ink. So too the Written Torah is unformed in a physical image, except through the power of the Oral Torah. That is to say, one cannot be explained fully without the other.[13] So too, the attribute of Mercy is not comprehended nor seen except by means of the attribute Severity. Now the hues of the mark of black (which are the hues of the attribute of Severity) rise and expand and spread over the hues of white (which are the colors of the attribute of Mercy) that rise and cover the blackness. This is similar to the image of the light of a glowing ember, for the force in the colors of the flame rises and strengthens until the light of the ember is invisible due to the intensity of the flame which envelops it. When the colors of the flame increase and spread out one from another then the physical eye rules over the essence of the ember [by] physical, sensible sight.

So too [we find] that in the grade of the crown of Mercy the hues of the luminaries are absolutely hidden and secret. [These luminaries] surround [Mercy] with a great intensity so that [Mercy] is not perceived by any worldly creature. But with the advent of Will (rason), the shades of blackness are weakened and dissipated and dispersed from the unreflecting mirror above the white hues which illuminate and sparkle and shine like the splendor of a white sapphire.[14] Then a few of the prophets, peace be upon them, were able to perceive this splendor by means of the crown of Kingdom, each according to their merit: a spiritual perception and vision appropriate to each prophet. The shades of blackness which spread forth and sparkle from it are similar to the image of the flame which sparkles from the light of the ember, like the intensity of the hues of the small luminary in the midst of the intensely strong light of the sun, and [the small luminary] shines because of [the sun's] strength. It darkens the face of one who peers into it, and blinds anyone who persists and continues his gaze. And if he escapes the blindness by distancing himself from the rays of the sun, he [still] cannot see the light of the ether until he calms down and rests nearly an hour or two. And due to the abundant intensity of its light and splendor, it is called the reflecting mirror. It illuminated the greatest of the prophets, peace be on him. For no other prophetic eye viewed it or united with it, save Moses our teacher, peace be upon him.[15]

And when it says that from three droplets the entire world was filled with water, so it is appropriate that all kinds of supernal waters are emanated from the [droplets], solidifying from their emanation by means of the ether which spreads over all the different lower waters. This is entirely akin to the Spirit of God which moves the [waters] and hovers above them. For it is known that the element of wind which permeates the ether surrounds the waters in order to press them down on the land. Therefore it is written, "And the Spirit of God hovered above the surface of the water" (Genesis 1:2).

When he saw light to the right and fire to the left, He called all that was emanated from the right side "light," and all that was emanated from the left side He called "fire." And this is the explanation: When the Holy One, blessed be He, saw the light which had emanated from the right side, the brilliance of the flaming light of the left side, and the splendor of the shining water below the hovering wind, He drew them together and combined them one to the other. He took fire and water and created from them the heavens; He took water and ether and created from them the Holy Hosts and the ministering angels. The force of their emanation is a brilliant and burning fire. And so it is written, "God by Wisdom founded the earth" (Proverbs 3:19). Wisdom in this instance is the Torah, which is also called a Torah of Lovingkindness.[16] By means of [the Torah] the living world and all that is below were emanated. "By understanding he established the Heavens" (Proverbs 3:19) signifies that by means of the Spirit of the living God the "heavens of God" (Psalms 115:16) were emanated. These [two heavens] are the upper heavens and the lower ones below them.

And, Wisdom *(H-K-M-H)* in numerology equals 73—the three powers which we mentioned as "droplets" and seventy holy Names [of God], each one capable of creating the world.[17]

AND DUE TO [HIS] ABUNDANT LOVE FOR ISRAEL HE GAVE THEM THE TORAH. And this is like, "For His love for us is great" (Psalms 117:2).

*   *   *

Up to this point I have acquired and found the interpretation of this legend, transmitted in the name of the venerable Rabbi Isaac, may his memory be blessed. And I do not know who he is.[18]

Notes

1. The Jewish tradition posits that there are 613 commandments in the Torah. The four letters of the Hebrew word Torah *(T-W-R-H)* have the numerical

value of 611. By adding to this sum two outstanding commandments, it then becomes possible to link the word Torah to the 613 commandments.

2. The sefirotic world is often described vertically as right side, left side, and middle pillar. The right side is linked with the *sefirah* Lovingkindness *(hesed)*, the left side, as we shall see, is linked with Strength/Severity *(gevurah/din)*, and the middle pillar is associated with Beauty or Mercy *(tif'eret or rahamim)*.

3. Isaac the Blind uses the term *Thought* for the most supernal *sefirah*, which in later Kabbalistic traditions became known as Crown *(keter)*. Isaac employs the word "crown" as a synonym for degree, attribute, and *sefirah*.

4. *Mahseb ha-teshuvah*, a reference to the *sefirah* Understanding *(binah)*.

5. These three letters ('-M-SH) are called the "three maternal letters" in the *Sefer Yesirah* 1:2, a cosmological work of unknown origin dating back at least to the sixth century C.E. From these three letters all the other letters and sounds of the Hebrew alphabet developed.

6. The three droplets of water are named after various permutations of the three-letter root for Lovingkindness, (H-S-D), based on the changing of the order of the three letters, like the changed order of '-M-SH and M-SH-'. The exact nature of the pattern is unclear.

7. Understanding is the ontologically third emanation, resulting from the inner workings of Thought and Wisdom.

8. The first name was drawn from Lovingkindness. From the antithesis of Lovingkindness—i.e., Strength—a second name was drawn forth. Strength is on the left side, and, in accordance with the imagery of severity, is associated with fire. (The more gentle Lovingkindness is associated with water.)

9. Angelic names based on a permutation of the four-letter root SH-L-H-V, meaning "flame."

10. Unclear. The combination of fire and water (= Strength and Lovingkindness) produces the synthesis of the heavens (usually associated with Beauty).

11. These angelic names are permutations of two words: "light" *('-W-R)* and "face" *(P-N)*.

12. These three lights correspond to three levels of creation. The first light brings forth a throne, resting on the *sefirot* Lovingkindness, Strength, and Mercy. This throne is in all likelihood *binah*, "Understanding." The second light brings forth the world to come, usually Foundation, here linked to Kingdom. The third light brings forth the physical "this-world" of creation.

13. The Written Torah is usually associated with Beauty/Mercy. From it a light was emanated, which formed the three "crowns" of Foundation, Endurance, and Majesty. The oral Torah is linked with Kingdom, and secondarily with Severity and the world to come. The two Torahs, both juridically and mystically, are intertwined.

14. Here we see the release and freedom that the divine flow exerts on the lower, entrapped *sefirot*.

15. The sun is associated with Mercy, and the Moon with Kingdom. Also, Mercy is known as "the unreflecting mirror"; while Kingdom/Moon, re-

flecting the light of the sun, is called "the reflecting mirror." Prophecy comes through being illuminated by these spiritual lights.

16. Cf. Proverbs 31:26.
17. On the rabbinic tradition of the seventy Names of God, see *Numbers Rabbah* 14:24.
18. Of course, this "Rabbi Isaac" is none other than Rabbi Isaac the Blind.

The Process of Emanation

IN THE BEGINNING *(Be-re'shit)*: The letter *bet* is the most elevated Crown *(keter)*, and therefore this *bet* is larger than all other *bets*.[1] The word "beginning" *(re'shit)* is in fact Wisdom *(ḥokhmah)*. In truth, then, two *sefirot* are encompassed in one word.

From whence do we know that Wisdom is called "beginning"? It states: "The *beginning* of *wisdom* is the fear of the Lord" (Psalms 111:10). With both Crown and Wisdom He created THE HEAVENS AND THE EARTH—that is: Beauty *(tif'eret)* and Diadem *('atarah)*. He also created the [two] *'ets*, and these are the supernal powers which are Lovingkindness *(ḥesed)* and Fear *(paḥad)*.[2] All of creation is summarized in this. Afterward, he explained the entire matter, beginning with the result of creation, Diadem, through which the entire Structure is made complete. And it states:

AND THE EARTH WAS UNFORMED AND VOID *(tohu va-bohu)*: Earth is Diadem. Before it was emanated from the Cause of causes, it was *tohu*, something that is astounding *(mathe')*, for it has nothing substantial within it, nor does it possess any form. But when it was emanated it then became a substance more ethereal than Spirit.

VOID *(bohu)*: This means "in it" *(bo)*—when it was emanated, something substantial was made in it. And our Rabbis, may their memories be blessed, explained that these [two] are called collectively "the foundation stone."[3]

80

RABBI ISAAC

AND DARKNESS OVER THE SURFACE OF THE
DEEP: This is the depth of above and the depth of below.[4]

AND A WIND FROM GOD SWEEPING OVER THE
WATER: Wisdom envelops everything, as in "sweeping over her
young" (Deuteronomy 32:11).

OVER THE WATER: Everything was called water, for Lovingkindness—the summit of five *sefirot*[5]—is water. More precisely,
[Wisdom] is the power of water, for water pours forth from its overflow.

GOD *(Elohim)* SAID, "LET THERE BE LIGHT." GOD—
This is Repentance *(teshuvah)*.[6] And thus he, may his memory be
blessed, said: "To wrap oneself—to wrap oneself in a prayer shawl,
and this means to wrap oneself in Wisdom."[7] And it states:

LET THERE BE LIGHT: This means Beauty, for the Torah
came forth from Wisdom.[8] From Nothing *(me-ayin)* spread forth the
thirty-two paths which stem from Wisdom. These [paths] are the
source and the derivatives of the Torah and all other sciences.

And He wraps Himself [with the Torah] and peers into it and
builds worlds and destroys worlds. He saw that all things were hidden and He said, "Let all these things expand from potentiality to
actuality, that they be actuated and uncovered," "they" being the
now actualized Beauty and Diadem.

AND THERE WAS LIGHT: It does not say "and it was so"
as in the case with all other created things,[9] because in the rest of
creation essences were emanated which themselves formed essences
but not forms. But here forms were developed. For this reason the
light of Beauty and Diadem is incomparable to the supernal light,
because when it states LET THERE BE LIGHT it refers to Beauty
and Diadem. And from this particular light spread forth all essences
and entities. Also, [God] utilized the light of Beauty and Diadem
until the fourth day, but He foresaw that the world could not endure
this light, due to [the light's] abundant merit. He therefore set it aside
for the righteous people of the future. This light is sevenfold more
intense than all the other luminaries of light, and thus it states: "And
the light of the moon shall become like the light of the sun; and the
light of the sun shall become sevenfold, like the light of the seven
days" (Isaiah 30:26).

AND GOD SAW THE LIGHT THAT IT WAS GOOD
(tov): This is derived from "when he tends *(be-hetivo)* the lamps" (Exodus 30:7). The matter is ignited as if one lights a candle one from

81

the other. Thereby He grants a power to the essences to expand and draw forth.

AND GOD SEPARATED THE LIGHT FROM THE DARKNESS: He delimited to each one the extent of their expansion and extension. And thus:

GOD CALLED THE LIGHT DAY: He likened the masculine power—which is Beauty—to the day; and so Diadem—which is feminine—to the night. Furthermore, neither became manifest until their effects came forth and the world was created.

LET THERE BE A FIRMAMENT IN THE MIDST OF THE WATER: This is Lovingkindness. Now we have already said that the water is from the overflow of Lovingkindness and from the FIRMAMENT. Likewise, Beauty in the midst of the water contains water which is Lovingkindness, part above and part below. Thus the order of all things can be likened to the skins of onions. For our Sages, may their memories be blessed, said that just as there is the divine Presence above, so too is the divine Presence below; and all things are like the skins of onions.[10] What they mean is this: Each attribute emanates [downward] and accepts from that which stands above it. Therefore Solomon said, "For one high official is protected by a higher one, and both of them by still higher ones" (Ecclesiastes 5:7).[11] Therefore I have written that each attribute mutually lends to the other, as is written: "A good man lends with a good grace" (Psalms 112:5). And it is at this moment that the endeavor [of creation] began.

AND GOD MADE FROM THE FIRMAMENT: He began to sketch within Beauty the form of space and limit, but He did not make material space like a man who would clear away an area in order to construct a building. And Scripture does not say regarding [the firmament] "for it was good" because Thought (*mahshavah*) had not finished [its work] until it had cleared away space for Diadem, which is the *nun*.[12]

On the third day [of creation], He said the verse LET THE DRY LAND BE SEEN. This is feminine, as it states: "It is not good for man to be by himself" (Genesis 2:18), and "man" is none other than Beauty.

AND GOD CALLED THE DRY LAND EARTH: The Will (*rason*), which is the furthest extension of Thought—the Supernal Crown that no one can comprehend—was drawn to the dry land, which is feminine. For the meaning of "dry land" is something which cannot bear fruit. It could not bear fruit until "man" was created so that he could draw the furthest reaches of Thought to [the land]. And this is the rule for all things. It is akin to what the Sages, may their memories be blessed, said: "The depth of the beginning and the depth of the end,"[13] meaning the beginning of Wisdom and its depth.

Put another way—highest Crown is above it. The "end" is feminine and thus our Rabbis, may their memories be blessed, said: "The entire world was created exclusively for the sake of Israel,"[14] and this means "due to the merit of Israel"—because of the unique qualities inherent in Israel. For [Israel] receives the divine overflow from the very root, core, and trunk of the Tree—from the middle pillar which draws from the branches.

AND THE GATHERING OF WATER HE CALLED SEAS: The middle pillar draws from the Source to Beauty like the spinal cord draws from the brain. This is similar to "All the streams flow to the sea" (Ecclesiastes 1:7). All the channels are drawn forth from Beauty to Diadem by way of the Foundation of the world (*yesod 'olam*), which is the Righteous One (*saddiq*), as in "For there shall be the seed of peace; [the vine shall give her fruit, and the ground shall yield its increase, and the heavens shall give their dew, and I will cause the remnant of this people to possess all things]" (Zachariah 8:12).[15]

LET THE EARTH BEAR GRASS: As it says—the setting aside of space for Diadem so it could shower abundance on all generations.

LET THERE BE LIGHTS: These are shapeless entities without form, and the overflow of the activities of Beauty and Diadem became visible. Therefore they are called "great [lights]" (Genesis 1:15), for they are the first [things] in history. Beauty is called the greater light and Diadem the smaller light. Now they were the first in history—this means they were the first of five material *sefirot*,[16] and in the fifth—

LET THE WATERS SWARM: It is the seed of the world; that is to say, "Let the supernal waters emanate by way of Beauty and Diadem."

SWARMS OF LIVING CREATURES: These are all the supernal forms derived from Beauty and Diadem and therefore He blessed them. And this is akin to the blessing that accepts from above and then descends to the lower realms.

AND LET THE FOWL FLY ABOVE THE EARTH: This

is the commissioning of Lovingkindness and Fear for Beauty and Diadem. This is the meaning of AND LET FOWL FLY ABOVE THE EARTH—let each one emanate from its respective power to Beauty and Diadem.

AND GOD CREATED THE GREAT SEA-MONSTERS: These are the four hosts of the divine Presence—Michael, Gabriel, Rafael, and Uriel. Until this [verse] the term "creation" had not been used. But from this point onward the world of separate entities begins. [The world of separate entities] is the separate intellects—the angels—and the living soul within the angels which is the ever-ascending Spirit.

WHEREWITH THE WATERS SWARMED, EACH TO ITS KIND: This is Lovingkindness. For we have already stated that water comes from the overflow of Lovingkindness. Those powers that receive from [Lovingkindness] must receive this overflow in accordance with each of their respective activities.

AND FILL THE EARTH: This is feminine, as it is stated: "in a stomach that is filled" (Ecclesiastes 11:5). All the channels are drawn to her and from her they are actualized.

AND LET THE FOWL MULTIPLY UPON THE EARTH: Included are all the powers which are drawn forth from Diadem. On the sixth day the Structure was completed in perfection, as it is stated, "In our form and in our image" (Genesis 1:26). This symbolizes the completion of the Structure so that it may bear fruit. This is what is meant by "Which God had created so it may do" (Genesis 2:3). Up to this point throughout the six days of creation the name *YHVH* had not been mentioned, for the ten *sefirot* are implicit in it. The letter *yod* (י) alludes to Wisdom and the coronet alludes to Crown. The first *H* alludes to Understanding *(binah)*. The *V* alludes to Beauty along with the six extremities, while the final *H* is a sign for Diadem.[17] Now how could the Tetragrammaton be mentioned before the completion of the Structure? Therefore the Sages, may their memories be blessed, said: "From IN THE BEGINNING to THEY WERE COMPLETED—'It is the glory of God to conceal a thing' (Proverbs 25:2); but henceforth—'Search out a matter' (ibid)."[18] These are Beauty and Diadem. Thus it is stated: "And on the seventh day He rested, and was refreshed" (Exodus 31:17). The soul extended into the body and the powers were formed and finalized. Then history began, as we already explained. And Scripture then continues THESE ARE THE GENERATIONS OF THE

HEAVEN AND THE EARTH—instead of "heaven and earth" read Beauty and Diadem.

AND BEHOLD, IT WAS VERY GOOD: On all the other days Scripture states that "it was good" (Genesis 10:4, 10, 12, 18, 21, 25), because on all the other days the illumination of Beauty and Diadem and their drawing forth continued to shine, for they are the furthest reaches of Thought. Finally, on the sixth day IT WAS VERY GOOD. The start of the matter is implicit in its end, for [the word] "very" *(me'od)* is Wisdom.

AND THE HEAVENS WERE COMPLETED *(va-yakhullu ha-shamayyim)* is derived from the word "bride" *(kallah)* and ornaments *(qishshurim).*[19]

A RIVER WENT OUT OF EDEN: Beauty comes forth from between Lovingkindness and Fear; from even higher, from supernal Wisdom.

TO WATER THE GARDEN: The garden is Diadem.

AND FROM THENCE IT WAS PARTED: The *sefirot* continue until Diadem. Diadem is to be counted among them, unique but inseparable. But from then on the world of separate entities branches off.

AND THEY BRANCHED INTO FOUR STREAMS: These are the four hosts of the divine Presence which we have already mentioned. Here they are mentioned as they become actualized. Corresponding to them are the four dimensions: the dimension of the East, the dimension of the West, the dimension of the North, and the dimension of the South.[20]

Notes
1. The letter *bet* is the first letter of the word *be-re'shit* and hence the first letter of the Torah scroll. It is a traditional orthographic feature of the written scroll that this *bet* be larger than all other *bets*, and its unique size is seized on by Rabbi Isaac as an allusion to the first *sefirah*, called by him either Crown or Thought.
2. Preceding the words "the heavens" and "the earth" in the Hebrew text is the accusative preposition *'et*, which is untranslatable. Each *'et* is taken by Rabbi Isaac as a symbol for two further *sefirot*: Lovingkindness and Fear. The latter is subsequently referred to in the later Spanish Kabbalah as Strength or Severity.
3. Source unknown. For the "foundation stone," see BT Yoma' 54b; Sanhedrin 26b.
4. See *Sefer Yeṣirah* 1:5.

5. Wisdom is situated directly over Lovingkindness, which here is likened to water. It is "the summit of five *sefirot*," first to receive emanation among the five *sefirot* that constitute the Beauty and its retinue.
6. Repentance is a designation for the third *sefirah*.
7. Cf. *Genesis Rabbah* 3:4, ed. Albeck, p. 20.
8. Beauty is often linked with the Torah, especially the written Torah.
9. Cf. Genesis 1:7, 9, 11, 15, 24, 30.
10. See the *Bahir*, ed. Margoliot, section 161.
11. An often quoted verse used by Kabbalists to describe the layered and unending nature of the emanative process.
12. The letter *nun*, in both its regular and final forms, is linked in classical Kabbalah with the tenth and lowest *sefirah*, Kingdom. For a summary of the Kabbalistic associations, see R. Moses Cordovero, *Pardes Rimmonim* (Munkacs, 1906), 26:17.
13. *Sefer Yesirah* 1:5.
14. See L. Ginzberg, *Legends of the Jews*, vols. 1:50 and 5:67.
15. This verse establishes the relationship between Beauty ("heavens") and Diadem ("ground"), with Foundation ("the seed of peace") as catalyst.
16. Between Beauty and Diadem there stand three other *sefirot*, making a total of five. What *sefirot gufaniyyot* indeed means is unclear.
17. The Tetragrammaton *(YHVH)* alludes to the entire sefirotic Tree. The "six extremities" are Beauty and the five *sefirot* directly surrounding it.
18. See *Genesis Rabbah* 9:1.
19. Rabbi Isaac understands "was completed" as "was joined to the bride." The heavens, a symbol for masculine Beauty, was wedded with the feminine bride Diadem. The meaning of "ornaments" in this context may have something to do with the decorations worn by a bride. The precise connection between *qishshurim* and the verse is unclear.
20. A second manuscript witness reads "king" *(melekh)* instead of "dimension" *(meshekh)*. In either case, the four represent the *sefirot* interlinked with the Presence.

Rabbi Azriel of Gerona

INTRODUCTION

The "Explanation of the Ten Sefirot" translated below was published as a prolegomenon to Meir Ibn Gabbai's *Sefer Derekh Emunah* in Warsaw (1850, pages 3–9). The translation is based on this printed edition, with corrections from the most reliable manuscript witness, ms. Milano, Bernheimer 53, B1, folios 113a–117b.

The *Commentary to Talmudic Legends* was published as *Perush ha-Aggadot le-Rav 'Azri'el* by I. Tishby (Jerusalem, 1943). "Amen" is found on pages 23–26 of that edition; "Wisdom and the Elements" is taken from pages 86–91.

Explanation of the Ten Sefirot

1. If a questioner asks: Who can compel me to believe that the world has a Ruler?

   Answer: Just as it is inconceivable that a ship be without a captain, so too is it impossible that the world be without a ruler. This Ruler is infinite *(eyn sof)* in both His Glory and Word, as in the matter that is written: "I have seen an end to every purpose, but Your commandment is exceedingly immense" (Psalms 119:96), and it is written: "For God shall bring every act into judgment—every *hidden* thing whether good or bad" (Ecclesiastes 12:14). That which is *hidden* is without end and limit; it is unfathomable and nothing exists outside it.

   The philosophers admit to this fact that the Cause of all causes and the Origin of origins is infinite, unfathomable, and without limit. According to the way of the Ruler we see that the end of every act is hidden from the probing of an investigator, as in the matter that is written: "So that no man can find out the work which God has made from the beginning to the end" (ibid. 3:11). And it is further recorded: "Should the wise man can say that he knows, even he will not be able to find it" (ibid. 8:17). . . .

2. If a questioner asks: Who can compel me to believe in Eyn-Sof?

   Answer: Know that everything visible and perceivable to human contemplation is limited, and that everything that is limited is finite, and that everything that is finite is insignificant. Conversely, that which is not limited is called Eyn-Sof and is absolutely undifferentiated in a complete and changeless unity. And if He is [truly] without limit, than nothing exists outside Him. And since He is both exalted and hidden, He is the essence of all that is concealed and revealed. But since He is hidden, He is both the root of faith and the root of rebelliousness. Regarding this it is written: "In his faith a righteous man shall live" (Habakkuk 2:4). Furthermore, the philosophers are in agreement with these statements that our perception of Him cannot be except by way of negative attribution.[1] And that which radiates forth from Eyn-Sof are the ten *sefirot*. [And this is sufficient for the enlightened.]

3. If the questioner persists: By what necessity do you arrive at the assertion that the *sefirot* exist? I rather say that they do not exist and that there is only Eyn-Sof!

Answer: Eyn-Sof is perfection without any imperfection. If you propose that He has unlimited power and does not have finite power, then you ascribe imperfection to His perfection. And if you claim that the first limited being that is brought into existence from Him is this world—lacking in perfection—then you ascribe imperfection to the force which stems from Him.

Since we should never ascribe imperfection to His perfection, we are compelled to say that He has a finite power which is unlimited. The limitation first existentiated from Him is the *sefirot*, for they are both a perfect power and an imperfect power. When they partake of the abundant flow stemming from His perfection they are perfected power, and when the abundant flow is withdrawn they possess imperfect power. Thus, they are able to function in both perfection and imperfection, and perfection and imperfection differentiate one thing from another.

Now if you were to claim that He alone willed the creation of the world without [recourse to] the *sefirot*, the response to this [assertion] is that the intention indicates an imperfection in the intender. Alternatively, if you claim He did not intend His creation—if such were the case, then creation was a random accident. All things which are the outcome of a random accident have no order. Yet we witness that creation is ordered, with the sun during the day and the moon and stars at night. They exist by an order and by order they are generated and pass away. This order by which they exist and pass away is called the *sefirot*, for they are the force behind every existent being in the realm of plurality. Since the existentiation of created beings is brought about by means of the *sefirot*, each one differs one from the other: some are elevated, some are lowly, while others are intermediate. This is the case despite the fact that they are all derived from one principle. Every being is from Eyn-Sof, and nothing exists outside of Him.

4. If the questioner persists and asks: Agreed, you have demonstrated the necessity of *sefirot;* but by what [argument] do you establish that they are ten and yet one power?

Answer: I have already informed you that the *sefirot* are the beginning and commencement of all that is subject to limitation. Everything subject to limitation is bounded by substance and place, for there is no substance without place and there is no place except by means of substance. There is at least a third force in substance, and this third force is manifest in length, width, and depth: Thus there are nine. Since substance cannot exist without place and since there is no space except by means of substance, the number is not complete regarding substance and place with anything less than ten. Thus it states: "ten and not nine."[2] And since we cannot complete the number without taking into account substance—itself bounded by substance and place—it states: "ten and not eleven."[3] Just as the three produce nine; the fourth—which is place—when added to the three, produces sixteen. But it is sufficient for us to use ten in order to hint to the fact that place is derived from substance, and substance is but one power.

5. If the inquirer continues to ask: How can you say that the *sefirot* are emanated? I say they were created like all the other created beings!

Answer: I have already informed you that Eyn-Sof is perfect without any imperfection, and that the agent which initially is brought forth from Him must also be perfect. Thus, the dynamic of emanation is fittingly the beginning of all creation, for the potency of emanation is the essence of the creation of all things. Had there been no emanative potency extracted form Eyn-Sof—lacking in nothing—how would we recognize the abundant perfection stemming from Eyn-Sof? How would the dynamic of the *sefirot* properly receive and subsequently circulate [the abundant flow] to all the needy beings without being diminished? For, when one draws from something in creation it is decreased and diminished. Since the *sefirot* are the first act existentiated from Eyn-Sof, it is appropriate that He be their dynamic, perfect without imperfection. Yet they are the ones who flow upon the impoverished, receiving from Eyn-Sof.

6. About this the inquirer persists: How can we possibly say that He is One and the multiplicity of ten unites within Him? By this we may preserve the truth in our hearts but certainly not in our statements.

Answer: I have already informed you that the One is the foundation of the many and that in the many no power is innovated—only in Him. He is more than them and each of them is superior to its antecedent, and the potency of one is in the other. Nevertheless, the first is the dynamic of all the others. Though this first is the dynamic of the other, it is not so specifically but only generally. The metaphor for this is the fire, the flame, the sparks, and the aura: They are all of one essence even though they are different one from the other and divisible into separate components.

7. If the inquirer persists after you have established that there are *sefirot* and that they are ten and they were emanated and not created and their multiplicity is derived from unity and asks: Now answer me, why should I [not] ascribe to them measure, limit, and corporeality?

Answer: I have already informed you that Eyn-Sof is perfection without imperfection, and that He has a finite power which is unlimited and that the limitation emanating from Him which delimits all existent beings is the *sefirot*, having the power to act in perfection and imperfection. Had He not existentiated for them limits, we would be unable to recognize that He has the power to existentiate limitation. As a testimony to the fact that nothing exists outside of Him, He brought into existence limitation, so that the confined beings could recognize their own boundaries. And though there are no limits above, the musings stemming from Eyn-Sof suggest that He is above and beyond extension in boundaries.

All that is limited, whether apprehended by the pondering of the heart or hinted at in thought extending below, can be found in speech and vision. Further, anything subject to limitation has magnitude and corporeality, because anything existent that is grasped by contemplation of the heart is called "body," not only spiritual things but even the *sefirot*. For they are [part of] the rule of all limited entities: They are the root of limitation. This limitation which is unlimited is emanated, and thus it states: "Their measure is ten without end."[4] Finally, the philosophers stated that man's intellect is finite, and that from the way of the Ruler we see that everything has limitation, magnitude, and measure.

8. If the inquirer continues: Now you must answer me—these *sefirot*, when did they come into existence? If you now answer me that they were almost contemporaneous with the creation of the world, then it may be countered: Why did He intend their emanation at that precise moment and not at some earlier point—would this not be a change of mind in Perfection? And if you answer that they are His eternality, then they would subsist in His undifferentiatedness; and if such were the case, what would be the difference between God and the *sefirot*?

Answer: Some of the *sefirot* existed in potentia within Eyn-Sof before they became actualized, like the first *sefirah* which is equal to all the others. There were some that were intelligible that were then emanated, like the second *sefirah* from which the preexistent Torah came forth. There were some that were perceived and some that were innate, such as those *sefirot* which were needed for this world and which were emanated almost contemporaneously with the creation of the world.

And since in the existentiation of the first two *sefirot* the hidden and intelligible powers [of the two] were totally intermingled, their reality nourished the other [*sefirot*]. As the Sages, may their memories be blessed, said, "Could not [the world] have been created with one statement?"[5]

As to your other question, "that they would subsist in His undifferentiatedness"—

Answer: Even though we should avoid coining metaphors regarding Eyn-Sof, in order to help you understand let us compare the matter to a candle. The candle lights a myriad of other candles. Each lit candle shines more, yet they are all equal in comparison to the first candle and they all derive from one principle. But one must not liken the latter to the former. Their phylogenesis should not be compared to His ontogenesis, for He is greater than them and their energy is brought forth from Him, because of His supra-preeminence. Furthermore, no change takes place in Him. Rather, the dynamic of emanation becomes revealed through the division of their existence. Thus, one cannot say that there was a change of mind in Him, even though nothing exists outside of Him.

9. If the questioner continues: What is the nature of [the *sefirot*]?

Answer: The nature of *sefirah* is the synthesis of every thing and its opposite. For, if they did not possess the power of synthesis, there would be no energy in anything. For that which is light is not-darkness and that which is darkness is not-light.

Therefore, we should liken their nature to the will of the soul, for it is the synthesis of all the desires and thoughts stemming from it. Even though they be multifarious, their source is one, either in thesis or antithesis. This is the case with every function of the soul: intellect, esthetics, love, and mercy—even though they are all [created] *ex nihilo*, their existence is not absolute.

But, by embellishing substance with imagination, we can liken the first power to the concealed light. The second power [can be likened] to the light which contains every color. This light is like *tekhelet*,[6] the essence *(takhlit)* of all colors in which there is no known hue. The third power [can be compared] to green light. The fourth power can be likened to white light. The fifth power can be likened to red light. The sixth power is composed of whiteness and scarlet. The seventh power is the power of scarlet tending toward whiteness. The eighth power is the power of whiteness tending toward scarlet. The ninth power is composed of whiteness and scarlet and scarlet tending toward whiteness and whiteness tending toward scarlet. The tenth power is composed of every color.

10. If the inquirer persists and asks: What are their names, their order, and their rank?

Answer: The name of the first power is Elevated Height *(rom ma'alah)*, for it is elevated above the probing of an investigator. The second is called Wisdom *(ḥokmah)*, for it is the beginning of conceptualization. The third is called Understanding *(binah)*. Up to this point is the world of intelligence *('olam ha-sekhel)*.

The fourth is called Lovingkindness *(ḥesed)*. The fifth is called Fear *(paḥad)*. The sixth is called Beauty *(tif'eret)*. Up to this point is the world of the soul *('olam ha-nefesh)*.

The seventh is called Victory *(nesaḥ)*. The eighth is called Majesty *(hod)*. The ninth is called the Righteous One, Foundation of the world *(saddiq yesod 'olam)*. The tenth is call Justice *(ṣedeq)*. Up to this point is the world of the body *('olam ha-guf)*.

Following is the order of their activity. The first is the divine power. The second is for angelic power. The third is for prophetic power. The fourth extends lovingkindness to the heights. The fifth passes judgment with the fear of His strength. The sixth has compassion in fear upon the lower worlds. The seventh nurtures and strengthens the vegetative soul. The eighth weakens and infirms it. The ninth draws together all their powers, sometimes for one purpose, sometimes for another. The tenth is the lower attribute of severity. It is composed of the power of all the others in order to judge the lower worlds.

The energy of the human soul is drawn from them and their powers in the following way:

Elevated Height exists as the power of that soul which is called "only one" *(yeḥidah)*; Wisdom exists in the soul as the animative soul; Understanding exists in the power of spirit; Fear in the power called "animus" *(neshamah)*; Beauty in the power of blood; Victory in the power of bone; Majesty in the flower of flesh; Foundation of the World in the power of the sinew; and Justice in the power of the skin.

And their placement above is as follows:

Elevated Height encompasses and encircles Wisdom and Understanding, which in turn surround all that is beneath them. Lovingkindness is drawn to Eternity, which is on the right side. Fear is drawn to Majesty, which are in the middle, and Justice is opposite them.

11. Should the questioner persist: You have now informed me as to their names, rank, and order. You have further informed me as to the position of Justice, which receives from all their power. Now tell me whether there is bestowing and receiving in each one.

    Answer: Know that no emanation is radiated forth except to proclaim the unity within Eyn-Sof. If the receptor did not unite with the bestower into one power, then it would not be possible to recognize that the two are really one. In their unity one knows that power of union. Upon seeing the uniting force made manifest, how much more so one should not ruminate upon it in secret. Thus, everything is both receptor and bestower. . . . [7]

Notes

1. See Maimonides, *The Guide of the Perplexed*, I:58.
2. *Sefer Yesirah* 1:4.
3. Ibid.
4. Ibid., 1:5.
5. Mishnah Pirqey Avot 5:1. The word "statement" *(ma'amar)* also signifies *sefirah*.
6. Traditionally a very dark blue associated with sky-blue.
7. The twelfth and final question seeks to establish biblical and rabbinic proof texts for the positions taken in the answers to the first eleven questions. Much of what presently constitutes the published answer to the twelfth question was added to Rabbi Azriel's original composition.

Commentary to Talmudic Legends

AMEN

We should extract and extend forth the Fountain of Blessing[1] to the attribute befitting it. Thus one should not forsake reading it;[2] nor should one skim over any of its letters nor hurry in reading them; neither should he respond with *amen* more than required.[3] Anyone who avoids all these [errors] and performs properly is analogous to one who opens the Source of Blessing within Him, may He be blessed.

One who makes the Fountain [of Blessing] flow is similar to a hero who emboldens his troops which are struggling with his adversary: When they overcome [his adversary], the battle thereafter is known by the hero's name. But if this is not the case, then all is in vain. This, then, is the reason that Blessing is known by the name of he who responds with *amen* in faith *(be-emunah)*. Just as the victorious warriors quickly take plunder and then gather the booty together so that the king may keep for himself the choicest parts, so too do those who bless hasten to be blessed from the expanding Blessing. Thereupon, he who answers *amen* is blessed from the very origin of the Source of blessing: By that attribute which he blesses he too is blessed. Finally, he who responds with *amen* is similar to one who proclaims "Let the power of God be increased" (Numbers 14:17).

Since Faith *(emunah)* stems from Eyn-Sof, one says *amen*, and in so doing he is like one who says "in Faith *(be-emunah)*, the Trainer *(ha-omen)* increases the Confidence *(imun)* from the Artisan *(oman)*, by means of *amen*.[4]

This means: *amen* increases Truth *(emet)* out of Faith *(emunah)*.[5] According to Rabbi Ḥiyya, *amen* causes Truth to grow forth from its origin so that it expresses God's Unity and Kingdom.[6] Thus, *amen* draws the power from Faith to increase the power of Truth, which nourishes everything. Furthermore, he who answers *amen* in faith increases the Source of Blessing. He not only is one who increases the blessing from Blessing, but from the Source itself.

The meaning of *amen* is to extol Truth, and therefore it is said, "From whence is it known that we should respond to one who makes a benediction with amen? Because it is written, 'Extol God with me' (Psalms 34:4)."[7] This exultation is immeasurable, as in "His greatness is immeasurable" (Psalms 145:3).

[One who answers *amen*] is akin to proclaiming "let it be established *(ye'amen)* and may Your Name be magnified from *amon*," as is written: "So let it be established *(ve-ye'amen)* that Your Name may be magnified forever" (1 Chronicles 17:24). If this be the case, why do we change the language of this verse? It speaks in the future tense, but we should choose an expression which encompasses all tenses and which also indicates the unending unity of *amen*, *omen*, and *amon*. That expression is the word *amen*, for they all unite in it.[8]

This is very much like *sekhel*, *maskil*, and *muskal* (intelligence, thinker, and concept), for from one point of view intelligence is thinker and from another it is the concept. They are three forms from one noun, for behold: *Amen* unendingly unites the fountain of Faith with its blessing and its point of acceptance. For *[amen]* is the divine flow which extends forth to Wisdom. Within Wisdom is the flowing extension of Wisdom, which in turn is the emanation of Blessing and also of Life *(hayyim)*,[9] as is written, "Thus I will bless you and I live" (Psalms 63:5), and as it is also written: "Wisdom enlivens those who possess it" (Ecclesiastes 7:12).

This is also the import of "Who is like You among the gods, O Lord; who is like You, glorious in holiness *(ne'edar ba-qo desh)*?" (Exodus 15:11). Holiness is the Fountain of Blessing, also known as the Beginning of Wisdom. Thus it is written: "Israel is holy to the Lord, the first fruits of His produce" (Jeremiah 2:3), and "Bless the Lord God *from the fountain* of Israel" (Psalms 68:27).

FROM THE FOUNTAIN means from the fountain of direct

power *(koaḥ ha-yoshar)* which Israel merits. This is the meaning of "Lift up your hands in holiness and bless the Lord" (Psalms 134:2). Thus when Scripture mentions power *(koaḥ)*, it refers to it as "glorious in power *(ne'edari ba-koaḥ)*" (Exodus 15:6), adding the letter *yod* to *ne'edar*.[10] But when Scripture states "glorious in holiness" (ibid., 15:11), no *yod* is written, for Holiness is the energizer and the flow in the Temple, and thus there is no need to answer with *amen* [in the Temple].[11]

The meaning of "who is like You among the gods?" can be found in the five united and supernal *sefirot*. They never descend, but are ever exultant. In opposition to them are the five names for the soul, namely: "only one" *(yeḥidah)*, living *(ḥayyah)*, spirit *(ruaḥ)*, soul *(neshamah)*, and animus *(nefesh)*. Thus the meaning is: Who is like You among the five *sefirot* that are specifically set aside to spread downward, for all of them are united in Holiness, which encompasses the entire decade.

It is furthermore written: "Say to Wisdom *(le-ḥokhmah):* You are my sister" (Proverbs 7:4a). The intention here is to bring about the convergence of Thought *(maḥshavah)* to Wisdom as if the two were one entity. The letter *lamed* of "*to* Wisdom" *(le-ḥokhmah)* is an allusion to the All, and to the drawing forth of the flow of Wisdom and the emanation of this flow, known as "the familiar of Understanding" *(binah)*. This is "and call her the familiar of Understanding" (ibid. 7:4b), and it means "draw forth the familiar of Understanding."

He who answers *amen* is one who draws forth the flow of Wisdom sanctified through the holiness of the power of intelligence. And he does it more explicitly than the one who says the blessing by the power of the word *amen*, which is an allusion to Wisdom from which the energy of each and every power grows. Thus it states: "I was by him as *amon*" (Proverbs 8:30).

One should answer *amen* after he who blesses, for it is written, "Ascribe greatness to our God" (Deuteronomy 32:3) and "So that he who blesses himself on the earth shall bless himself by the God of *amen.*" (Isaiah 65:16).

Notes
1. The "Source of Blessing" denotes one of the inner aspects of the *sefirah* Wisdom dealt with in this section.

2. The word *amen*.
3. One responds with *amen* to all blessings.
4. This passage is extremely difficult to translate, let alone explain. As the transliteration suggests, all these words, which encompass the whole divine realm, are derived from the Hebrew root '-*M-N*. Tishby suggests the following reading: "In Wisdom, Crown increases Beauty from Foundation by means of *amen*."
5. Truth, a symbol for the *sefirah* Beauty *(tif'eret)* grows forth from Wisdom, here called Faith.
6. See BT Shabbat 119b.
7. Source unknown. But see BT Berakhot 45a.
8. The stative noun *amen* encompasses all tenses.
9. All these terms refer to Wisdom.
10. The *yod* stands for *yosher*.
11. *Sifre, Ha-azinu*, sec. 306.

WISDOM AND THE ELEMENTS

Rabbi Simeon bar Yohai said: " 'A *man* has joy in the answer of his mouth' (Proverbs 15:23a). 'A *man* has joy'—this is the Holy One, blessed be He. For Scripture states: 'God *(YHVH)* is a *man* of war, God is his name' (Exodus 15:3).

" 'In the answer of his mouth'—it is written 'And God said, "Let there be light" ' (Genesis 1:3). This reminds one of what is recorded: 'The light of the righteous rejoices' (Proverbs 3:19).

" 'And a word in a season, how good it is' (Proverbs 15:23b)— 'And God saw the light, that it was good' (Genesis 1:4)."[1]

It is indeed the case that all light is the light of the animus; it enlightens the eyes and is also the countenance of the face. For Scripture states, "A man's Wisdom makes his face shine" (Ecclesiastes 8:1). It also is the life of the spirit, as it is written, "Wisdom enlivens those who possess it" (ibid. 7:12); and "But there is a spirit in man" (Job 32:8); and [the phrase] "the spirit of Wisdom and Understanding" (Isaiah 11:2).

This Understanding *(binah)*, which possesses different aspects, is Life *(hayyim)*, as it is written, "And the breath of the Almighty has enlivened me *(tehayyeni)*" (ibid. 33:4). Knowledge *(da'at)*, by which Wisdom differentiates and comes to know the Truth *(emet)*, is referred to as "the spirit of Knowledge" (ibid. 11:2).

In *The Chapters According to Rabbi Eliezer* it states:[2] By ten sayings (ma'amarot) was the world created and the ten are encompassed in three, namely Wisdom, Understanding (tevunah), and Knowledge. For it is written, "The Lord established the earth in Wisdom, by Understanding He founded the heavens and by His Knowledge the depths were split asunder" (Proverbs 3:19–20). With these three the Tabernacle was built; and by these three the Temple was constructed; and by these three it will someday be rebuilt. These three will be given over to the King Messiah, as Scripture states: "And the spirit of the Lord shall rest upon him, the Spirit of Wisdom and Understanding, the spirit of Counsel ('esah) and Strength (gevurah), the spirit of Knowledge and of fear of the Lord" (Isaiah 11:2).

They also said:[3] The Holy One, blessed be He, took counsel with the Torah—which is also called "Counsel"—in order to create the world. The Torah responded to God and said, "If there be no army for the king and if there be no camp for the king, then over what does he reign? If there be no people to praise the king, where be the king's honor?" The Holy One, blessed be He, heard this and it pleased Him. The Torah said, "With me did the Holy One, blessed be He, take counsel to create the world, as it is said: 'Counsel is mine, as well as Advice; I am Understanding; I possess Strength' (Proverbs 8:14)." Hence [the Sages] said, "A kingdom without advisors is not a true kingdom."

They also said:[4] "He covers Himself ('oteh) with light as a garment" (Psalms 104:2)—HE COVERS HIMSELF really means "He counsels Himself" as in "with counsel ('etah) and discretion" (Daniel 2:14). LIGHT is the Torah as in "And the Torah is light" (Proverbs 6:23). Thus, [the verse] should be rendered "The Holy One, blessed be He, took counsel with the Torah as did Solomon." When the Holy One, blessed be He, saw that the Torah was in agreement with His designs, the heavens were immediately unfurled like a screen [or: garment].

Another interpretation of HE COVERS HIMSELF WITH LIGHT—when the Holy One, blessed be He, undertook to create His world, He did so by three Names derived from His Great Name, as it is written, "He established the earth in Wisdom" (Proverbs 3:19). Rabbi Yohanan said: "It is a cipher—the numerical value of the letters in the word Wisdom (H-K-M-H) is 8, 20, 40, and 5 respectively. These are the seventy-three Names that were inscribed in God's arm before the world was created. Upon finding Himself alone, He yearned to create the universe. For Scripture states, "But

101

He is unchangeable [literally: alone] and who can turn Him? What His soul desires He does" (Job 23:13).

God extracted one of the seventy-three Names and from it He drew forth three droplets of water and the entire world filled with water, which He then placed below Himself. For it is written, "And the wind of God hovered above the surface of the water" (Genesis 1:2).

He extracted a second Name and drew forth from it three droplets of light and the entire world became permeated with light. This is the sevenfold light, as Scripture states: "Let there be light" (ibid. 1:3). He set the light to His left, for the verse states HE COVERS HIMSELF WITH LIGHT, and one always covers oneself from the left side.

He extracted a third Name and from it drew forth three droplets of fire. The entire world filled with fire, which He then placed to His right. For it is written, "From His right side is a burning law for them" (Deuteronomy 33:2).

Light, fire, and water—all were created from the Wisdom of Torah. Whence is it known that the light issued forth from the Torah? It is written, "And the Torah is light" (Proverbs 6:23). Whence is it known that fire bursts forth from the Torah? It is written, "Is not My word like fire?" (Jeremiah 23:29). And whence is it known that water pours forth from the Torah? It is written, "Where there were no depths, I was brought forth; when there were no fountains glorious with water (*nekhbedey mayyim*)" (Proverbs 8:24). Do not read "glorious with water" but rather "caches of water (*nivkhey mayyim*)".

How, from the resplendence of Wisdom, Understanding, and Knowledge, and from the Splendor that radiates forth from them all, do substantial, real entities cluster together and come into being? The force that brings this about is their motion—the motion of fire, which is both warm and dry. As the warmth [of the fire] becomes distanced from its resplendence and its source, the heat diminishes. From this is generated [the element] air, which is both warm and humid. In the aftermath of its generation, the air continues to become distant from the source of the fire. Thus the warmth continues to decay. Then it stabilizes and weakens, all the while becoming more pervasive and humid. From this is generated [the element] water, which is cool and humid.

As a result of its generation, the water becomes more removed from the air. The warmth and humidity diminish further. It cools and solidifies, thereby forming dregs and clods and sediments, which are dry. From this [process] comes the generation of earth, which is cold and dry.

It is by these four elements that the first principles combine and mix. From these the combination of heat, cold, dryness, and humidity result in the generation of animals, vegetables, and minerals, each one drawn to its dominant element.

Such are the views of the philosophers.

But the Torah Sages said:[5] Three things preceded the creation of the world: water, spirit [literally "wind" or "air"; Hebrew *ruaḥ*], and fire. The waters conceived and gave birth to darkness; fire conceived and gave birth to light; spirit conceived and gave birth to Wisdom. It is with these six created entities that the world is maintained: with spirit, Wisdom, water, fire, light, and darkness.

The meaning of "spirit conceived and gave birth to Wisdom" can be found in the above-mentioned seventy-three Names, for they are derived from the principle underlying all letters, which is *ruaḥ*. By the chill of wind/spirit, ice is formed, as it is written, "By the breath of God ice is given" (Job 37:10a). From ice emerges water, as it is written, "and the breadth of the waters is *solidified*" (ibid. 37:10b). The word "solidified" means a place into which one can pour water. This is also found in "and He weighs the water by measure" (ibid. 28:25)—that is, He gathers the water into a place. He weighed out the mass of that which was to be filled. For some He [arranges them] to accept the whiteness of the light so that they do not take on a greenish appearance.

Some become dark due to the ice in them, as it is written, "His pavilion round about him was dark water" (Psalms 18:12). This, then, is the meaning of "the waters conceived and gave birth to darkness." For just as wind/spirit emanates from wind/spirit, so too does water emanate from water, rarefied matter from rarefied matter, this from that and this from the midst of that. But the paths of all essences flow from water.

There are stones of water, as Scripture records, "Water is hidden as stone and the surface of the deep solidifies" (Job 28:30). . . . Just as there are stones of water there are also stones of darkness, as it is written, "the stones of darkness and the shadow of death" (ibid. 28:3). Everything recorded about the [stones of darkness] provides all that is written about the structure of water.

From the emanation of water came forth the fire and every appearance of fire: fire within fire and fire from the midst of fire. The paths of all essences [are grounded] in fire which flashes from one to the other and back again. All that is written about the structure of fire [applies], as it is written, "In the midst of fiery stones you have walked" (Ezekiel 28:14). This, then, is the meaning of "The fire conceived and gave birth to light"—from [fire] all the flashing lights spark to and fro, and all essences are encompassed in these lights. Concerning this Scripture states "the light was good *(tov)*" (Genesis 1:4). This means that it is befitting for this light to emanate forth from many lights—this is derived from the expression "when he cares *(be-hetivo)* for the lamps" (Exodus 30:7), which is translated [into Aramaic] as "when he ignites."

From wind, water, light, and fire—each emanated one from the other—and from that which is emanated from them, all that ever was or ever will be was created. At first dimension, measure, place, and time were created for each existent being. A delimited and established dimension is called "division" *(hilluq)*. This is what was made between each dimension, measure, place, and form, between all existent beings and a thing and its opposite. If this were not the case—were there not some kind of separation between things—then one thing would be indistinguishable from the other. Everything would have been united and undifferentiated, and then dimensions were made to separate one thing from another and to allow for the combination of separate parts and the relation of one thing to another. Divisions inform form to a thing, and correct and place it in a condition such that it may be recognized.

It is well known that form cannot exist without a substratum. Furthermore, all things [occupy] united space, because at first all compound objects were in a state of unity, for in the beginning there were no perceptible dimensions, or divisions.

Before the existence of dimension, however, He sent forth upon dimension the straight line in order to separate the undifferentiated. This is the "unformed" [*tohu* of Genesis 1:2]; within it was nothing of substance. What it did contain, however, were essences without dimension, form, or corporeality. These essences then assumed corporeality in both dimension and form. The refuse and dross were separated to one side and the effulgence and purity to another, whereupon the green line—which surrounds and darkens—was created.[6]

Then the elements—the powers that exist one inside the

other—were deposited and submerged into the nethermost depths, their structure ascending to the highest depths. These elements constitute the beginnings of the various structures of water, and they are known as the stones of the void [*bohu* of Genesis 1:2], for a tangible substantiality permeates them in dimension—all beings are perceived in them.[7]

From these void-stones come forth water and dark water. From the water there is snow, from the snow there is dirt and from dirt there form rocks, iron, and brass. As Scripture states, "Iron is brought forth from earth, and brass is molten from stone" (Job 28:2).

*　　*　　*

In *Genesis Rabbah* it states:[8] A builder requires six things: water, earth, timber, stones, reeds, and iron. And if you were to say, "He is wealthy and has no need for reeds," surely he needs one for a measuring rod, as it is written, "And a measuring reed in his hand" (Ezekiel 40:3). The Torah existed prior to the following six preexistent things: undifferentiatedness, void, darkness, water, and [the two] depths, which altogether make six. . . .

A king of flesh and blood builds a palace and roofs it over with timber, stones, and earth. But the Holy One, blessed be He, roofed His world with nothing other than water, as it states, "who roofs your upper chambers with water" (Psalms 104:8).[9]

Rabbi Yoḥanan said: The Holy One, blessed be He, took all the primeval waters and placed half in the firmament and half in the ocean. And so it states, "the river of God is full of water" (ibid. 65:10).[10] Here, "river" is the sea.

Rabbi Judah said: The upper waters exceed the lower waters by about thirty pints . . . our Sages said they are equal.[11]

The order of these statements is as follows. Everything was brought into existence from the Root of all Roots *(shoresh ha-shoreshim)*, as is stated, "Wisdom is founded from Nothing *(me-ayin)* and *Ey* is the place of Understanding" (Job 28:12). It is further written: "God understands [Wisdom's] way and He knows its place" (ibid. 28:23).

He then drew forth its paths in Understanding; and in Knowledge everything was created. From the Spirit of Wisdom He brought forth Water, as it is written, "A river flowing from the fountain of Wisdom" (Proverbs 8:14). From the Spirit of Understanding He brought forth the Light of Intelligence; from the Spirit of Knowledge, Fire. Since Understanding is linked to the heavens and was not entrusted to earthly inhabitants (as were Wisdom and Knowledge), its product—namely, the light of Intelligence—was not mentioned by the Sages when they enumerated the three things which preceded the world.[12] Furthermore, everything is included in the statement "Wind/spirit conceived and gave birth to Wisdom," for the unfolding expansion of spirit is an exceedingly subtle and fine [process]. The unfolding [of Wisdom] in the ethereal wind/spirit is not unlike the permeation of ethereal spirit in coarse matter, and this image of spirit from spirit continues infinitely. In spirit are the paths of all beings, each encompassed by another. In this entire process of spirit these [paths] are known as Wisdom.

God then took these three—namely Light, Fire, and Water—and mixed them together. Taking Light and Fire, He created a Tabernacle and a Throne and the four heavenly beasts and the curtain and the angels. He then took fire and water, creating from them the heavens, the angels that stand outside the inner sanctum, and the vicious angels placed in charge of the portals of each of the heavens.

Rabbi Eliezer said:[13] The heavens were made from the light of His garment, as Scripture states: "He covers Himself with light as a garment and stretches out the heavens like a screen" (Psalms 104:2). Another interpretation: HE COVERS HIMSELF WITH LIGHT AS A GARMENT—this informs us that the iridescence was created first and only afterward did the heavens come into being.

This iridescence is the subject of the previous statement "He extracted a second Name and drew forth from it three droplets of water." But when it states "fire conceived and gave birth to light," the subject [of the sentence] is the Light of the Fire. This Light was not [ontologically] first, for both Fire and Water preceded it.

With regard to the Light that emanates from the Name, Rabbi Eliezer said that they were created from the Light of His garment. This means that they came only from the fineness of the Light, unmixed, for this Light is the Light of Intelligence, the attribute of Mercy.

The Sages who proclaimed that the heavens were created from Fire and Water also admitted that they were created from the Water's foam and the Fire's glow. How did this occur? First, a measure and an edge and a space were formed into which the Water could gather. When the Water was gathered into this space, it accepted the brilliance of the Light and exited therefrom by a channel. It was then gathered into another space, as it is written: "who has divided a watercourse for the torrent of rain" (Job 38:25). From the prevailing warmth of the Fire a very white congealment formed—white due to the whiteness accepted from the Light. From the fineness of the Water a kind of white salt was extracted, formed by the Water's foam and the pure, distilled quality of the fineness.

The lower waters, which did not receive any of the iridescent Light, appear green. This water evaporates and freezes like icicles. The ice within freezes further and then becomes earth.

In the Talmud [we find]:[14] R. Yudah b. Pazi sat and expounded: In the beginning the world was water within water, as it is written, "And the wind/spirit of God hovered upon the surface of the water" (Genesis 1:2). He then made snow of the water, as it is written, "He casts forth His ice like morsels" (Psalms 147:17). Out of the snow He made land, as it is written, "For He says to the snow, 'Be earth!' " (Job 37:6). The land then floats upon the water, as it is written, "He who placed land upon the water" (Psalms 136:6). And the water lies upon the mountains, as it is written, "The water stood above the mountains" (ibid. 104:6). The mountains stand above the wind, as it is recorded, "Behold the Former of mountains and the Creator of winds" (Amos 4:13). The wind is tied to storms, as Scripture states, "Stormy wind fulfills His word" (Psalms 148:8). The storm He made as a kind of amulet to hang on His arm, as in "And beneath are the arms of the world" (Deuteronomy 33:27).

We further find:[15] From the outset the world was water within water. He decreed upon the water and drew out the wind from its midst. He conquered the water, which submitted to His decrees and gathered together as an ocean. The ocean is now known as the Dead Sea, and He surrounded the Sea with beach and sand. He adjured it not to exceed beyond the sand, as it is written, "I have placed sand as a boundary to the sea" (Jeremiah 5:22).

Notes
1. *Genesis Rabbah* 3:3.
2. *Pirqey de-Rabbi Eli'ezer* (Warsaw, 1852), ch. 3.
3. Ibid.
4. This verse is also discussed in *Pirqey de-Rabbi Eli'ezer*, ch. 3, but in a slightly different context.
5. *Exodus Rabbah* 15:22.

6. Cf. BT Hagigah 12a.
7. *Sefer ha-Bahir*, sec. 2.
8. 1:8–9, with many variants and lacunae.
9. *Genesis Rabbah* 4:1.
10. Ibid. 4:4.
11. Ibid. 4:5.
12. See above, p. 103.
13. *Pirqey de-Rabbi Eliezer*, ch. 3.
14. JT Hagigah 2:1.
15. While the Midrashic reference to the Dead Sea is found in *Exodus Rabbah* 15:22, the source for the other half of the paragraph is unknown.

Rabbi Jacob ben Sheshet of Gerona

INTRODUCTION

The texts presented in the following section come from two works by Rabbi Jacob ben Sheshet of Gerona. The first work is entitled *Sefer ha-Emunah ve-ha-Bittaḥon* (The Book of Faith and Reliance), a work that for generations was attributed to another Geronese Kabbalist, Rabbi Moses ben Naḥman (Nahmanides; c. 1194–1270). In fact, the most recent edition of this book is published in the Nahmanidean corpus edited by H. Chavel, *Kitvey Rabbenu Mosheh ben Naḥman* (Jerusalem, 1964) 2:353–448. The four sections presented below are selected from the first, third, fourth, and fifth chapters of the work (pages 353–358 and 360–370), with many lacunae.

Afterward, sometime between 1230 and 1240, ben Sheshet composed the *Sefer Meshiv Devarim Nekhoḥim* (Response of Correct Answers), in response to Samuel Ibn Tibbon's pro-Maimonidean *Ma'amar Yiqqavu ha-Mayyim*. The *Meshiv* was edited by G. Vajda (Jerusalem, 1968). The translation below of the second and third chapters of the *Meshiv* correspond to pages 74–86 of Vajda's edition, with some lacunae.

Vajda wrote extensively on the *Meshiv*. See his "An Analysis of the Ma'amar Yiqqawu ha-Mayim by Samuel b. Judah Ibn Tibbon" in *Journal of Jewish Studies* 10 (1959): 137–149; and his *Recherches sur la philosophie et la Kabbale dans la pensée juive du Moyen Age* (Paris, 1962), pp. 13–113.

The Book of Faith and Reliance

CHAPTER ONE: FAITH AND RELIANCE

Faith and reliance are two matters wherein the latter requires its counterpart while the former does not depend on the latter. For faith precedes reliance and endures in the heart of the believer even though reliance is not present. To exist, faith does not need reliance; therefore faith is not an indication of reliance. But reliance points to faith, for it is impossible for reliance to exist before faith, nor can it endure without faith.

All who trust are called believers, but not every believer can be called reliant, for faith is like a tree and reliance like a fruit. Now the fruit is dependent on the tree or the plant which nurtures it. But the tree or plant is not dependent on the fruit, for there are some trees and many plants which do not bear fruit. Nevertheless, fruit cannot exist without some tree or plant.

This is similar to piety, [for piety] is indicative of wisdom and it is impossible to be pious unless one is already wise. Thus [the Sages] said: "A boor does not fear sin, nor is an ignoramus pious."[1] But wisdom does not depend on piety, for it is possible to be both brilliant and evil.

And so it is with faith and reliance: every trusting person is a believer, for a man cannot have trust except in whom he believes has the ability to fulfill his own requests. But not every believer is reliant, for occasionally (the believer) will fear lest his transgression [has turned God away from him] or lest he had already received miracles from the Creator for his meritous acts [and is not deserving of any more]. When he finds himself transgressing and erring against the benevolence of the Creator, may He be blessed, he does not arouse himself to trust in Him that He will save him from his misfortune or that He will grant him his wishes and desires. Therefore, he will exert himself in worldly ways for deliverance from his misfortune or to attain his wishes and desires. Were it not for his fear lest he cause transgression, his effort to be delivered through worldly means would detract from his faith. For it is written: "I have not seen a just man forsaken nor his progeny begging for bread" (Psalms 37:25). Even Hillel and Rabbi Ḥanina ben Dosa and their colleagues—who were all exceedingly impoverished and who had little money[2]—were never forsaken, since they never amassed property in the first place. For the term "forsaking" applies only to someone who had support and then was abandoned; but someone who never was dependent cannot be forsaken.

Being abandoned is not a random occurrence, without relation to transgression or iniquity. Therefore it is impossible to find the fear of God in an individual who is smugly certain that he has not sinned. He who fears sin might be apprehensive lest a calamity befall him because of the transgression [that they fear]. Now he who knows in his being that he is a righteous man but still has the intention of what was said, namely: "You should have assisted me";[3] then behold, his heart is inclined toward heaven and he does well and his faith is not lacking.

Also, he who fears his own transgression believes that he has the ability, but also knows that before Him there is no preferential treatment and that the Holy One, blessed be He, can fulfill His promises one way and collect what is due Him in another way—this kind of individual fears lest he cause transgression that will not be delivered from his anguish. This is like when our patriarch Jacob, peace be upon him, was assured by God, saying: "Behold, I am with you" (Genesis 28:15). But he feared Esau, as it is written, "And Jacob was greatly afraid and distressed" (Genesis 32:8). And he offered presents and divided his servants into two camps and he was fearful lest he cause a transgression. And we also find that David was a believer upon seeing the goodness of God and he was fearful lest he cause transgression, as our Sages, may their memories be blessed, said: "Why is the word lule' ("were it not that" of Psalms 27:13) dotted? Because he feared lest he cause a transgression."[4] Evidently the believer may fear lest he cause a transgression, but the reliant never fears lest he be the cause of transgression. As David said: "He shall not be afraid of evil tidings: his heart is firm, trusting in the Lord" (Psalms 112:7), and another verse says: "In God I have put my trust—I will not be afraid" (Psalms 56:12). This verse does not contradict the words of our Rabbis, peace be upon them, for it was said referring to this world, while "Were it not that I believed" refers to the World to Come. . . .

These two issues—Reliance and Faith—have been mentioned together in one verse, as it is written, "Trust in the Lord and do good; dwell in the land and enjoy faith" (Psalms 37:3). He first warns about reliance and afterward mentions good deeds to teach that reliance is trusting God that He will assist one in the performance of the commandments. Had the text said, "Do good and trust in the Lord," I would have said that this trust about which we are warned refers to the reward of the good deed and not to the necessities of this world which a person requires in order to exist. By this I mean those causes and matters which establish a good deed. Therefore he first said, "Trust in the Lord": trust that He will help and support any individual so that he may fulfill both his own desires and God's commandments. Afterward he stated "And do good," which means pursue the commandments and exert yourself in their performance, and never be slovenly in doing good due to your lack of ability, for God will support you and help you. This, then, is the meaning of "Trust in the Lord and do good." And this was [David's] intention when he placed the command for reliance before the command for meritorious deeds.

This particular interpretation is much better than the one that states that this reliance refers to the reward for a meritorious act. For there is no distinction between one who trusts God that He will reward him because of a commandment he has observed and one who trusts that God will grant the plea of his heartfelt prayers.[5]

This entire matter is a sign of iniquity; as our Rabbis, may their memories be blessed, said: "Three things are signs of the iniquities of man and they are: a shakey wall, expectation of prayer, and calling on heaven to strike down a neighbor."[6] This passage refers to a man who examines his prayer and then claims that he prayed a perfect prayer and that he expects that his request will be answered from on high.

Long ago, Antigonus of Socho reprimanded his students, "Do not be like slaves who serve the master in order to receive a gift."[7] This means: When you serve Him do not allow your trust in Him to be conditional upon immediate reward, for if you do, you compel your soul to be reminded of its iniquities, like the one who examines his prayers.

On the other hand, he who contributes a *sela'* to charity so that his son will thrive or that he will merit life in the World to Come is not part of this class of people.[8] For at the outset, when he performs this commandment it is in his hands whether he reduces or increases the performance of the commandment, and it is for this reason that he observes the commandment. This is in no way similar to someone who eats unleavened bread on Passover or purchases for himself a palm branch[9] or observes the Sabbath or other similar [commandments]. Regarding them Scripture states, "Trust in the Lord and do good." Furthermore, it is well-nigh impossible to interpret "Trust in the Lord" as referring to the reward for the observance of a commandment, neither in this world or the World to Come. For no warning had yet been given regarding the whole matter; anyhow, how could He warn us to rely on Him in order that He reward us with good? And after reliance—which is the effect—was mentioned, then faith—which is the cause—was mentioned; and thus it says, "Dwell in the land and enjoy faith."

Furthermore it states, "Trust in the Lord and do good." This means: Even though you are not able to do anything and you know in your heart that you are wicked—despite all this, "Trust in the Lord," for He is the master of mercy and He will have mercy upon you. As Scripture states, "His mercies are upon all His works" (Psalms 145:9), and by this is meant [both] the righteous and the wicked. And [the Sages] said: "When a man is punished what does the *Shekhinah* say? 'I feel lighter than my head, I am lighter than my arm.' "[10] Therefore Scripture first states "Trust in the Lord"— whether you be of the righteous or of the wicked, trust in the Lord. Then afterward it states: "and do good"—even though He be merciful and compassionate, do not impulsively assure yourself that you will never be witness to evil. For God, may He be blessed, "has a long-suffering Spirit and back."[11] If He forgives you once, twice, or three times—as Scripture says, "Lo, God does all these things twice or three times with a man" (Job 33:29)—afterward He will abandon you. Therefore, when you see that He has compassion toward you and fulfills your requests, you will be compelled to do good.

Afterward, the verse reads "Dwell in the land." It means this: Perhaps you might think that the statement "do good" means that you should forsake your work and business by which you earn your living and you fear lest you die of hunger. Therefore it states "dwell in the land," meaning that despite all this, you should repent and pursue the commandments and not withdraw from your bodily life. "It is good that you take hold of this; but do not withdraw your hand from that either" (Ecclesiastes 7:18).

This is the opinion of Rabbi Ishmael as we find (in the Talmud):

Our Rabbis learned: "And you shall gather the corn" (Deuteronomy 11:4) . . . you are to combine the study (of Torah) with a worldly occupation. This is the view of Rabbi Ishmael. Rabbi Simeon ben Yoḥai says: Is that possible? If a man plows in the plowing season and sows in the sowing season and reaps in the reaping season and winnows during the windy season, what is to become of the Torah? Rather, when Israel performs the will of the Omnipresent their tasks are carried out by others, as it says, "And strangers shall stand and feed your flocks, and the sons of foreigners shall be your farmers and vinekeepers" (Isaiah 61:5). But when Israel fails to perform the will of the Omnipresent their tasks are carried out by themselves, as it says, "And you shall gather your corn." Nor is this all, but the work of others is also done by them, as it says, "You shall serve your enemies" (Deuteronomy 28:48). Said Abaye: Many have followed the advice of Rabbi Ishmael.[12]

Afterward, the verse says "and enjoy faith." Maybe you will say that when I am busy in my work I am thereby free of the Torah and busy in the dealings of commerce. Therefore it says "and enjoy faith." This means be strong and make certain that all your deeds are performed in faith. And you will find that you are never—not even for one hour—free of the obligation to do good.

The word "enjoy" (re'eh) has two interpretations derived from the verse "And you shall love your neighbor (re'ekha) as yourself" (Deuteronomy 28:48). It is a command, meaning: Join with supernal Faith or Wisdom, whose names are interchangeable. Cling to it, for it encompasses all 613 commandments. As the Rabbis said: "Habakkuk came and based them all on one principle, as it is said, 'A righteous man shall live by his faith' (Habakkuk 2:4)."[13] In another place it says, "Wisdom gives life to those who have it" (Ecclesiastes 7:12). It is the case, then, that Faith is Wisdom and Wisdom Faith, and it is round about the Holy One, blessed be He. As it says, "Who is strong like you, O Lord; and faith surrounds you" (Psalms 89:9). It further states, "In your faith and justice, answer me" (Psalms 143:1), as if he were swearing Him. This I have heard from the mouth of the pious Rabbi Isaac, son of the great Rabbi Abraham, peace be upon him. And he said it on the authority of his father.

The Prophet said: "Trust in the Lord forever, for the Lord God is an eternal Rock" (Isaiah 26:4). First he mentioned the Name of God and afterward said FOREVER. This (construction) signifies something endless. Thus, you are informed that "forever" Praises the Name, like "For the Lord most high is terrible" (Psalms 46:3). Thus, "Trust in the Lord who is forever": He is eternal and exists without end. It is as if he said: "(Trust) in the God who is faith and truth."[14]

After all this he said: "for the Lord God (YH YHVH) is an eternal Rock." The import here is that He is unique like an eternal rock in each and every one of His attributes. Furthermore, in many places the attribute of Severity is alluded to as YH, as in "God (YH) has chastised me severely" (Psalms 118:18); "Because God (YH) has sworn by His throne" (Exodus 17:16); and "If you, God (YH), watch over iniquities . . ." (Psalms 130:3).

This is what the Sages said in *Genesis Rabbah:* " 'Happy is the man chastised by you, God (YH), and taught by You from Your Torah' (Psalms 94:12). The verse does not read YHVH but rather YH. It is as if one were standing before a court while the judge makes his ruling."[15]

Furthermore, by the attribute of Mercy, the esteemed Tetragrammaton, He is made unique in each of the (attributes), and all are unique in Him. This, then, "for the Lord God is an eternal Rock."[16]

Notes

1. Mishnah Pirqey Avot 2:5(6).
2. For some of the rabbinic traditions regarding the impoverishment of these two Talmudic scholars, see BT Yoma' 35b and BT Ta'anit 28a.
3. In an aggadic passage, God says this statement to Moses. See BT Shabbat 89a.
4. The verse in Psalms reads: "Were it not that I believed I should see the goodness of the Lord in the land of the living." In the traditional Masoretic

Hebrew text, the first word of the verse is marked with dots above the letters. This orthographic peculiarity demanded an explanation. The comment is from BT Berakhot 4a.

5. For both worship, hoping to be rewarded.
6. BT Berakhot 55a.
7. Mishnah Pirqey Avot 1:3.
8. See BT Ro'sh ha-Shanah 4a.
9. A ritual object used in the celebration of Sukkot, or the Feast of Tabernacles.
10. Mishnah Sanhedrin 6:5. The sense of a joint sadness shared by the punished man and the Shekhinah is conveyed by this *aggadah*.
11. Cf. JT Ta'anit 2:1.
12. BT Berakhot 35b.
13. BT Makkot 4a.
14. Cf. Isaiah 25:1.
15. 92:8. The convicted man, on hearing his sentence, cries out "Yah, Yah!"
16. The two names in combination—*YH* for Severity, *YHVH* for Mercy—represent God as one eternal, perfect being.

CHAPTER THREE: HEAR O ISRAEL

. . . Just as all the above-mentioned matters testify to His unity,[1] so too each of His Names and attributes testify to His unity, as Scripture states, "Hear O Israel, the Lord is our God, the Lord is One" (Deuteronomy 6:4). This verse proclaims His unity in all His attributes by three words, and they are "The Lord, our God, the Lord" *(YHVH elohenu YHVH)*. The letters are "Water from Spirit and Fire from Water,"[2] and the inner meaning of the reflecting mirror and the unreflecting mirror.[3] I will only hint to this in the sum of my words, but if you seek it out carefully you will find it.

I said "inner meaning" above, for I have found two [conflicting] verses. One verse says, "And the light dwells with Him" (Daniel 2:22), and the second states, "He made darkness his secret place" (Psalms 18:12). But it is taught that there is no problem: "One is invisible, one is visible."[4] The meaning of "visible" is "the light" and it is the light created on the first day [of creation]. "It dwells with Him" and it is the reflecting mirror. And the "visible" is the fifth of the five lights recorded in the story of creation.[5] It is "the darkness of his secret place" and it is called the unreflecting mirror. The meaning of "reflecting" is that it gives light to those who gaze into it. Thus, the skin of Moses' face shone when he received revelation through the reflecting mirror. And it is called "day" for it is written, "And

God called the light day" (Genesis 1:5). Therefore, God only spoke with him during the day. The unreflecting mirror is called "night." Therefore it is written, "I make myself known to him in a vision, and I speak to him in a dream" (Numbers 12:6).

This verse—and I mean "Hear O Israel, the Lord is our God, the Lord is One"—proclaims His unity from the heights to the depths, and from the depths to the heights. If we explicate this verse [as proclaiming His unity] from above to below, we would say that the first name is not a symbolic attribute but rather a proper noun. In the word OUR GOD allusion is made to two attributes, and the second name is likewise an attribute. If we instead expound this verse as [proclaiming His unity] from below to above, we would say that the first name is an attribute. Similiarly, OUR GOD makes allusion to two attributes as in the first interpretation. But it is not like the arrangement of the first [interpretation], in that this descends while the former ascends. And the second name [in this second interpretation] is a proper noun.[6]

Thus we find that in the first interpretation these three words start above and conclude below, while in the second interpretation they commence below and end above. Four matters are mentioned: the Creator, may He be blessed, and three attributes, which are Lovingkindness *(ḥesed)*, Severity *(din)*, and Mercy *(raḥamim)*, and through these all the [ten] attributes in their totality [are mentioned]. I will now lay out the two systems—you should be aware that our Rabbis, may their memories be blessed, established that one should say "Blessed be the name of the Glory of His Kingdom *(kevod malkhuto)* forever and always" in the recitation of the *shema'*.[7] They established that it should be said because Jacob said it, but it should be said in a whisper because Moses, peace be upon him, did not say it.

They told a parable: To what is this compared? To the king's daughter who smelled minced meat pudding [and desired it]. If one mentions the odor, she will be embarrassed. If she says nothing, she will suffer. Then her servants began to secretly bring her some of it.[8]

Now their words are words of the living God, and about them Scripture says, "To understand a parable and a figure of speech, the words of the wise and their riddles" (Proverbs 1:6). The understanding of the parable is clear to one who understands for what reason they likened a particular matter to a particular symbol. The understanding of a figure of speech entails comprehension of the various components of a parable and the issues alluded to by the parable. This also entails contrasting the parable with the subject. Now take this principle and you will thereby understand the two systems, especially if you pay close attention to why Jacob said it and then why Moses did not say it.[9]

I am of the opinion that the reason Jacob was compelled to declare ["Blessed be the name . . ."] was that the *Shekhinah* departed from him. When he desired to reveal the end [of days] to his sons the *Shekhinah* departed from him. Then he said, "God forbid! There is something unworthy in my offspring, like Abraham who begat Ishmael and like Isaac who begat Esau." His sons burst out and proclaimed, "HEAR O ISRAEL, THE LORD IS OUR GOD, THE LORD IS ONE. Just as in your heart there is only the One, so too in our hearts there is only the One." Jacob thereupon exclaimed, "Blessed be the name of the Glory of His Kingdom forever and always."[10] He drew down Blessing and Will from above to below according to the order first mentioned by his sons. This is the system I have written about above, and because of it, the *Shekhinah* dwelled upon him. Therefore, we ought to say that it is from above to below.

But when Moses was about to declare this sentence, he was not compelled to say, "Blessed be the name of the Glory of His Kingdom for ever and always" for the *Shekhinah* was already with him, and he wrote by divine inspiration. But he needed to rise and ascend into holiness. Therefore one can say he began below and concluded above. . . .

Now the meaning of "Israel"[11] is Severity and contention, as in, "For you have contended with God and with men and have prevailed" (Genesis 32:29). Whether it is from above or below, such is its interpretation without a doubt.

In a legend [we read]: "There was one beast who stood in the midst of the firmament and its name was ISRAEL."[12] This refers to the holy throne room facing toward the center. Law and fire are to his right, as in, "From His right went forth a fiery law for them" (Deuteronomy 33:2). The Holy One, blessed be He, is above them all and rules over them all.

We unite Him in [the word] ONE. If it began from above, it has already drawn forth, and then it seems appropriate to include everything and finish in Blessing. If it began from below, then when it reaches ONE, Blessing and Kingdom shower down.[13]

As for the word "One" (*eḥad* [root: *'ḤD*]): the *alef* (א) is an allu-

119

sion to that which thought cannot fathom.[14] The *ḥet (Ḥ)* signifies Wisdom *(Ḥokhmah)*. The *dalet (D)* is well known.[15] Therefore we should quickly pronounce the *alef* so that the mind not dwell on it for long. Such is what Solomon wrote under divine inspiration: "And do not become too wise; why should you destroy yourself?" (Ecclesiastes 7:16). But be sure not to hasten the pronunciation of the *ḥet*. We are permitted to contemplate it. Since one has to express unity with the *dalet*, we dwell on it and unite it with the six extremities.[16] See, now, how fine and becoming at last is "Blessed be the name of the Glory of His Kingdom forever and always," for one should draw divine sustenance over it. And now he is prepared and ready for just this purpose, as was the situation when our patriarch Jacob said it.

Another interpretation: The *ḥet* is Wisdom through Foundation inclusive,[17] the *dalet* is the end,[18] while the vowel seat[19] is without [symbolic] meaning. This tradition I have heard in the name of the pious Rabbi Isaac, Son of the great Rabbi Abraham, may his memory be blessed.[20]

This verse—by which I mean HEAR O ISRAEL . . .—was not needed in the Torah were it not for the accusation of Aḥer and his comrades who claimed that there are two powers in heaven.[21] They also chopped off the shoots in order to make one of the branches a tree unto itself and the root a tree unto itself [thereby asserting a dualistic heresy].

I am of the opinion that this chopping is of ten things: each one of the ten [*sefirot*], either between the tenth and the ninth or the ninth and the eighth and so on until between the first and Eyn-Sof itself. Regarding this, the *Sefer Yeṣirah* states: "Ten *sefirot belimah*; ten and not nine, ten and not eleven."[22] And the pious Rabbi Isaac interpreted "ten and not nine" in a different way.[23] Any interpretation which dissuades one from stating that they are nine or that they are eleven is to be commended. How much more so does this apply to eight or six or five or less, or alternatively twelve or thirteen or more.

Even though the chopping is of one of the ten entities, it is as if one were chopping in Eden, to uproot it from the garden in which it was planted, as in, "And God planted a garden in Eden" (Genesis 2:8).

But Jeroboam son of Nebat sinned, in my opinion, because he severed five from five.[24] Thus one of his comrades is called one who steals from his mother and father,[25] and therefore he made the form of a golden calf. Our Rabbis, may their memories be blessed, further said in the tractate Ta'anit: Rava said that [the angel] Ridya' has the image of a calf . . . he stands between the upper depths and the lower depths.[26] This [Ridya'] is the name of the angel appointed over the rains. It is my opinion that [Jeroboam] did not make the calves for themselves but for local needs. Had he needed another one to erect in a different place he would have made a third and a fourth. But [his] intention was to combine the two forces to sever the right power from the center, for the power is drawn to that material within which form is joined.

Notes

1. Chapter 2 had described God's unity in all his biblical apellations, particularly as male and female.
2. *Sefer Yesirah* 1:11, 12.
3. Terms for *Tif'eret* (Beauty) and *Malkhut* (Kingdom) respectively. The "reflecting mirror" both receives and transmits light, while the "unreflecting mirror" is only a receptacle of light. This imagery is applied to Beauty, in that it both receives and emanates the divine energy; and then to Kingdom, the tenth *sefirah* that can only receive energy from above.
4. BT Ḥagigah 13a. The Aramaic terms used here also mean "within" and "without."
5. The term "light" is mentioned five times in Genesis 1:1–5. According to the homilist, each "light" is a reference to a different aspect of the divine world.
6. The terms "noun" (*'esem*) and "attribute" (*middah*) are not just grammatic distinctions, but references to the emanated divine powers (*middot*) or the Emanator Himself (*'esem*).
7. The verse "Hear (*shema'*) O Israel . . ." is included in the morning prayer liturgy, along with Deuteronomy 6:5–9, 11:13–21, and Numbers 15:37–41. This complex, along with accompanying blessings, is known technically as "the recitation of the *shema'*." The Rabbis instituted the declaration "Blessed be the name . . ." between Deuteronomy 6:4 and 6:5.
8. BT Pesaḥim 56a.
9. The two systems are the interpretations of *YHVH elohenu YHVH* of the *shema'*: one by considering the verse as an ascent through the sefirotic tree, and one as a descent.
10. BT Pesaḥim 56a.
11. In Deuteronomy 6:4.
12. See the *merkavah* work *Pirqey Heikhalot* 31:4. The "beast" (*ḥayyah*) is one of the celestial creatures that carry the Chariot in the vision of the prophet Ezekiel.
13. Either way, unity of the *sefirot* is achieved and the flow of divine energy is maintained.
14. A stock phrase for the highest and least conceivable *sefirah* of the Provençal mystics. See below, Jacob ben Jacob's *Explanation of the Letters*.

15. The *dalet* symbolizes the complex of the lower 6, from Lovingkindness *(hesed)* to Foundation *(yesod)*, and is also called the six extremities.
16. In traditional practice, one is to prolong the pronunciation of the consonant *dalet* of the word "one" *(ehad)* during the recitation of Deuteronomy 6:4. The homilist provides a new tradition to justify this unusual enunciation.
17. Eight *sefirot*, equal to the numerical value of the letter *het*.
18. *Malkhut.*
19. The letter *alef.*
20. Rabbi Isaac the Blind.
21. *Aher* is the rabbinic defamation for Rabbi Elisha' ben Abuyah, a Rabbinic master of the second century C.E. who apparently became a gnostic dualist.
22. *Sefer Yesirah* 1:4.
23. See G. Scholem, *Ha-Qabbalah be-Provans* (Jerusalem, 1963), p. 3 of appendix.
24. Jeroboam son of Nebat was the first king of Israel (ruled c. 922–901 B.C.E.). According to 1 Kings 12:28f., he set up two golden calves in his kingdom.
25. Cf. BT Sanhedrin 102a.
26. BT Ta'anit 25b.

CHAPTER FOUR: PEACE—THE NAME OF GOD

. . . Thus, according to this matter, we may say according to the literal explanation that the name of the Holy One, blessed be He, is known as Peace *(shalom)* for it reconciles *(hishlim)* two systems.[1] But by the method of the Kabbalah, it appears to me that He is called Peace for He fosters peace between the principle of Severity and the principle of Lovingkindness which are neither fire nor water, nor the two angels about which Scripture states, "*Dominion* and *fear* are with Him, He makes peace in His heights" (Job 25:2). To this the Sages, may their memories be blessed, said: "*Dominion* is Michael and *fear* is Gabriel. One is water and the other is fire and the Holy One, blessed be He, makes peace in the heights. Never has the concavity of the moon been seen by the sun so that the moon not feel humiliated."[2]

Know that the pronouncements of our Rabbis, may their memories be blessed, are words of the living God and one should never contradict them. But it is also a commandment for each wise man to make innovations in the Torah according to his ability. From the previous material, the way of Kabbalah (says) that the Rabbis' intent was to hint to the springs which burst forth and are drawn to the secrets of the principles that are understood from the allusion that I have hinted. Then the Rabbis called them by the name of the angel which resembles them. And he linked it to the humiliation of the moon and the opinions of sun-worshipers.[3] My intention is to join the principles and combine them and this is the unity of the cosmos.[4]

The enlightened person will understand both opinions and know that they are really one and the same. There is some difficulty in understanding the words of Rabbi Yoḥanan, but they are clarified through the rabbinic statement: "Two witnesses came and said, 'We have seen (the new moon) at its proper time, but the next night it was not to be seen' and Rabban Gamliel accepted their testimony. Rabbi Dosa ben Harkinas said, 'These are lying witnesses! How can one testify that a woman gave birth and the next day she remains pregnant?' Rabbi Joshua said to him, 'I see your point.' "[5] This, then, is the power of domestic tranquillity (shalom bayit), as Scripture states: "And you shall know that your tent is at peace; and you shall visit your habitation and miss nothing" (Job 5:24); and it (further) says, "He makes peace in your borders" (Psalms 147:14). I say the word YOUR BORDERS (gevulkha) is derived from "he mixes" (megabbel) and from the expression "mix (gabbel) for the ox."[6] The intended meaning of the verse is to the extension and emanation radiating forth from Peace to Righteousness (sedeq) and that which is adjacent[7] to it, for it is written, "Righteousness and Peace have kissed" (Psalms 85:11), and this is the literal sense of the word YOUR BORDERS. Furthermore: Every occurrence of the word Solomon (Shelomoh) in the Song of Songs is holy except for one; and [Solomon means] the king to whom peace belongs [i.e., God].[8] This, then, is "He makes peace in your borders" and afterward "and fills you with the finest wheat"—the inundation of white and red waters along with the shells of wheat and its finest portion.[9]

Domestic tranquillity also comprises peace between men, for it encompasses everything. Therefore, it is not astonishing to find that the Name of God, may He be blessed, was effaced by water so that peace could be established between a man and a wife.[10]

I am certain that if you understand all this you will also understand why God gave Phineas peace, as it is written, "Behold, I give him My covenant of peace" (Numbers 25:12). Now know that [the Rabbis] said that Phineas is none other than Elijah.[11] The numerical value of the name Elijah ('LYHW) is 52, or twice the value of the Tetragrammaton.[12] If you pay close attention to the episode in Shittim[13] from "And Phineas saw . . ." (Numbers 25:7) until the end, you will know full well what our Rabbis, may their memories

123

be blessed, meant. You will also discover that God gave him the covenant of peace measure for measure.

Now if you want to say that Life is included in Peace, you will find, "My covenant was with him for *life* and *peace*" (Malachi 2:5). This (opinion) is likewise correct and one and the same.[14]

Scripture states, "Hear my voice according to your Lovingkindness; Lord! Enliven me according to your judgment" (Psalms 119:149). MY VOICE is well known.[15] YOUR JUDGMENT is the Foundation of the world *(yesod 'olam)*. Behold, I have explained everything to you such that no doubt can remain.

Notes

1. Of letters. Peace, as well as the phrase "the Holy One, blessed be He," refers to *tif'eret*, the sixth *sefirah*.
2. *Yalqut Job*, loc. cit. Cf. *Genesis Rabbah* 12:7 and BT Ro'sh ha-Shanah 23b.
3. He spoke of the concavity of the moon. In a discussion of the appearance of the new moon (BT Ro'sh ha-Shanah 23b), Rabbi Yoḥanan said that the sun is never witness to either the concavity of the moon (for the moon would be humiliated) or the concavity of the rainbow (lest sun-worshipers liken it to a cosmic bow by which the sun/god destroys enemies).
4. I.e., God.
5. Mishnah Ro'sh ha-Shanah 2:8.
6. BT Berakhot 40a.
7. Peace signifies *tif'eret*, and it radiates to Righteousness, a symbol in the *malkhut* symbol complex. *Malkhut* is adjacent to Foundation *(yesod)*, the mediating and phallic *sefirah* that unites the male *tif'eret* with the female *malkhut*.
8. BT Shabu'ot 35b.
9. I.e., the Red and the White, the two divergent principles.
10. See Numbers 5:23 and BT Sukkah 53b.
11. *Yalqut Shim'oni*, section Phineas, no. 771. In this passage, Phineas, who brought peace to the Israelites after they worshiped Midian gods at Shittim, is identified with Elijah, who upon announcing the Messianic epoch will bring peace to the world.
12. *YHVH* = 26.
13. See Numbers 25:1ff.
14. Life *(ḥayyim)* is one of the symbolic attributes of *yesod*.
15. "Voice" *(qol)* is linked with *tif'eret*.

CHAPTER FIVE: THE MYSTICAL PRAYER

Herein you will understand what is found in the words of our Rabbis, may their memories be blessed: "Rabbi Ḥisda' said: 'A man should always *enter* two doors and then pray.' What is the meaning of two doors? Rather say: 'The distance of two doors.' "[1] The verb "to enter" is often used when speaking of Wisdom, as when they spoke of "the four who *entered* paradise"[2] . . .

We ought to note that it was Rabbi Ḥisda's intention to allude to the matter of prayer and how prayer is derived. His statement— "a man should always enter"—(means) to draw forth and emanate Blessing and Will into that which is drawn forth and emanated and bursts forth from spring to spring, like a candle lit by (another) candle. Thus a man should enter through two doors as mentioned above.[3]

Afterward he should pray with Thought and the emanation of the (letter) *yod* which hints to the attribute of Humility. [The letter *yod*] appears in its small and bent shape in order to indicate its origin; like the bend of the letter *bet:* by this I mean that its bent shape indicates that to which all else bow down. And by (the letters) *YV* the Holy One, blessed be He, is called: "I dwell *on high* and in *a holy place* and also with the *depressed and low in spirit* in order to revivify the spirit of the lowly and the heart of the dispirited" (Isaiah 57:15). That is to say, to draw the power of Fear toward the Wisdom that is alluded to in the statement "Fear the Lord your God" (Deuteronomy 10:20).[4] For Fear precedes Wisdom, as it is said, "The beginning of[5] Wisdom is the Fear of God" (Psalms 111:10).

ON HIGH [of Isaiah 57:15] is Severity and A HOLY PLACE is Mercy, and the AND of the verse denotes the divine emanation. DEPRESSED AND LOW IN SPIRIT is derived from "And He came from holy multitudes" (Deuteronomy 33:2), meaning "I can be found in everything."

Afterward, [in Deuteronomy 10:20] he said "He shall you serve." After he mentioned fear and service, he said "in Him shall you cling"; then he said "and in His name you shall swear *(tishave'a).*" In all these [clauses] ten are found.[6]

The next verse reads "He is your praise and He is your God" (Deuteronomy 10:21). Knowing why these two verses are joined is a most profound and hidden secret.[7]

In any event, we have learned that [the verse] begins with Fear, an allusion to Wisdom, as when [the Sages] said: "FEAR THE LORD YOUR GOD—this includes wise students."[8] Then it says "him you shall serve." (About this verse) the Jerusalem (Talmud states): Both Him and His Torah.[9] Thus, it alludes to the Torah created two millennia before the creation of the world. About this I will soon write, since afterward it says "in Him shall you cling." Up to this point one cannot unite with Him. Then it says "you shall swear," which is derived from the word "vow" (shevu'ah). And this is the bent yod in which both Humility and holiness are hinted.

With regard to the exultation of the Creator, may He be blessed, through this particular attribute, it is said that the Holy One, blessed be He, prays. Rabbi Yoḥanan said, "From whence is it known that the Holy One, blessed be He, prays? It is written, 'And I will make them joyful in the house of My prayer' (Isaiah 56:7). It does not say 'their prayer' but rather 'My prayer.' "[10] This (above cited verse) refers to "the sons of strangers who accompany God," which are mentioned in the preceding verse (Isaiah 56:6).

First (Isaiah 56:7) says "(I will bring them) to my holy mountain," and this is also known as the community of Israel.[11] Then it states "and I will make them joyful in the house of My prayer."

I say that the word HOUSE (bayit; in the construct state: bet) alludes to the letter bet (‏ב‎). It is therefore not to be taken as HOUSE. From this we understand what is written in Genesis Rabbah:[12] "They said to the letter bet: 'Who created you?' He showed them the tip (of his form) that is above—'That which is above created me.' 'And what is its name?' He showed then his point that is to his back, pointed toward the letter alef—'One is His name.' " Therefore it is fitting that the bet alludes to Thought which itself is hinted at in the letter yod.[13]

Do not be troubled by what you find in the book Bahir:[14] "Why is the letter bet closed on all sides but open to its front? It teaches that it is the abode[15] of the world."

The meaning (of this expression) is: The Holy One, blessed be He, is the abode of the universe, and the universe is not His abode. Do not read (the letter bet), but rather 'house,' as is said, 'With Wisdom the house will be built' (Proverbs 24:3)." This is identical to what I have written. A confirmation of this is what is written there (Sefer ha-Bahir): "Rabbi Amora' sat and expounded: Why is the letter alef the first (in the alphabet)? It was prior to everything, even the Torah. And why is the bet next to (alef)? It too was before the beginning. Why does (the letter bet) have a tail? In order to indicate its origin. And there are those who say that through (the letter bet) the universe is maintained."[16]

After (the above) is recorded, the verse continues, "Their burnt offerings and sacrifices will be accepted on my altar" (Isaiah 56:7). What is the reason for all of this? For "My house" which is mentioned "shall be called a house of prayer for all nations" (ibid.). This language is reminiscent of an invitation. Then "I will pour out My Spirit on all flesh" (Joel 3:1). Furthermore, it states, "For then I will convert the peoples to a purer language, that they may all call upon the name of the Lord, to serve Him with one consent" (Zephaniah 3:9).

Another interpretation (of Isaiah 56:7): MY HOLY MOUNTAIN is the community of Israel, as I have already recorded. IN THE HOUSE OF MY PRAYER refers to the inner aspects of the central pillar facing the Temple.[17] And the meaning of I WILL BRING THEM is similar to "I will cause them to enter."

"For I will pour water on the thirsty land and floods upon the dry ground" (Isaiah 44:3). FOR I WILL POUR WATER from the right side. ON THE THIRSTY LAND—these are the souls, about which it is said, "My soul thirsts for God, for the living God: When shall I come and appear before God?" (Psalms 42:3). FLOODS come from the left side. UPON THE DRY GROUND—each and every [sefirah] receives from its power. Understand who is called thirsty and who is called dry ground.[18]

After you understand this, then comprehend why [the Rabbis] instituted the recitation of "O Lord, open my lips and my mouth will speak of Your praise" (Psalms 51:7) before the prayer of eighteen benedictions.[19] In my opinion, MY LIPS means "edge/limit," like "the river's edge." They are further known as "foundations," as in "Lean me against the foundations (ashishot)" (Canticles 2:5). I am of the opinion that these are the elements—by which I mean the supernal powers which correspond to the elements. This is quite similar to what [the Sages] said in the Midrash to Canticles: "LEAN ME AGAINST THE FOUNDATIONS—[this means] against two fires (eshot), the supernal fires and the lower fire. Another opinion is that the two fires are the Written Torah and the Oral Torah. Another opinion is '(lean me) against many fires,' the fires of Abraham, Isaac, and Jacob, and the fires of Moses and Hannah and Elijah and Hananiah, Mishael and Azariah."[20]

Now apply your mind and understand that every one of these opinions gave the meaning "fire" for "foundations." Understand the implication. The fire of above and below are both undoubtedly from Severity. The Written and Oral Torah are one, and everything is encompassed in each one. There is no reason to be astonished [at this interpretation] of the Written and Oral Torah. Its implication is well known, and thus the intent of this statement likewise refers to the two fires. Also, comprehend the structure of [this statement]: It is arrayed from groom to bride and from bride to groom.[21]

[As for the interpretation] "against many fires": this includes the three fires recorded in the first two opinions. Then it adds four more, namely Elijah, Ḥananiah, Mishael, and Azariah. Thus, there are seven altogether.[22]

The word "will speak (yagid)" [of Psalms 51:17] means "to issue forth," as in "A fiery stream issued (naged) and came forth from before him" (Daniel 7:10); it further states, "Lift up your hands in the sanctuary and bless God" (Psalms 134:2).

It is required that the benediction for redemption be joined to the (standing) prayer,[23] not because redemption is the outcome of prayer—prayer, after all, is in Eyn-Sof and redemption is the end (sof) of all that is—but rather because its end is inextricably contained within its beginning.[24]

(The Rabbis furthermore) instituted the recitation of "May the words of my mouth and the meditation of my heart be according to Your will (le-raṣon) before You, O God, my Rock and Redeemer" (Psalms 19:15) after the (standing) prayer. The "to" (le of le-raṣon) fulfills a variety of uses—you may choose the best one. I am of the opinion that the reason for the inclusion of "May the words . . ." is in order to unite everything into Eyn Sof. Then one draws the divine emanation even while leaving [the standing prayer], so that one does not appear to be "cutting off the shoots."[25]

Furthermore, know that the Will is the cause of all things, and it is hidden and secreted, only comprehended by means of a meditation. Expanding forth from it is an entity which is perceptible. This is Wisdom, which clarifies and refines Will. It is through Wisdom that Will is perceived, and not through itself.

After saying "according to Your will" one says "before You (le-paneykha)," and this is because each and every thing is called "Faces" (panim). Thereupon one says, "O God, My Rock and Redeemer," and through this [clause] you know that the purpose of all existence is redemption. For example, when Jacob blessed Ephraim and Menasseh he concluded with redemption, for it states "The angel who redeemed me" (Genesis 48:16).

When one finishes and completes the [standing] prayer, one

takes three steps backward. At the outset the worshiper entered two doors and now he exits with two paces and with the third step he returns to his starting point. Yet even though he steps back three paces, the divine Presence always remains above him, for it says "His Glory fills the entire world" (Isaiah 6:3). Then one proclaims *"shalom"* as if one were a student departing from one's master. First one greets the left—which is the right side of the Holy One, blessed be He—and then the right, which is His left side.

I have two opinions [about this salutation] and I will now record them. But before I do, I would like to make two preliminary remarks. The first point is that Scripture refers to south by (the word) "right" and to north by "left," as is written, "If you take the left then I will take the right" (Genesis 13:9). And this is translated as "If you take the north I will go south."

The second point is what the Rabbis, may their memories be blessed, said: "One who seeks wisdom should turn south and one who desires wealth should turn north; a sign (that this is the case) is that the table is in the north and the lamp is in the south."[26] With regards to these two directions—by which I mean south and north— it is written, "Upon your right hand stands the queen in gold of Ophir" (Psalms 45:10) and "His left hand is under my head and his right hand embraces me" (Canticles 2:6).

Now if [the worshiper] faces south he first greets his left side with peace and then his right, as if they are fire and water.[27] A precedent [for this interpretation] to this says, "Dominion is [the angel] Michael and fear is Gabriel."[28] We already know that Michael is to the right and Gabriel to the left, the former of water and the latter of fire, and the Holy One, blessed be He, fosters peace between the two.[29]

If [the worshiper] faces north he first greets his left side and then his right, for the Torah is to the right of the Holy One, blessed be He, and the phylacteries are to His left. It is customary to greet [them] at the outset. These, then, are the two opinions I have regarding greeting the left side first.

There is another aspect. When he faces south, he directs himself to the right attribute in order to beseech from there the King of kings. When he faces the north—the left—he also requests Him from [the left attribute].

Another point: [The worshiper] turns the throne southward to the attribute of Lovingkindness, as in "And in lovingkindness a throne was established" (Isaiah 61:5). He turns to the north with a similar meaning—he turns the throne north, as in "From the north comes gold" (Job 37:22).[30] . . .

The sage Rabbi Ezra,[31] may his memory be blessed, wrote:

It does not say one prays in the south, but rather that one *turns* southward. This means he directs his heart to the southern attribute, the bright light. Because of this he who desires wealth should turn north to the northern attribute from which comes wealth. Therefore it states: "Why are (the prayers of) Israel not answered? Because they do not know how to pray with the Holy Name."[32] This means that it applies to that very entity and that very Thought, and it derives from the unity of all.

That is his statement.

But this doesn't appear to me to be its meaning whatsoever. For when (the Sages) said that (Israel) does not know how to pray with the Holy Name, they did not say it except for the fact that Israel, accompanied by the divine Presence, is in exile. They do not know how to awaken love, for the stirring fountains have been closed to Israel, as in (God's) promise not to incite the end of days when it says "I charge you, O daughters of Jerusalem, by the gazelles and by the hinds of the fields that you stir not up, nor awaken My love till it please" (Canticles 2:7). But with regard to all other matters there can be no doubt that they are answered. For prayer has been efficacious for our patriarchs and ourselves since the exile from Jerusalem. Also, a covenant has been made by the thirteen attributes that [Israel] will not be turned away empty-handed.[33] With the increase of good deeds prayer becomes more effective with all things that are fit to be revealed.

The story in the Talmud about Rabbi Ḥiyya and his sons does not contradict our words.[34] Quite possibly they had that power for that moment only. As [the Sages] said, "There is not a man who does not have his moment."[35] And the proof of this is that every day Rabbi Ḥiyya and his sons prayed the same prayer, even though they never together descended to the dais to bring our Messiah. Furthermore, how can it possibly be claimed that from the destruction of the Temple until the time of Rabbi Ḥiyya and his sons or in following generations there was not anyone else great in wisdom and deeds like Rabbi Ḥiyya and his sons? I am also of the opinion that Elijah was punished only because he revealed [to them their] moment. Also, it is a tradition in our hands that with regard to mercy and supplications, it is just a drop of water from the ocean, which is Wisdom, as I shall explain in a special treatise.

Because of all of this we know that in fact there is power in prayer. Scripture also states: "I will set him on high, for he knows My Name" (Psalms 91:14). The text does not say "My names," but rather "My Name." Immediately following it says, "He will call Me, and I will answer him" (ibid. 91:15). If what [Rabbi Ezra wrote] is a traditional law, we will accept it. But if it is [his] judgment, then we have a response. The truth is what I have written.

Another aspect [of the statement] that we do not know how to pray: It is a well-known fact that every word of the Torah can change by the modification of its diacritical points even though the letters remain unaltered. If you vocalize some words one way, then all the letters are linked to the root. If you take these same words and vocalize them differently, its content changes and one of the letters becomes a connective. So we can say that the Tetragrammaton must be expressed with its correct vocalization. If one knows how to construct its structure, he directs himself to the structure that this vocalization teaches. His prayer will be accepted and he will be answered from heaven. Do not regard this as far-fetched, for had I not discovered this in my heart I would have said it is a direct tradition from Moses at Sinai. It is quite likely that this was also the opinion of the sage Rabbi Ezra, may his memory be blessed.

Notes

1. BT Berakhot 8a.
2. BT Ḥagigah 14b.
3. This portion of chapter 4 is not translated. Citing the verse "waiting at the post of my *openings*" (Proverbs 8:34; note the plural form), Ben Sheshet suggests that all doors have a twofold function as both entrance and exit.
4. Fear the Lord your God, He shall you serve, and in Him shall you cling, and in his name you shall swear.
5. Or: "Before . . ."
6. "Fear" here is a symbolic attribute of *keter*, "service" is related to *hokhmah*, "clinging" to *binah*, and "you shall swear" to the seven *(sheva')* lower *sefirot*.
7. I.e., not to be revealed in this popular work.
8. BT Pesahim 22b.
9. JT Berakhot 9:5.
10. BT Berakhot 7a.
11. A term for *malkhut*.
12. 1:14.
13. The upper tip of the *yod* denotes the first and highest *sefirah*.

14. Ed. Scholem no. 11; ed. Margoliot no. 14.
15. Or: house.
16. Ed. Scholem no. 13; ed. Margoliot nos. 17, 18.
17. The pillar denotes *kenesset Yisra'el*, the tenth *sefirah*.
18. Both refer to the tenth *sefirah*, *Malkhut* (Kingdom).
19. Also known as the *'amidah*, "the standing prayer."
20. *Canticles Rabbah* 2:14.
21. A reference to the divine unity between the sixth and seventh *sefirot*.
22. Combined, they represent the seven lower *sefirot*.
23. BT Berakhot 9b.
24. A phrase from *Sefer Yesirah* 1:6.
25. I.e., committing the heresy of separating between the *sefirot*.
26. BT Bava' Batra' 25b.
27. Fire is *din*, water *hesed*.
28. *Yalqut Job*, loc. cit.
29. The Holy One, Blessed be He, or *tif'eret*, mediates between fire and water.
30. North, left, and gold—all symbols of *Gevurah* (Strength), the source of evil.
31. Rabbi Ezra ben Solomon of Gerona.
32. *Yalqut Psalms*, 843.
33. BT Ro'sh ha-Shanah 17b.
34. See BT Bava' Mesi'a' 85b, where Rabbi Ḥiyya and his sons are invited to the prayer dais and perform wonderful deeds by simply reciting the prayers. In response, God punishes Elijah for involvement in such awesome feats.
35. Mishnah Pirqey Avot 4:3.

Response of Correct Answers
THE HOLY THRONE AND THE COMMANDMENTS

CHAPTER TWO

Since we have explained in what way man is a microcosm in both soul and body, we will now explain in what way the world is a macrocosm.

All creation may be divided into four parts: The first part is the throne of Glory *(kisse' ha-kavod)*; the second is made up of the angels; the third constitutes the spheres, stars, and constellations; and the fourth is the sublunar world. As Scripture states: "God has established His throne in the heavens, and his kingdom *(malkhuto)* rules over all" (Psalms 103:19). This "throne" which we link to the Creator, may He be blessed, is that part which can be understood through intellectual contemplation by metaphors. It is alluded to by one of the letters in His Name, which is the letter *vav* (‫ו‬).[1] Therefore Scripture calls the heavens the throne of the Omnipresent; similarly the Prophet said: "The heavens are my throne, and the earth is my footstool" (Isaiah 66:1).

Since [the heavens] were created from the light of His garment,[2] it is appropriate that they should be nearer to Him than the rest of creation. That which is near Him ought to be called His throne, and it is an allusion to the light created on the first day—the intent here is not to the worldly heavens. The FOOTSTOOL is the Glory which unites with the throne and is included with it in order to be one name. It descends to become visible to the prophets, and it is called by the name "Glory" or by one of the other names. . . .

In the statement AND THE EARTH IS MY FOOTSTOOL there is a hint to that Throne of the Glory, and the Glory is alluded to by one letter of His Name, and it is the second *he* (ה) of the Tetragrammaton. And this is an allusion to the fifth light of the first day of creation, according to the order of the rabbinic interpretation. And that which is attached to His throne in a singular and uninterrupted communion is called THRONE; while that which is attached to the Glory and Presence is called FOOTSTOOL. Thus the throne and the footstool are called by their names.

This is the rule—the attached entity is called by the name of the thing to which it is attached; and the thing by the name of that which is attached to it. So too the guard [is called by the name] of that which is guarded, as when the verb is called by the name of the act, and the guarded by the name of the guard.

Since the Holy One, blessed be He, guards all creation, the text says, "Every one that is called by My name, for I have created him for My Glory" (Isaiah 43:7). Even though the Sages of the Kabbalah explain [the Glory] by measurement,[3] the [above interpretation] does not contradict it. A proof for this is what is said in the *aggadah* regarding the angel of the covenant: "Why is his name Sandalfon? Because the Sandalfon of the Holy One, blessed be He, is in his hand."[4]

And the intention of Solomon—who said by divine inspiration: "A women of valor, who can find her?" (Proverbs 3:10)—is well-known and widely famous among all Israel as a reference to the gathering of Israel *(kenesset yisra'el).*

And when [Solomon] said, "And deliver girdles to the Canaanite" (ibid. 31:24): It is well known that girdles are for the hips—the middle of the human body—as in what is written: "Gird thy loins" (2 Kings 4:29). Similarly, the land of Israel lies in the middle of the world, the very navel of the world.

And it appears to me that this was the intention of Rabbi Abraham Ibn Ezra when he wrote that "The Canaanite was then in the land" (Genesis 12:6). For after that verse it is written "And God appeared to Abram and said, 'To your seed will I give this land'; and there he built an altar to God" (ibid. 12:7) to inform us about the matter therein. Like this is "And behold, Egypt marched after them" (Exodus 14:10). And relating to this matter it is also written, "This is Jacob that seek your face" (Psalms 24:6). And also what Israel/Jacob said,[5] and also what was said: "Three are those that are called by the name of the Holy One, blessed be He, and they are the righteous, the Messiah, and Jerusalem. The Messiah for it is written, 'And this is his name whereby he shall be called: God *(YHVH)* is our righteousness' (Jeremiah 23:6). Jerusalem, for it is written, 'And the name of the city from that day shall be: God *(YHVH)* is here' (Ezekiel 48:35)[6] . . . All these instances prove that that which is attached to a thing is called by the thing's name, and the thing by the name of that which is attached to it.

And never forget this lesson whenever you find "the hand of God," "the face of God," "the ears of God," or "the eyes of God." For even though it is my own innovation that I have written, know that in truth it is important and traditional. And the philosophers cannot refute it; how much more so the masters of the true Kabbalah! It is a major principle by which one can understand many difficult things, and it resolves some [difficult] verses like "The hand of God was upon me" (Ezekiel 37:1) and "The eyes of God, they rove to and fro through the whole earth" (Zachariah 4:10), and "And his feet shall stand in that day upon the Mount of Olives" (ibid. 14:4), and many other verses of a similar vein. Also, one can understand the significance of several rabbinic statements such as the above-mentioned legends in Bava' Batra' said by Rabba Bar Bar Ḥana', and the [legend] in Bekhorot that once upon a time an egg of Bar-Yokam fell from its place and swamped seventy cities and shattered 300 cedar trees,[7] or stories of that nature which cannot be reconciled through a literal reading. About this issue Scripture states: "For let all people walk everyone in the name of his god, and we will walk in the name of God our Lord for ever and ever" (Micah 4:5)—which means: each and every one in his god to which he is attached in this world.

We will now return to the issue of the verse we were studying and we say: When the verse states THE HEAVENS ARE MY THRONE maybe the intention is to those who dwell in the heavens, as in "The heavens declare the Glory of God and the firmament proclaims his handiwork" (Psalms 19:2). There can be no doubt that one verse refers to the heavens and the second to those who dwell in the heavens—whether they be the stars as some commentators suggest; or they be angels, which is our explanation.

Now [Scripture] refers to these as "heavens" or "firmaments," and we already know that the firmament is called "heavens" as when

Scripture states: "And God called the firmament heavens" (Genesis 1:8). Thus when the Torah states THE HEAVENS ARE MY THRONE the reference is to those who dwell in the heavens.

And when Torah states THE EARTH IS MY FOOTSTOOL it means those who dwell on the earth, as in "All the world shall prostrate before you and shall sing to you, they shall sing your name" (Psalms 66:4); and also "And the earth came to Egypt to Joseph to buy corn" (Genesis 41:57); and many other similar verses whose true meaning is *the inhabitants of the earth*.

The Torah calls the union of the angels with the Creator, may He be blessed, by the word THRONE; and the union of man to the angelic union is FOOTSTOOL. Now instead of only mentioning the Throne of Glory without the interpretation of heavens and earth and angels, it is possible to interpret it according to this method, and thus these two unions themselves [are apparent]. For our Rabbis, may their memories be blessed, said: "one (throne) to Severity and one to Charity, one to him and one to David," and so forth.[8]

And where the two are mentioned, the text calls that in which man unites a FOOTSTOOL in relation to what the angels—or spheres [by the other interpretation]—are united. This is to teach that there is a superior quality to the union of the angels—or spheres—to the Creator than that of man to the Creator; and it is the superiority of a THRONE in contrast to a FOOTSTOOL. For man is incapable of uniting with the Creator in a permanent, unmoving union, for man is composed of the four [finite] elements and is subject to their rule. [Man's essence] differs from the essence of the angels and the spheres, for they are not compound entities; rather they are simple substances. With regard to them it is said, "He makes his messengers of air; his messengers of burning fire" (Psalms 104:4).[9] Therefore they are united to Him in a perfect and unending union.

Thus, it may be said that the attachment of the spheres in him can be called FOOTSTOOL in comparison to the union of the angels, while their union can be called THRONE since the angels are form without body while the spheres are material, though of an uncompound substance. Previously *the Rabbi*, the author of the [*Book of*] *Knowledge*,[10] wrote that the spheres—also referred to as the heavens—recognize and apprehend more of the reality of the Creator, may He be blessed, than does mankind; and that above the spheres are the separate intellects, and they recognize and apprehend more than do the spheres.[11] And, no doubt, the union of the spheres in the apprehension of His reality is continual and uninterrupted.

And were it to occur to you to say: For what reason are not the angels explicitly called the Throne of the Omnipresent, as are the heavens? Do they not in fact recognize and apprehend the reality of the Creator, may He be blessed, to a greater extent than the spheres? And is not their union continual and uninterrupted? But know that the answer to these questions is twofold and behold, I will explain the matter and ascertain the undisputed truth. The first reason is that you already know that the Torah is explicated by thirteen and thirty-two hermeneutical principles; one of them is *a minori ad majus*, that is, that we can infer a minor proposition from a major proposition and vice versa. The Torah relies on this famous principle: Since it had already called the heavens THRONE it was not necessary to call the angels THRONE, for we can infer the major from the minor. Therefore we say that since the heavens are called His throne because of their abundant and uninterrupted apprehension of and union in Him, then undoubtedly the angels also should be called His throne since their apprehension of His reality is greater than that of the spheres, and their union is a union without interruption. Therefore the text did not call the angels the Throne of the Omnipresent and for this reason the text does not explicitly call the heavens FOOTSTOOL. Furthermore, if we interpreted and said that the heavens and the spheres are His footstool we would have to interpret who exactly is the throne, in this context: on this the verse is silent for the reason which I have explained.

The second reason that the heavens and not the angels are called the Throne of the Omnipresent is that the creation of the heavens is before the creation of the angels. The heavens were created on the first day, as is explicitly stated in the Torah: "In the beginning God created the heavens and the earth" (Genesis 1:1). The angels were not created until the second day according to the opinion of Rabbi Yohanan, or the fifth day according to the opinion of Rabbi Ḥanina, as is explained in *Genesis Rabbah*:[12] "When were the angels created? Rabbi Yohanan said: on the second [day], etc. Whether it is the opinion of Rabbi Yohanan or Rabbi Ḥanina, everyone agrees that nothing was created on the first day, etc."

It is for this reason that the heavens and not the angels were explicitly called *His Throne*. They are called so only by inference, according to the interpretation I provided to the verse "The heavens are My throne" (Isaiah 66:1).

And if you were to ask: How is it possible to assert that when God said THE HEAVENS ARE MY THRONE He hinted to the light created on the first day (according to the first interpretation), or to the angels (according to the second interpretation)? Or furthermore, when He said THE EARTH IS MY FOOTSTOOL, that He hinted to the light of the fifth day (according to the first interpretation), or to the inhabitants of the earth (according to the second interpretation)? Did not our Rabbis say that the Throne was created before the world and that all these, the light and the angels, were created during the six days of creation? Would it not have been more appropriate to allude to something that preceded all of creation, that which is called "the Beginning"?[13]

The answer to your question, based on the first interpretation, is that the light created on the first day already preexisted [creation], before the statement "Let there be light" (Genesis 1:3), as I shall soon explain. And the five lights are one entity; just as the Pentateuch is fivefold yet it too is one entity—one composition that is incomplete in the absence of any of its component parts. So too are the five lights.

And the answer to your question according to the second interpretation is based on what I have already written—namely, that which is united is called by the name of that to which it is united. Even though they were created during the six days of creation, because of their union in the Throne that was created before the creation of the world, the angels—or mankind—are called THRONE or FOOTSTOOL. But they are not His Throne in truth; in truth they are like the light which is the Torah (as I shall soon write). And [Samuel] Ibn Tibbon[14] wrote that the angels were not created during the six days of creation, and I will soon quote his words and write an appropriate reply to his words in a separate chapter.

CHAPTER THREE

I will return to the Psalm that I was interpreting and say: the Throne that we are linking to the Creator, may He be blessed, is not a real throne like the construction of a corporeal throne; but rather it is a partial concept of His true Reality through the application of speculative thought by similitude. When we come to investigate the

Throne of the Holy One, blessed be He, in a thorough way, we find seventy thrones which correspond to the beliefs of the seventy nations. For there can be no doubt that the beliefs of each nation have as their ultimate goal the Divine. Thus the Torah states: "For from the rising of the sun until it goes down, My Name is great among the nations; and in every place incense is burnt and sacrifices are offered to My Name, and a pure offering: for My Name is great among the nations, says the Lord of hosts" (Malachi 1:11).

Do not drift off when reading this verse, but read and understand its meaning: for His *Name* is great among the nations, and they offer incense to His *Name*. But it does not say *I* am great or that they offer to *Me;* rather everything is linked to His Name, may He be blessed. Therefore I say that their intention was to the Name of God, but they followed in error after the messengers appointed over them. These messengers were their celestial leaders and they reversed what was written—"Do not provoke Him *(al tammer bo)*" (Exodus 23:21)—into what our Rabbis, may their memories be blessed, said [of them]: "Do not exchange Me for him."[15]

And the sum of all these thrones is the Torah, which is the belief of the truth and the unity [of God]. You will not find a single belief in the world which is not alluded to in the Torah. Rather, at every place where [the seventy nations] commit heresy, a refutation of their beliefs is found nearby.[16] But each one of them has a verse which they can utilize.

For example: "Let *us* make man" (Genesis 1:26) implies dualism; but a refutation follows: "And *God* created" (ibid. 1:27); that is to say, the Creator, may He be blessed, is none other than One. Similarly: "For the Lord thy God is a consuming fire" (Deuteronomy 4:24) is used by the fire worshipers; and the rejoinder is explicit: "And upon the earth He showed you His great fire" (ibid. 4:36); that is to say, the fire belongs to Him, but He is not the fire. And there are many more, like: "God was not in the fire" (1 Kings 19:12). Likewise the belief of Edom reveals their rejoinder and it is well known in every place that they find fault and such is the case with each of the seventy beliefs of the seventy nations.

And there is not a single science in the world that does not have confirmation from the Torah, neither astronomy nor medicine nor geometry nor any other science. Not even dream interpretation: All of them have a basis in the Torah. Thus it is written, "And he said, 'If you will hearken diligently . . . I will put none of these diseases upon you which I have brought upon Egypt: for I am the Lord that heals you' " (Exodus 15:26)—thereby implying that in the commandments there is the healing of bodies. And it is written, "Keep them and do them: for this is your wisdom and your understanding in the sight of the nations" (Deuteronomy 4:6), and [the Rabbis] said: "Which wisdom and understanding in the sight of the nations? Say it is the calculations of dates and the constellations."[17] According to their statement it was not necessary to write "Keep them and do them"; rather, "Keep them and learn them." But [the verse] alludes to the commandment of guarding and observing the practice of the commandments included in the calendrical and astronomical sciences: Without a doubt this applies to the other verses.

Therefore [the Torah] is called perfect, for it is written, "The Torah of God is perfect" (Psalms 19:8). But if the Torah were lacking in something, He would not call it "perfect."

King David, peace be upon him, would consult the Torah with every action he took. Thus he said, "Your testimonies are also my delight; they are my counselors" (ibid. 119:24). Therefore I said that [the Torah] is the true Throne, encompassing all other thrones. I have brought myself to the point of saying that all sciences and beliefs are alluded to in the Torah, because of that which the Rabbis said—"[God] peered into the Torah and constructed the world."[18] We find that the world was created in such a way that it would be possible to derive all sciences and beliefs from the Torah. But the world would not have been created in this fashion—namely, to receive the sciences and beliefs—unless the sciences had already been alluded to in the Torah.

And in *Genesis Rabbah* it is stated with regards to LET US MAKE MAN: "He said before Him, 'Master of the universe, you are providing a pretext for the heretics to utilize.' "[19] Now heretics in this passage are those who believe in dualism. And it is impossible that He would provide a pretext for them or believers of other creeds, for then their position would be strengthened in professing that their beliefs are true. But when He hints in the Torah to all beliefs—with the rejoinder nearby—it becomes clear that they are all lies and falsehoods, save for our own faith. And these heretics exist solely to tyrannize Israel when Israel sins, to fulfill "And there you shall serve gods, the work of men's hands, wood and stone, which neither see nor hear nor eat nor smell" (Deuteronomy 4:26). And when Israel enslaves the heretics, they are fulfilling the

Will of the Omnipresent to fulfill "And you will consume all the peoples which the Lord your God shall deliver to you; your eye shall have no pity on them: neither shall you serve their gods; for that is a snare to you" (Deuteronomy 7:16); and "And you shall reign over many nations, but they shall not rule over you" (ibid. 15:6). And God said, "You shall utterly destroy all the places which you are about to possess where the nations served their gods, upon the high mountains and the hills and under every green tree" (ibid. 12:2). And there are many similar verses. . . .

The physicians prohibit all food which is not mixed. Similarly, it can be asked for what reason did the Torah prohibit impure fowl? Because they are gossipers and revealers of the secret of the universe. Now the Torah previously warned "Do not gossip" (Leviticus 19:16), and this means that if you eat impure fowl their nature will mix with yours. Now I have heard from a wise sorcerer that one does not divine except by means of an impure bird. Furthermore, any bird that has an advantage in attack also is efficacious for divination and should be reliable. This is what he told me.

And though they do divine with pure fowl, like a cock which crowed in the evening or a chicken which crowed like a cock[20] and others of like nature, it is not necessary to forbid this bird out of hand, for two reasons. The first is that the essence of sorcery is in the act that the bird does and not in his crowing, for crowing is not at all effective in sorcery. In fact, it is the action—not the chirping or the warbling—by which one divines. But if he chirps and calls out all day and does nothing else, nor returns to his place, then one does not divine by it.

Now everything that pure fowl reveals is by crowing and chirping. And in any event even with impure fowl it is not called sorcery but rather wisdom, like the speech of palm trees[21] and the speech of trees. And regarding this, Solomon in his wisdom said, "For a bird of the sky shall carry the sound, and that which has wings shall tell the matter" (Ecclesiastes 10:20). And in only the rarest of instances does a pure bird reveal anything in the world through action, and one should not rely on what it does reveal; and then only in simple matters which are quickly grasped with little consideration by people who can foresee events. Now I wrote that one does not divine except on the basis of actions, and I have [found] a great proof for this in what [the Rabbis] said: "His bread has fallen out of his mouth . . . a deer has crossed his path."[22] Likewise, both the pure beasts and animals were not forbidden because of sorcery, for they do not exist in order to reveal these matters. Rather, they are like "His bread has fallen out of his mouth," and various similar matters.

Maybe you will say the matter hinges on the revelation of a secret, whether [it is revealed] by action or by sound. But know that there is a substantial difference between the two. The impure fowl alters its action and its posture in conjunction with the changes that take place. Everyone knows and recognizes that it is revealing something, and he that knows the ways of sorcery understands it, while everyone else does not. That is not the case with sound. It is like what Scripture states: "And your ears shall hear a word behind you, saying, 'This is the way, walk in it, when you turn to the right or the left' " (Isaiah 30:21).

The reason that there is a prohibition of beasts is another matter entirely. The core of it lies in the interpretation of the fourth animal which Daniel saw,[23] and what the Rabbis, may their memories be blessed, said: "Why is it called pig *(ḥazir)?* Because in the future the Holy One, blessed be He, will return *(yaḥzir)* it to Israel."[24] Now the masses understood this to mean that someday the pig will be pure for Israel. "Who can bring purity from impurity? Not one" (Job 14:4). But in their pronouncement that the Holy One, blessed be He, would in the future return *it* to us, they really referred to the pig's power, which is troubling to Israel now. In the future it will return along with all the other forces to facilitate and support Israel. Then peace will be abundant in the land, as in "The wolf shall dwell with the lamb, and the leopard shall lie down with the kid" (Isaiah 11:6). And Scripture further states: "The cow and the bear shall feed" (ibid. 11:7). And Scripture says: "They shall not hurt nor destroy in My holy mountain" (ibid. 6:9). Furthermore, Torah states: "Let the mountains bring peace to the people; and the hills by righteousness" (Psalms 72:3); and: "Let there be abundance of peace till the moon is no more" (ibid. 72:7). Scripture also states: "For you shall go out with joy and be led forth in peace: The mountains and the hills shall break forth before you in singing, and all the trees of the field shall clap their hands" (Isaiah 55:12). And just as the pig is distressing to Israel during the time of the dispersion, so too the other animals distress them and are detestable. Therefore they were prohibited so that their nature would not blend with [Israel's]. But this is not similar to the abomination of Egypt, for they are not distressed by this—instead the Egyptians worship their form.

RABBI JACOB BEN SHESHET

We have already received a tradition that the beginning of the creation of the pure beasts was in the attribute of Lovingkindness *(ḥesed)*, and that some of them remain tied to that attribute. The pure animals seem to me to be "the deer, the gazelle" (Deuteronomy 14:5): "by the gazelles and by the hinds of the field" (Canticles 2:7); "the fallow deer *(yaḥmor)*" (Deuteronomy 14:5): "The heap *(ḥomer)* of great water" (Habakkuk 3:15); "the antelope *(dishon)*" (Deuteronomy 14:5): "And your threshing *(dayish)* shall reach to the vintage" (Leviticus 26:5); "the bison *(te'o)*" (Deuteronomy 14:5): "And you shall point out for them *(ve-hit'avvitem)*" and "You shall mark out *(tita'u)*"; "and wild sheep *(zemer)*" (Deuteronomy 14:5): "Sing to Him, sing songs *(zamru)* to Him" (Psalms 105:2). And the reason for the impure fish appears to me to be that in the future the Holy One, blessed be He, will make a feast of the Leviathan—which has fins and scales—for the righteous in the future world. . . .[25]

Another answer: The reason that the impure beasts, animals, fowl, and fish are forbidden is based on common sense. We have been commanded to seek union in Him, as Scripture states, "that you listen to His voice and cleave unto Him" (Deuteronomy 30:20), and as it also says, "You shall cleave unto Him and swear by His Name" (ibid. 10:20).

Now it is manifestly evident that the meaning here is not a corporeal joining but rather a joining of spirit. Furthermore, any thoughtful person understands that when the soul is united with the Creator all bodily sensations are eliminated such that it has no need for food nor drink nor any other bodily need. His limbs will be inactive and the food already in his stomach will be preserved so that he lose nothing because of the energy expended while he is united with Him to the extent that his intellect reaches in union with Him. And when his energy for union is expended, the soul awakens easily and quickly to bodily sensations like a slumbering individual awakened from his sleep. His limbs do not accept [awakening] suddenly; rather it is like the flame of a wick which has not yet completely caught fire, easily extinguished at the moment of ignition—much more so than a well-burning fire. Such is the soul when a man awakens from his slumber: He finds himself somewhat weak until he gains back a bit of strength, and this is what happens when one unites in Him. Therefore, when one is about to leave his senses, if he were to eat impure food—which, according to the medical experts, causes illness—there is no doubt that he would incur sickness. But He has already assured us—"If a man keeps [the statutes], he shall live in them" (Leviticus 18:5).

This matter is alluded to in the Torah by the statement "All the diseases I have put upon Egypt I will not put on you for I am God that heals you" (Exodus 15:26). That is to say: Do not be neglectful of the commandments because they are commandments which are oppressive to the body. Do not fear that they may produce sickness in you. FOR I AM GOD THAT HEALS YOU—I will charge you to perform another commandment which will heal you. And by this method you will find an opening to the remaining issues until it becomes clear to you that the Torah includes all sciences and beliefs, and it is the Throne of the Holy One, blessed be He.

I am aware that among the pious and the Sages of Israel there will be those that reproach me because I have written explanations for two or three of the commandments in the Torah and that these [explanations] are a pretext for providing explanations for many commandments by way of science. Behold, I will put forward a proof that any wise man can provide an explanation to any commandment whose explanation is not given in the Torah, and that his reward will be great, for he has made the commandments more beautiful in the eyes of the nations. "They will say, 'Surely this great nation is a wise and understanding people' " (Deuteronomy 4:6). For they challenge us: What is the reason for this or that commandment—are not they all nothing but parables? But when we provide for them a reason by means of wisdom, they will have no way to deny the commandments. They will say, "Come, let us go up to the house[26] of the Lord and to the house of the God of Jacob; and he will teach us of his ways and we will walk in his paths; for from Zion the Torah shall go forth, and the word of the Lord from Jerusalem" (Micah 4:2).

Our patriarch Abraham, peace be upon him, who was not charged with all the commandments but only with eight—how did he come to know them all if not through wisdom; for he was wise in all sciences. Maybe you will respond to me and say that the Creator, may He be blessed, imparted to Abraham the entire Torah and revealed to him all 613 commandments. But look at what our Rabbis, peace be upon them, said: "At the age of two or three Abraham recognized his Creator."[27] They did not say that the Holy One, blessed be He, was revealed to Abraham; rather that Abraham recognized his Creator. There can be no doubt that this recognition came by wisdom and not prophecy. Not only for Abraham did wisdom precede prophecy; for wisdom preceded prophecy in all the prophets, as [the Sages] said: "The *Shekhinah* dwells only upon him that is wise, valiant, wealthy, and tall."[28]

Now once our patriarch Abraham had recognized his creator by wisdom, how much more so was he able to recognize those commandments which were fitting for him and his Torah. Therefore it should not be an impediment in the eyes of any pious or wise man to provide an explanation for commandments whose reasons are not explicitly stated in the Torah. Only one should not say that the explanation itself is the object of the bestowing of the commandment; rather one should say, "If this commandment had not been given, it would have been appropriate to be given for this and that reason, and would be binding because of this wisdom."

Now should it occur to you to say that our Rabbis already said that the Torah precedes the Throne of Glory;[29] therefore how can it possibly be stated that the Torah is the Throne? I have already written about this matter in detail—behold, it is fully explained and there remains not a doubt nor a problem regarding it. All we need to do now is meticulously explain the difference between the verse which states, "He has established his Throne in the heavens" (Psalms 103:19) and between "God is in His holy throne room; God, whose throne is in the heavens" (ibid. 11:4) and the verse which says, "The heavens are My Throne" (Isaiah 66:1). In the statement GOD HAS ESTABLISHED HIS THRONE IN THE HEAVENS it would appear that the Throne is something other than the heavens and the heavens are something other than the Throne. In the statement THE HEAVENS ARE MY THRONE it would appear that the Throne is the heavens and the heavens are the Throne. These two verses must be interpreted this way—the first is about the angels, which are understood to be THE HEAVENS; while the second is about the heavens themselves.

According to the way of the true tradition, one should interpret THE HEAVENS ARE MY THRONE as the Written Torah, which is the light created on the first day. HE HAS ESTABLISHED HIS THRONE IN THE HEAVENS is the Oral Torah, which is already encompassed by and alluded to in the Written Torah—it is the fifth light mentioned in Genesis. The interpretation of the verse should be thus: When He established His Throne in the heavens, His Kingdom ruled over all. Or it can be said that HEAVENS is a name for the attribute of Lovingkindness *(ḥesed)*, and therefore he said HE HAS ESTABLISHED HIS THRONE IN THE HEAVENS.

And the Sages said: "If one dare say it, the Throne was buckling until it was propped up by Lovingkindness, for it is said, 'And in Lovingkindness a throne was established' (Isaiah 16:5)."[30] From this we may say that HEAVENS is a name for the attribute Lovingkindness, and therefore he said HE ESTABLISHED HIS THRONE IN THE HEAVENS. And in the statement THE HEAVENS ARE MY THRONE we find that HEAVENS is a term for the Throne. A third verse comes to reconcile them—"O God, in the heavens (be-ha-shamayyim) is your Lovingkindness (hesed)" (Psalms 6:6). HEAVENS is here mentioned along with two other letters.[31] We learn from these three verses—namely THE HEAVENS ARE MY THRONE; HE HAS ESTABLISHED HIS THRONES IN THE HEAVENS; and AND IN LOVINGKINDNESS A THRONE WAS ESTABLISHED—that HEAVENS is a term for the Throne and Lovingkindness. We further learn from the verse IN THE HEAVENS (be-ha-shamayyim)—and not ba-shamayyim—that hesed is a term for the Throne. Therefore we find that it reconciles between THE HEAVENS ARE MY THRONE and between HE HAS ESTABLISHED HIS THRONE IN THE HEAVENS and other similar verses. This, then, is what is clear to me regarding the Throne which we ascribe to the Creator, may He be blessed.

Regarding the statement "His Kingdom (malkhuto) rules over all" (Psalms 103:19): The word malkhut sometimes acts as a description of sovereignty, as in "Your kingdom is an everlasting kingdom" (ibid. 145:13)—meaning: your rule is an everlasting one. Sometimes it acts as a description of the area over which he rules, as in "And when the king's decree which he shall make shall be heard throughout his empire" (Esther 1:20)—here the cities and lands are being discussed; so too in "The hundred and twenty seven provinces of the empire of Ahasuerus" (ibid. 9:30). Also, "And the beginning of his empire was Babel and Erech and Akkad and Calneh" (Genesis 10:10).[32]

Now [Samuel] Ibn Tibbon was most precise about this, but he did not explain correctly when he wrote that HIS KINGDOM RULES OVER ALL applies to the spheres, stars, and separate intelligences, as he explained ad nauseum in his book.[33] Would that he hold his peace! For where have we found that He is called the King of the angels, like He is called "the King of Israel and his redeemer, the Lord of hosts; I am the first and I am the last; beside me there is no God" (Isaiah 44:6)? Or with the nations it is said, "God is king over the nations: God sits upon the throne of His holiness" (Psalms 47:9). And the prophet said, "Who would not fear you, King of the nations? For to you it is fitting: for among all the wise men of the nations and in all their kingdoms there is none like you" (Jeremiah 10:7). But he did not link His Kingdom to the heavens as we find it linked with the earth, as David, peace be upon him, said, "For God is the King of all the earth; sing a skillful song" (Psalms 47:9).

Now listen to the unambiguously true [meaning of] HIS KINGDOM RULES OVER ALL. This refers to the Glory to which His Kingdom is linked, as when David, peace be upon him, referred to God as "the King of the Glory" when he said, "Lift up your heads, O gates! And be lifted up, O gates of the Eternal for the King of the Glory is coming!" (ibid. 24:7). . . .

The Creator, may He be exalted, Himself is called the King of the Glory and He is also called "the God of the Glory" as when David said, "The God of the Glory thunders" (ibid. 29:3). And about this Glory Scripture states HIS KINGDOM RULES OVER ALL. And this is what the Sages said in the first chapter of [the tractate] Megillah: "Now it came to pass on the third day that Esther clothed herself in royalty *(malkhut)*" (Esther 5:1). Surely it should say "royal apparel"! Rabbi Eliezer said: Rabbi Hanina said: "She was dressed with the Holy Spirit. It is written here AND SHE CLOTHED and it is written in another place 'Then the spirit clothed Amisai, chief of the captains' (1 Chronicles 12:19)."[34]

Regarding this Glory Scripture states: "May the Glory of the Lord endure forever" (Psalms 104:31), as if it said may the Glory endure and continue eternally—or may it be unlimited: This is what is hinted at by FOREVER. Therefore Scripture continues: "Let the Lord rejoice in His works" (ibid.). This means may God always rejoice in His works. Thus the intent of this verse is a prayer that the world not be destroyed. . . .

Now since the verse MAY THE GLORY OF THE LORD ENDURE FOREVER is a plea and supplication, our Rabbis, peace be upon them, said: "This verse was said by the angel of the universe."[35] That is to say: He requests before the Omnipresent mercy and compassion that the world not be destroyed. . . .

MAY THE GLORY OF THE LORD ENDURE FOR-

147

EVER: now the proof for the interpretation of the Rabbis, peace be upon them—namely that the verse was said by the angel of the universe and that it is a plea and supplication—is in the end of the verse, which states "Let the Lord rejoice in His works." It is as if it provides a reason for the first part of the verse, saying, "It is fitting for you that mankind acknowledge Your grace and beauty and that they exult You for Your works and that You be happy with them." This is like the matter that is written: "My son, if your heart is wise, my heart will also rejoice" (Proverbs 23:15). "And when did the angel of the universe say this verse? When the Holy One, blessed be He, said 'after its kind' (Genesis 1:11) on the trees, the plants applied to themselves an *a fortiori* argument, saying, 'If the Holy One, blessed be He, desired a motley growth, why did He say AFTER ITS KIND to the trees? Moreover, is there not here an *a fortiori* argument? If upon trees which by nature do not grow up in a motley growth, the Holy One, blessed be He, enjoined AFTER ITS KIND, how much more so does it apply to us!' Immediately each plant came forth after its kind. Thereupon the angel of the universe declared, MAY THE GLORY OF THE LORD ENDURE FOREVER."[36]

And it may be said [that this verse was said then] because the creation of man and the rising of the mist are connected and that one interrupts the other. For Scripture states: "And there was not a man" (Genesis 2:5). Scripture then should have attached to it: "And the Lord formed man" (ibid. 2:7). But it instead states: "And no plant of the field was yet in the earth . . . *and there was not a man*" (ibid. 2:5). *Then* it states: "There went up a mist from the earth" (ibid. 2:6). And only then does it state: "And the Lord formed man of the dust of the ground" (ibid. 2:7). Now they already said that the clouds of the Glory were strengthening and rising. And by saying THE EARTH—the "known" one, and not just the material one—this is to include the land, the spheres, and all that is beneath them. . . .

And with all this it is a prayer and supplication and teaches favor and provides a reason for the first half by virtue of the second half, which is LET THE LORD REJOICE IN HIS WORKS. And this also [intimates to] the clouds of the Glory which strengthen and rise upon each other.

Notes

1. *Vav* = Beauty *(tif'eret)*; the sixth *sefirah* = "heavens."
2. See the description of creation in Rabbi Azriel of Gerona's *Commentary to Talmudic Legends.*
3. A reference to *Shi'ur Qomah* speculation.
4. Source unknown.
5. *Genesis Rabbah* 68:11.
6. BT Bava' Batra' 85b.
7. BT Bekhorot 57b.
8. BT Hagigah 14a.
9. Simple substances.
10. Maimonides, simply "the Rabbi." This quotation is from his massive legal code, the *Mishneh Torah.*
11. *Hilkhot Yesodey Torah* 2:8, 3:1.
12. *Genesis Rabbah* 1:3.
13. Also Wisdom *(hokhmah)* = *re'shit*, "beginning."
14. Translator of Maimonides *Guide for the Perplexed.* This composition by Ben Sheshet is in part a polemical answer against Ibn Tibbon's own composition, the *Ma'amar Yiqqavu ha-Mayyim (MYM).* See *MYM*:10.
15. BT Sanhedrin 38b.
16. Cf. ibid.
17. Cf. BT Shabbat 85a.
18. *Genesis Rabbah* 1:1, ed. Albeck, p. 2.
19. *Genesis Rabbah* 8:8, ed. Albeck, p. 61.
20. BT Sukkah 28a.
21. BT Sanhedrin 65b. The passage reads: "Our Rabbis taught: A sorcerer is one who says: 'His bread has fallen out of his mouth; his staff has fallen out of his hand; his son called after him; a raven screamed after him; a deer has crossed his path.' "
22. See Daniel 7:3–8, especially 7. This fourth animal is viewed by the cited Midrashic text as a pig.
23. *Leviticus Rabbah* 13:5; *Ecclesiastes Rabbah* 1:9.
24. BT Bava' Batra' 75a.
25. BT Hullin 67b.
26. The biblical text has "the mountain."
27. BT Nedarim 32a.
28. See BT Shabbat 92b. In medieval Jewish prophetology, the presence of the *Shekhinah* is an indication of prophetic consciousness. Since wisdom is a prerequisite for such an event, Ben Sheshet concludes that wisdom precedes prophecy.
29. *Genesis Rabbah* 1:4.
30. *Midrash Psalms* 89:2.
31. Normally, both the preposition *in (be-)* and the definite article *the (ha-)* would elide into one syllable—*ba*. In the Masoretic text, however, the elision does not take place. Such an anomaly is a perfect springboard for further comment.

32. The last verse quoted does not contain the word *malkhut*, but a derived form: *mamlakhah*.
33. *MYM*:57f.
34. BT Megillah 14b.
35. Cf. BT Ḥullin 60a.
36. Ibid.

The Kohen Brothers

INTRODUCTION

Gershom Scholem published all the writings of these two brothers in *Mada'ey ha-Yahadut*, vol. 1 (1926), pp. 165–293, under the title "Qabbalot R. Ya'aqov ve-R. Yiṣhaq."

Rabbi Jacob's "Explanation of the Letters" is published on pages 201–219 of Scholem's edition. Translated below are the comments to the letters *alef*, *dalet*, *he*, *ṭet*, *yod*, and *kaf*.

Rabbi Isaac's "Treatise on the Left Emanation" is published on pages 244–264 of Scholem's edition, and appears here with some lacunae.

Explanation of the Letters

RABBI JACOB BEN JACOB HA-KOHEN

Concentrate on the image of the letter *alef* (א) with your eyes and understand it in your heart. You will find that many hidden truths concerning the shapes of other letters are depicted and encompassed in the shape of the *alef*—something you will not find in any other letter. Now we should seek out and investigate why all the shapes of all the letters of the alphabet are depicted in the *alef*.

You know full well that all the letters are pronounced in specific places in the mouth. The *alef* is the first letter pronounced in the mouth with air, without any strain or effort, to teach that the Holy One, blessed be He, is one with no other partner, and that He is hidden from all creatures. Just as the *alef* is pronounced in a hidden and concealed spot at the back of the tongue, so the Holy One, blessed be He, is hidden from visible sight. Similarly, just as the *alef* is ethereal and imperceptible, so the Holy One, blessed be He, denied to all creatures the ability to comprehend Him, save by means of thought, for thought is pure and unblemished and subtle as the ether. But not even thought can grasp the Holy One, blessed be He, so hidden that He is.

That you see all the letters depicted in the *alef* is because the powers of all created things are hidden within the power and awesomeness of the Holy One, blessed be He. Every single power emerges from the divine Will when He so desires. Thus we learn from the image of the *alef*, within which the shapes of all the letters are hidden, that there is no creature without a Creator, no handiwork without a Maker, and no depiction without an Illustrator.

Now you should examine the form of the *alef*, the inner white form and the external black form. You will discover that it is as if the inner [form] bears the external [form], and that the inner [form] is the abode of the external [form]. This teaches you that the inner [form] corresponds to the Holy One, blessed be He, completely hidden from the sight of all creatures and unbounded in His interiorness. The external form corresponds to the world, dangling from the arm of the Holy One, blessed be He, as a charm on the arm of a hero.[1] And just as the inner form is the abode of the outer (form), so too the Holy One, blessed be He, is the abode of the world, though the world is not His abode.

When I said to you that the white form and not the black exterior form in the *alef* corresponds to the exaltedness of the Holy One, blessed be He, I said this to you as a principle and a great secret: The white form corresponds to the white robe. And the Sages, may their memories be blessed, said: "From whence was the light created? It teaches that the Holy One, blessed be He, wrapped Himself in a white robe whose sparks shone forth from one end of the world to the other. As it is written, 'He wraps Himself with light as a garment' (Psalms 104:2), and 'the light dwells with Him' (Daniel 2:22)."[2] Thus, you cannot pronounce the word light *(or)* without the letter *alef* at the beginning.

When we say that He WRAPPED HIMSELF IN A WHITE ROBE, do not take this literally. For it is known that the Holy One, blessed be He, is not a body nor does He wrap like one of flesh and blood. Rather, the Sages, may their memories be blessed, spoke in human terms, for this wrapping is mentioned solely to teach that there was nothing [standing] before Him except light. And this is what David, peace be upon him, said, "Even the darkness is not darkness for you" (Psalms 139:12).

When you observe the four directions from which the letter *alef* extends forth from the center point, know that they correspond to the four directions of the heavens and the four letters of His great and holy name and the four holy animals and the four encampments of the Chariot.

As the inner white form encircles the four directions of the outer form, so the Holy One, blessed be He, encompasses all the degrees we have already mentioned, all resting upon His right hand. When you observe that all the shapes of the letters are included in the *alef*, it is to teach you that the Holy One, blessed be He, appears in various images and visions to His prophets and servants. This is what is meant when it is said, "To whom then will you liken me that I should be his equal, says the Holy One" (Isaiah 40:25), meaning: "I can reveal myself to My prophets and worshipers in various guises, for the power of all the forms and images and similitudes, both the encompassed and depicted, are within my ability, power, and strength." Even though Scripture states that the Holy One, blessed be He, reveals himself in various manifestations, do not think that such is the case. Rather there are at His disposal fluctuating forces which change into various manifestations. These are the powers of angels, as it is written, "He makes the winds His messengers, the flames of fire His ministers" (Psalms 104:4). But the Holy One, blessed be He, is one and utterly unchangeable, as it is written, "For I the Lord do not change" (Malachi 3:6). This (lesson) you can learn from the *alef*: for though the *alef* contains all the shapes, it never ceases to remain an *alef*. Similarly the Holy One, blessed be He, reveals Himself to His prophets in a variety of images and visions, yet He never varies in His unity. Therefore the numerical value of *alef* is one, since it partakes of the image of the unity of the Holy One, blessed be He.

Furthermore, the shape of *alef* acts as a witness to the name of the Holy One, blessed be He. The tip of the *alef* is in the shape of a *yod*, the middle stroke is in the shape of a *vav*, while the foot of the letter is shaped like *yod*. Now add *yod*, *vav*, *yod* (10 + 6 + 10) and you will get 26, which equals *YHVH* (10 + 5 + 6 + 5). The letter *alef* is established at the beginning of the word "one" *('ehad)*, because it is a witness that the Lord our God is One.

We should now consider and know why this particular letter is called by the name *alef*. You will find that the tip of *alef* resembles a *yod*, as we have already stated. Now multiply the *yod* ten times in accordance with its numerical value and the resulting product is 100. Now multiply *yod* a hundredfold and the product is 1,000 *(alef)*. It is for this reason that (the letter) is so called. Similarly you will find that the product of *alef* equals the product of ',*Y*,*Q* (1, 10, 100), for *alef* is computed along the same lines as ',*Y*,*Q*. The *alef* is one, and from the one comes ten and from the ten comes 100 and after 100 comes 1,000—the same as the letter *alef*. Furthermore, one can discern *alef* in its shape: In it you will find the shapes of an *alef* (א), a *lamed* (ל), and a final *pe* (ף).

When you see that the tip of *alef* resembles *yod*, you learn that the Holy One, blessed be He, is One, that He created and brought forth in His wisdom and understanding ten celestial spheres (*galgalim*), and that He bequeathed to His people Israel the Decalogue corresponding to the ten Utterances with which the world was created. At the beginning of the first commandment the letter *alef* was placed, as is written, "I (*'anokhi*) am the Lord thy God" (Exodus 20:2). The middle stroke which resembles *vav* comes to teach you of the six directions, which are east, west, north, south, up, down, and the Holy One, blessed be He, is One, ruling over all these directions.[3] For this reason you will find that the verse "Hear O Israel, the Lord is our God the Lord is One" (Deuteronomy 6:4) is composed of six words,[4] corresponding to the six directions. The verse is closed with the word "One" to teach that the Holy One, blessed be He, is One without partner and that He rules over these six worldly directions.

Add up the letters in *alef* (' = 1, *L* = 30, final *P* = 800) and it equals Supreme God (*el ram;* ' = 1, *L* = 30, *R* = 200, final *M* = 600). This teaches that it is fitting that He be called Supreme God, for He who has no partner is supreme over all.

Now look at the shape of *alef* and discover that it contains the shape of man with his head, his hands, and his feet. The tip resembles *yod*, which corresponds to the ten parts of the human head, namely: the four temples of the head, the two ears, two eyes, and two nostrils—behold ten corresponding to the value of the shape *yod* (י) in the tip of *alef*. It also corresponds to the ten fingers in the human hand. The middle stroke resembles *vav* (ו), which corresponds to the six directions of man. For man is a microcosm, and just as the world possesses six directions, so too does man possess six directions. They are: front, back, left, right, head, and feet. The front corresponds to the east, the back to the west, left to north, right to south, the head corresponds to up, and the feet to down—behold six directions in man which equal the shape of *vav* in *alef*. The foot of *alef* resembles *yod* corresponding to the ten toes of man. Now you have discovered that the shape of *alef* is like the shape of man. Therefore the *alef* is placed in the word man (*adam*), is a great wonder (*pele'*), as Scripture states: "terrible in wondrous deeds, doing wonder (*pele'*)" (Exodus 15:11)—reverse it to (read) *alef*.

Gaze at the form of the *dalet* (**T**) and behold that because of its height it is called "hunch-backed." In the *Sefer Yesirah* it states that *dalet* is wisdom (*ḥokhmah*).[5] Thus, the form of *dalet* indicates that just as the inner side of *dalet* is a hollow and empty space and that, conversely, its outer stroke is like a hunchback, so too is the wise man (*ḥakham*). For he fears heaven and his inside is like his outside. He distances his heart from profanity and untruths and totally eschews them. Thus his inside is like his outside.[6]

Similarly, the shape of *dalet* teaches you that just as it is empty and lacking on one side and complete on the other, so too in every respect is the wise man. He may be empty and deprived of the goodness of this world, but he will eventually inherit the life of the World to Come which was created in the letter *yod* and lies at the top of *dalet*. When you see that the shape of *dalet* appears from the back to be a man carrying a burden on his shoulders, it is to teach you about the wise man, who has awe of the Word of God, and is lowly and worthless in his own eyes. "For the world persists by (the wise man's) rights and he seems as if he were bearing the world" (Proverbs 10:27).

And when you see that *dalet* faces the *he* and not the *gimel*, it is a hint of the four holy creatures corresponding to the numerical value of *dalet*. The *yod*-shape on the upper stroke of the *dalet* is an allusion corresponding to the Holy One, blessed be He, riding upon the Chariot. And since the *dalet* does not turn toward the *yod* which is facing its rear, therein is an allusion that even though the Holy One, blessed be He, rides upon the four holy creatures, they are unable to view the face of the divine Presence (*shekhinah*), for they both fear and tremble from viewing. Therefore they are equipped with wings so that they may shield their eyes and thereby avoid viewing the face of the divine Presence.

When you notice that the *yod*-shape is behind the *dalet* and not before the *dalet*, you learn that the Throne and Presence of the Holy One, blessed be He, are in the west. West is called "back," therefore Scripture states: "And you shall see My back, but My face shall not be seen" (Exodus 33:23), which is on the western side. Thus you will find that man's brain is toward the back of the head and the spirit is in the brain. The brain represents the Throne of Glory while the soul, fluttering like a dove upon the brain, corresponds to the divine Presence in the West. For this reason we place the *dalet* of the *tefillin* behind the head, corresponding to the west. And thus within the form of the *dalet* is contained the form of the *yod* of the arm *tefillin*, placed above the vein [of the arm]. And the enlightened will understand.[7]

Observe the form of the letter *he* (‎ה) and see that it contains the shape of *dalet* and *vav*. The *dalet*, as we have stated, corresponds to the four holy creatures. The *vav* is the six directions of the world. The *dalet* found in the letter *he* is the *dalet* of "one" *(eḥaD)*, and the *vav* found in *he* corresponds to the six words of "Hear O Israel, the Lord is our God, the Lord is One" (Deuteronomy 6:4). This is reliably attested by the *vav*, of which the *Sefer Yeṣirah* states: "*He* is vision: *vav* is hearing,"[8] corresponding to HEAR O ISRAEL.

Now, focus your heart and comprehend the *dalet* formed in the *he*: It corresponds to the four holy creatures. One of these four creatures is named Israel.[9] This creature is the form of the image of our patriarch Jacob, peace be upon him, about whom it is said, "Your name shall no longer be called Jacob, but Israel: for you have struggled with God and men and prevailed" (Genesis 32:29). This particular creature whose name is Israel—as is our patriarch Jacob, peace be upon him—rules over the six directions of the world by the command and Will of the Holy One, blessed be He.

Just as the top of the *he*—which is similar to the *dalet*—rules and rises above the lower *vav* stroke, so this particular creature whose name is Israel is the judge of the entire world; to acquit or convict according to the command and holy pronouncement of the Creator. In response we say HEAR O ISRAEL—here meaning: Hear O Israel who is inscribed upon the Chariot! Behold we unite the Name of the Holy One, blessed be He, with a perfect heart and a willing soul. We further accept the yoke of the rule of heaven with love and fear, awe and dread, terror and trembling. Then [the creature] responds, "I am a witness when you unite the Name of the Holy One, blessed be He, whether you do so in love and fear or not. For this reason the *'ayin* of HEAR *(shema')* and the *dalet* of ONE *(eḥaD)* are written big, for the two letters together spell "witness" *('ed).* This teaches that this creature functions as a witness whenever we unite the Name of the Holy One, blessed be He.

This creature called Israel stands at the head of the four holy creatures. He leads and guides the others, as it is written, "In whatever direction the front one went the others followed" (Ezekiel 10:11). Thus you will find that the opening between the upper and lower stroke takes the shape of the opening in the eye of man. This upholds what was said in the *Sefer Yeṣirah* [5:2]: "*he* is vision," and there can be no sight except with an eye. Thus, this creature sees everything that man does, according to the Will of the Holy One, blessed be He. The *vav* formed in the inner part of *he* is in the form of the inner heads which reside in the ear. There cannot be hearing without an ear and for this reason the *Sefer Yeṣirah* says: "*vav* is hearing." This creature hears the prayers of Israel and brings them before the King of all kings, the high and lofty God. Therefore Scripture states HEAR O ISRAEL. And for this reason we close this verse with the *dalet* of ONE *(eḥaD)* and extend its pronunciation, for it corresponds to this creature to whom we say HEAR O ISRAEL, and so forth. [10]

Observe the shape of the *ṭet* (ט) and you will discover that it contains the shape of the *pe* (פ) and *zayyin* (ז). The sign for this is *PZ*, as it is written: "His head is the finest gold *(ketem paz)*" (Canticles 5:11). This is the head of the holy creatures of the Chariot and it takes the form of the image of our patriarch Jacob, peace be upon him. Thus the upper stroke of the *ṭet* alludes to Diadem, for this head (creature) of the holy creatures is crowned with the prayers of Israel, and this letter indicates the Diadem with which the above-mentioned angel is tied.

When you notice that the head of the *ṭet* is bent and hidden like a man hides his face from sight, it teaches you a great thing: Despite the fact that this head creature leads and guides the Chariot, even though it holds rank and rule over the entire heavenly hosts, it still must hide its face so that it does not see the face of the divine Presence. Furthermore, it comes to teach you that the four holy creatures cover their faces lest they view the face of the Presence, yet the antlers[11] of the creature ascend upward to the Throne of the Glory, just as you find that the head of the *ṭet* rises upward. Now the antlers of the holy creatures of which we speak are none other than the antlers of the morning doe.[12] Thus Scripture states, "The voice of God makes the does to calve, strips the forest bare; and in His Temple everyone speaks of Glory" (Psalms 29:9). The holy creatures are called does for the reason we have already put forth: Their antlers resemble those of the morning doe. This morning doe of which we speak is the star which shines in the morning: Its rays resemble the antlers of a morning doe.

159

Similarly, the holy creatures are called does because they continually stand upright, running to and fro while never tiring. This is similar to the female wild does which run to and fro and stand upright, for they possess in their legs an incredible ability to withstand [pain] to a greater degree than male rams. Thus King David, peace be upon him, said, "He makes my feet like does' feet" (Psalms 18:34). He did not say "like rams' feet," for he knew that the strength in does' feet is much greater than in the feet of rams.

These antlers of the holy creatures which we have mentioned do not think in your heart that they are truly antlers. In truth, they are brilliance and light and splendor. Thus, they are the antlers/rays of the creatures. The word "rays/antlers" *(qeranim)* mentioned here is derived from "and rays *(qeranim)* issued from His hand" (Habakkuk 3:4) and "the skin of Moses face radiated *(qaran)*" (Exodus 34:35).

Now I will inform you about how we can learn that the *tet* refers to the head creature in conjunction with the image of our patriarch Jacob, peace be upon him. Know full well that our patriarch Jacob, peace be upon him, has two names—Israel and Jacob—and in these two names you will discover nine letters, corresponding to the numerical value of *tet*.[13] From this fact you then learn that the *tet* informs us regarding stature of the creature whose name is Israel. About him Ezekiel, peace be upon him, said, "This is the living creature that I saw by the river Chebar beneath the God of Israel" (Ezekiel 10:20).

Similarly I will enlighten you as to how you can discover that the letter *tet* informs us about the holy creatures. Know that the *tet* equals nine and that there are nine degrees of holy creatures. They are: man, lion, ox, snake, wheel of man, wheel of lion, wheel of ox, wheel of snake, and one wheel in the earth. Thus you have nine degrees corresponding to the value of the crowned *tet*. Corresponding to these nine degrees the prophet, peace be upon him, recorded nine visions of the first and second Chariot.[14]

And when I stated to you that in the shape of the *tet* you will find a *pe* and a *zayyin*, and that its sign is HIS HEAD IS THE FINEST GOLD *(paz)*, it is because the Holy One, blessed be He, suspended the entire world upon the head, as it says "He suspends the earth upon nothing *(belimah)*" (Job 26:7). Know that the value of *belimah* equals the value of *PZ*. Thus it is Scripture's intent to say HE SUSPENDED THE EARTH UPON *PZ*.[15]

I will further inform you that when you observe that one tip of the letter *tet* is crowned and that the other is hidden like a man hiding his face so that he looks not, it is a great and significant matter. Know that this teaches us about that which our Sages, peace upon them, said: "The righteous ones sit in the World to Come, their crowns upon their heads, enjoying the brilliance of the divine Presence."[16] Why do they deserve this? In this world they hide their eyes from the sight of any sinful thing, just as the tip of the *tet* is hidden.

Furthermore, you will find that the tip of the hidden *tet* resembles a man secretly giving charity to a poor man, and then the Holy One, blessed be He, establishes for him in the World to Come a beautiful crown in the shape of the higher, crowned tip of the *tet*. In addition, the Holy One, blessed be He, repels away from him the angel of destruction known as "anger" *(af)*, as in, "A gift in secret pacifies anger" (Proverbs 21:14).

Know full well that the *yod* is tiny in its shape, more so than any of the other letters. And behold, we find a reaffirmation for what we have explained regarding the letter *tet*.

Observe and behold that the shape of the *yod* (**᾿**) is similar to the shape of the initial tip of the *gimel*. This teaches us that the Holy One, blessed be He, adorns the crowns of majesty and beauty upon the righteous in the World to Come because they observe in this world the Ten Commandments, equal to the numeric value of the *yod*. You will also discover that the *yod* appears in its shape quite similar to the tip of the *alef*. This teaches that at the moment when the righteous depart from this world and journey to the World to Come, they perceive and recognize and know the unicity of the Holy One, blessed be He, who is hidden from the eye of every other creature. This is like the *yod*, which is neither recognized nor perceived from a distance, in contrast to the other larger letters.

Furthermore you will find that the shape of the *yod* is similar to the shape of *zayyin*, only smaller. This teaches that anyone who does not regard himself humbly *(maqṭin 'aṣmo)* and who does not conduct himself in the paths of fear and humility "will not behold the majesty of the Lord" (Isaiah 26:10) at the time of his departure from this world. Nor will he merit "beholding the beauty of the Lord and visiting His palace" (Psalms 27:4); nor will he be able to say, "He is my God and I will extol Him" (Exodus 15:2). It is for this reason that our Sages, may their memories be blessed, said: "Every one who regards himself humbly in this world merits life in the World to Come and inherits life in this world."[17] Why did they say that through such belittlement of oneself one would merit and inherit both this and the World to Come? They observed that the World to Come was created through no other letter than the little *yod*.[18] Thus they proclaimed that anyone who belittles himself like the *yod* through which the World to Come was created will merit life in the World to Come.

In addition, know that the Torah—which is the Decalogue and corresponds to the numeric value of the *yod*—was given on only one of the seven mountains created by the Holy One, blessed be He, namely Mt. Sinai. Why? Because it was lowlier than the other mountains, and thus it was called Sinai, for it was more scorned and despised and hated *(sanuy)* than other mountain.[19] So the Holy One, blessed be He, said: "I created the World to Come with a small letter. As for the Torah"—which is the life of the World to Come and whose sum total equals the value of the *yod*—"I will give it in no other place that this lowly and despised mountain."

It is for this reason that King David, peace be upon him, merited becoming king over Israel and Judah. A son come from his loins to build the Temple, for (David) belittled himself and did not make himself haughty all the days of his life, as it is written: "And David was the smallest *(qatan)*" (1 Kings 17:14). Our Sages commented: Was David truly small? Was he not the head of all the tribes of Israel? Rather it is to teach that he belittled *(maqtin)* himself in this world— thus it states "And David was *qatan*."[20]

You will further find that the *yod* is similar to a tiny *resh*, which stands for "high" *(ram)*. This is the Holy One, blessed be He, as it is written: "The high *(ram)* and lofty One who inhabits eternity and whose name is holy . . ." (Isaiah 57:15). This teaches that the loftiness of the Holy One, blessed be He, is accompanied by the lowly and the despised. Thus the *yod* is similar to the *resh*.

Observe and behold the shape of the initial and medial *kaf* (כ) and see that it is similar to the shape of the Crown of Kingdom *(keter malkhut)*. It is thus an allusion that at the moment when the Holy One, blessed be He, is sanctified in the heavens and earth and when the heights and depths enthrone Him, they all become one crown from a stupendous brilliance and iridescence. They reside on the head of the Crown of His Kingdom and this Crown is called the Crown of Holiness *(keter qedushah)*.

It is for this reason that every Sabbath we say: "They gave You a crown, O God our Lord."²¹ The name of this crown is Katri'el, meaning the Crown of God. Another meaning is that the crown says: Even though I am my own crown, I am still the Crown of God.²²

You will discover that the word "throne" *(kisse')* is based upon the *kaf*. How is this so? Observe and behold that the *kaf* is covered *(mekhusseh)*, and so too is the throne covered.

As you note that the letter *kaf* is closed and complete only in three directions and open and incomplete in the fourth, so too the Throne of Glory is complete in all its supports. But in the fourth side the throne is as if it were imperfect, and such a state will persist until the memory of Amalek is utterly erased. As it is written, "For he said: Because the Lord has sworn by the throne of the Lord *(kes YaH)* that He will wage war on Amalek from generation to generation" (Exodus 27:16).²³ And just as the *kaf* is circular, so too the throne encircles all. Heaven forbid if we imply that the image of the *kaf* is actually that of the Throne of Glory, for there are no images as such in the supernal realms. Instead, we mean to say that the stature of the throne of the Holy One, blessed be He, is to be considered like the image of the *kaf*.

Also observe and behold that three sides of the *kaf* are visible, discernible, and exposed to the human eye, yet the fourth side is neither visible nor discerned. This situation comes to teach you that these three correspond to the camps of the Chariot, which are water, fire, and earth. These elements are exposed, discernible, and visible. The fourth side of the *kaf* is totally indiscernible and corresponds to the fourth camp, which is air. This air is hidden and obscure and not discernible. It is for this reason that the *kaf* is placed next to the *yod*, for they explain both the Diadem of beauty *('ateret hen)* and the Crown of Kingdom.

These two letters are also linked in that their sum is identical. When you compute the sum of the letters in the word *yod (Y, V, D)* the total which you achieve is the equivalent of the value of *kaf* [= 20]. Therefore it is included in the reverse alphabet, to teach that in the Throne of Glory ten wheels are united, and that the tenth is holy unto God.²⁴

Notes

1. JT Hagigah 2:1 (77a). This theme is found in the *Shi'ur Qomah* literature and in the *Sefer ha-Bahir*, sec. 142. See G. Scholem, *Das Buch Bahir* (Leipzig, 1923), p. 110.

2. Genesis Rabbah 3:4. Cf. *Pesiqta' de-Rav Qahana'* 145b.
3. In Hebrew numerology *vav* equals six. On the six extremities corresponding to six of the seven lower *sefirot*, see *Sefer Yesirah* 1:5.
4. *Shema' Yisra'el YHVH elohenu YHVH ehad.*
5. See BT Yoma' 72b.
6. Alluded to in 4:1.
7. On the Throne and the *Shekhinah* in the west, see BT Bava' Batra' 25a. The
   phylacteries for the head have a large square knot, which is placed at the
   base of the skull behind the cranium, and this know is now likened to the
   letter *dalet*. A smaller knot on the phylacteries for the arm, placed over the
   large muscle of the arm, is now likened to the *yod*.
8. 5:1, 2.
9. *Heikhalot* mysticism reports this statement of a celestial beast called Israel.
   Rabbi Jacob combines this older motif with the Kabbalistic usage of the
   symbol Israel as the sixth *sefirah*, *tif'eret*.
10. The traditional custom is to overenunciate the *dalet* of *ehaD* whenever re-
    citing the *shema'*.
11. Hebrew *qarney*. This word can also mean "rays of," and should be read with
    both meanings throughout this text.
12. Hebrew *qarney ayyelet ha-shahar*. This phrase figuratively means "the rays
    of the morning star." According to BT Yoma' 29a, the diffraction of the
    dawn light is likened to the spreading antlers of a doe.
13. Y, S, R, ', L + Y, ', Q, B = 9.
14. According to Rabbinic tradition Ezekiel mentions nine separate visions in
    Ezekiel 43:3. See *Leviticus Rabbah* 1:14.
15. Or upon *tet*, the letter whose shape is comprised of P and Z joined.
16. BT Berakhot 17a.
17. This idea first appears in BT Bava' Mesi'a' 85b and was subsequently in-
    corporated into the *Treatise of the Palaces*. See A. Jellinek, ed., *Bet ha-Midrash*
    (Jerusalem, 1938), vol. 2, p. 46.
18. Ibid.
19. This legend is also expressed in the *Midrash to the Decalogue*. See Jellinek,
    Bet ha-Midrash, vol. 2, p. 66.
20. See the *Treatise of the Palaces*, Jellinek, *Bet ha-Midrash*, vol. 2, p. 46.
21. In the Sefardi rite, this is recited at the beginning of the service that con-
    stitutes the public reading of the Torah.
22. The text here is corrupt.
23. The vocative "by the throne of God" of Exodus 17:16 is for the sake of this
    interpretation spelled incompletely. *Kes*, "throne," is normally *kisse'*. *Yah*,
    "God," is usually *YHVH*. From these defective spellings is derived the no-
    tion that the Throne of God is incomplete until the nation of Amalek is
    thoroughly blotted out.
24. The "reverse alphabet" *(alfa' beta' de-TaSHRa"Q)* is a common way of ex-
    pressing the Hebrew alphabet in reverse order. Scholem states that the text
    at this point is "apparently corrupt."

Treatise on the Left Emanation
RABBI ISAAC BEN JACOB HA-KOHEN

1. I have noted your tremendous desire to ascend to the ladder of wisdom and perceive enigmas and grasp the cunning ways of the ancient Sages, the masters of inscriptions,[1] those who expounded upon the secrets of the souls. And having noted that the Lord God, may He be blessed, bestowed upon you an attentive and understanding heart, I have decided with much fondness to answer your question and fulfill your request. . . .

[I will do this for you] even though you are quite aware that this path was not trod upon except for "two or three berries in the top of the uppermost bough" (Isaiah 17:6)—these are the ancient elders, the scholars of Spain who delved in the palace of Samael. It is a long and deep path and it eludes all masters of wisdom who are not willing to descend into the depths of the wisdom of the hidden emanation, the "depth of good and depth of evil."[2] [It is known] only to those few solitary individuals, "the remnant who the Lord shall call" (Joel 3:5). Moreover, to the best of my ability I will not stray my steps from the path[3] in order to grant your wish and quench a bit of your thirst. May His most beloved assist me in His mercy and Lovingkindness.

2. You have already dealt with the roots of the emanation of the degrees, from the top of Supreme Crown *(keter 'elyon)* to the secret of the Blessing *(sod ha-berakhah)* of life everlasting.[4] Now it is time to be awakened to the secret of the emanation radiating forth from

them, an emanation of degrees like the image of bodies to souls, specified with names received from the ancient Sages and from the book of Rabbi Ḥamai. I have not seen this book in all Provence, save for [copies] belonging to three pietists. One was in Narbonne, belonging to a wondrous, skilled scholar. It was transmitted orally from an elder rabbi. This holy and venerable rabbi testified that Elijah, may his memory be blessed, would appear to him on the Day of Atonement. The other two copies were in Arles, the large city.

The first emanation—like the image of a spiritual entity—corresponds to the primal emanation. Its name is Sabi'el, and we call him the prince of the Exalted Heights.

The second of the [emanations] is the emanation of Wisdom. Its name is Peli'i'el. He is the prince of the wonders (pela'ot) of Wisdom. We have received [a tradition] about him that the name by which his emanation is revealed is Zequni'el. His name is also Sagsagel, equal to the numerical value of "you shall honor the face of an *old man*" (Leviticus 19:32).[5] He is the planting of Wisdom, "the planting of the Lord, that he may be glorified" (Isaiah 61:3). His sign is "In the day of your planting make it grow (tesagsegi)" (Isaiah 61:3). The *samekh* and *sin* are interchangeable, deriving from the same [sound].

The third is the prince radiated forth from the emanation of Repentance, the hidden treasure trove to all those who know Understanding and have great fear (yir'ah). His name is Yerui'el.

Scripture alludes to all three of them in one verse: "You shall rise up before the hoary head and honor the face of the old man and fear your God" (Isaiah 19:32). These three are considered like bodies to souls, each one interlinked with the other like a flame to an ember, inwardness to inwardness.

The remaining seven degrees also have seven degrees which radiate forth like bodies to souls, and they too are spiritual. The name of the first is Memeriron. He is the prince of Lovingkindness and is associated with water. The second is Geviriron. He is the prince of awesome and invincible Strength (gevurah).

The name of the third is Yedideron. He is the prince of Mercy, the beloved (yedid) of God.

The name of the fourth is Satriron. He is the prince of the Foundation of the world which is concealed and secreted (nistar) in the middle pillar and is called the secret place of the most high (seter 'elyon). Thus "He that dwells in the secret place of the most high shall abide under the shadow of the Almighty" (Psalms 91:1). This should be sufficient to the enlightened.

The name of the fifth is Nashiriron. He is the prince of triumph and the victory *(nesaḥ)* of Israel.

The name of the sixth is Hodiriron. He is the prince radiating forth from the emanation of Majesty *(hod)*.

The name of the seventh is Seforiron. He is the prince radiating forth from the last *(sof)* emanation of all the degrees.

These, then, are the names of the ancient mighty ones. We have further received that the first three end their names with "-'el" and the latter end with "-ron" because the first three are powers from the forces emanating from within the power of the great and mighty Will, towering above all else: the Cause of all causes and the Reason of all reasons; while the seven are like ignited candles, each one lighting his own candle *(nero)* from the seven inner [candles]. They correspond to the image of inner souls and spiritual bodies.

3. Regarding this we have also received the following: The attribute Kingdom possesses three further currents. These are like three pillars faced toward her, doing her work and guarding her watch round and about the Throne in fear and trembling and silence, from emanation to emanation up to the beloved of God who embraces her and kisses her by means of the Foundation of the world. At this point the princes of Lovingkindness and Strength receive her in great and glorious fear and trembling and in awesome silence. Then Lovingkindness and Strength—which are the inner emanations—receive her and revolve like powerful torrents of water and "coals of fire which burn intensely" (Canticles 8:6). She remains hidden and concealed in the midst of all the emanations until the approach of the prince of Understanding accompanied by his troops. They receive her with incomprehensible fear and dread and silence until they approach the throne next to the Throne of Glory associated with Repentance. From there the multitude of his warriors appear. Overseeing them all is the prince of Wisdom. Then they set down the Throne with trembling terror and great quaking into the bosom of ancient Wisdom, who accepts her with the proclamation "Come my beloved."[6] He plays with her like a father doting on his only daughter among many sons. The Exalted Heights pours forth his blessing on her by means of the Father [i.e., Wisdom], for it is impossible for any emanation to apprehend or perceive spiritual vi-

sion or supernal perception except through the mediation of Wisdom and Understanding.

After the acceptance of the Blessing and after the delights bow and prostrate themselves before the awesome and sublime Throne of Glory, the Throne of Kingdom, by means of these unique princes, whirls and revolves back from emanation to emanation to its origin, resting between the two cherubs which are her arms.

This great outpouring—a joy to the inner souls and a delight to the spiritual bodies—was in effect when the land of Israel was inhabited and the holy nation dwelled in her. [Earthly] Temple is mirrored by [celestial] Temple and attendant High Priest is mirrored by a High Priest of holiness and purity, of fear and trembling, knowing how to direct perfect meditations to each of the outer and inner emanations, knowing how to draw forth the secret of the holy seraphim, awakening the Holy Spirit with the beauty of poetry and music. The singers [of the Temple], each according to their position and their perception, concentrate with their fingers upon the strings of the harp and the tones which awaken the song and the chant. They direct their hearts to the Omnipresent. Then Blessing is stirred and the divine Presence dwells upon them, each according to his worship and perception. Then Jerusalem and the earthly Temple fulfill [every] desire and are a delight to all the nations, and the fear and trepidation for her inhabitants rule over anyone who sees or hears of her. As it is written: "And all the peoples of the earth shall see that you are called by the name of the Lord and they shall be afraid of you" (Deuteronomy 28:10). Happy is the eye that beholds all this.

4. Now let us return to the point of our departure, namely the three princes who are the three pillars to the Throne which in turn is exalted by the four encampments of the divine Presence. The first one is named Malki'el, derived from the attribute of Kingdom (malkhut). The name of the second is 'Aturi'el, derived from the great Diadem ('atarah), like the image of gold which is likened to the attribute of Severity. The name of the third is Nashri'el, derived from the name of that emanation which is angry and chastises its children when they fail to conduct themselves along the straight path before their heavenly Father. But when they tip the scales toward merit by way of repentance, then they have peace and divine benevolence, and she has mercy upon her children "like an eagle (nesher) that stirs up its nest, that flutters over its young" (Deuteronomy 32:11). And

then "the mother of the children is joyous, reclining on her beloved."[7]

These three are in fact three pillars emanated from the power
of the attribute of Kingdom: Each one is an emanation in its own
right. Therefore, the emanation is derived from the thirteen
branches which draw upon one root, for all unity depends on it.
Therefore, the verse "God is one" (Deuteronomy 6:4) equals it.[8]

Another indication is [the mnemonic] *Na'amharon* for "the
beauty of the Diadem of Kingdom" [*hen 'ateret malkhut*]. "Ron" [of
Na'amharon] is the image of our patriarch Jacob, peace be upon him,
a simple man, a lower form inscribed parallel with a celestial one.
He is linked to the heavens and Jacob. The indication of this is "Sing
(ranu), O heavens" (Isaiah 44:23) and "Sing *(ranu)* with gladness for
Jacob" (Jeremiah 31:7). Thus the union is complete.[9]

The thirteen are completely spiritual emanations and they are
active, and the thirteen divine attributes mentioned in "And the
Lord passed before [Moses], and he proclaimed; 'YHVH, the Lord,
merciful and gracious God . . .' " (Exodus 34:6) are activated [by
them]. The active ones are causes, the activated ones are effects.
They are without limitation and there is no perception of their true
origin nor is there anyone who can know with a certainty their end.
Only the unique Lord of all who is hidden and concealed from His
creatures [can do so]. Even the thought which can never be
apprehended[10] is incapable of perceiving His very reality. . . .

These are three [emanations] encompassed in the Crown of
Kingdom, appointed and prepared to forgive and pardon the
transgressions and their perpetrators, who are nothing more than
rebels and sinners. These three are included in one name by virtue
of their various activities. "And this is the name by which he will be
called" (Jeremiah 23:6): *Na'amharon*—pardoning transgression, rebelliousness, and sin *(Nose' 'avon Mered Hata'ah)* so that the wrath
(haron af) of God turns away from Israel and He pardons and has
mercy upon those who turn away from their sins. . . .

5. Now we shall turn to the system of accusing hosts which reside in heaven, those which were created and then suddenly annihilated. When I was in the great city of Arles, a master of this
tradition showed me an extremely old booklet. Its handwriting was
crude and is different from our own. It was transmitted in the name
of a great Rabbi and gaon. They referred to him as the Rabbi Mas-

liah. Now the venerable Gaon, our Rabbi Pelatiaḥ, was from the holy city of Jerusalem. And this booklet was brought by a great scholar and pietist known as Rabbi Gershom of Damascus. He hailed from Damascus and lived in Arles for approximately two years, and people there told stories about his great wisdom and wealth. He showed this booklet to the elder sages of that generation. I copied from it some things, things which the sages of that generation had understood. For they were not familiar with its handwriting as were the earlier sages who had learned it directly from that scholar and pietist.[11]

Then I returned to Beziers, a city of Sages, where my pious brother of blessed memory had become ill. I have neither added nor subtracted from all that my brother explained, not even in the slightest detail except for stylistic concerns. Occasionally there is a small variation, but the intent is always identical.

With this I will begin to set down the system of the princes and their forces, from the first to the last. They were all created from a single emanation flowing forth from the power of Repentance. This emanation acts as a screen, separating the emanation of all the holy degrees in which there are no alien emanations. Each is a spiritual degree, pure and refined and lutescent, engraved out of the power of the Will of the hidden Lord. This dividing screen, emanated from the power of the emanated Repentance, was initially brought forth on the condition that various diverse emanations, some good and some evil, some of endless existence and others of horrible and utter disgrace, would stem forth from it. There is no one in creation, neither lofty nor low, who can perceive the secret of these worlds. Only the spiritual degrees and princes emanating therefrom [can be perceived]. There was a tradition already in the possession of the ancient Sages and studied by my brother of blessed memory, written in the composition of that perfect pious man, to the effect that the name of the ruler of this emanation is Masukhi'el, since he is a dividing screen (masakh).

The first emanation which flowed forth from him comprised the pure and splendorous souls. And from these souls the party of angels was emanated, all but the four encampments of the divine Presence.

These souls, which are angelic emanations, existed potentially within the recesses of the Emanator, hidden from all. But before they could become actuated, another world was emanated from alien forms and destructive images. The name of the ruler of this emanation, the prince of all its warriors, was Qamti'el. These are the cruel ones who began to rebuke and confound the emanations. Immediately a proclamation *(keruz)* went forth from Keruzi'el, the prince and voice of Repentance. He said: "Masukhi'el! Masukhi'el! Destroy what you have created and gather back your emanations, for it is not the wish of the King of kings, the Holy One, blessed be He, that these emanations remain in the worlds."

[The emanations] then returned to their original state and were obliterated: Just as they were brought forth, so were they annihilated. The Sages of tradition likened the matter to a wick saturated with oil. When one desires to extinguish [the fire], one immerses the wick into the very oil which kept it lit. Thus it returns [to its original state] and it is extinguished: so it is annihilated.

Afterward, another world was emanated, comprised of strange forms and alien images. The name of the ruler of this emanation and the prince of its warriors was Beli'el. These were even more evil in their plotting and their disruption of the various emanations. Then a decree came forth and the word of the King of kings went forth. They were annihilated in a flash, just like the first.

Thereupon a third world was created, comprised of even stranger forms than those of the first and second worlds. The name of the ruler and prince of its warriors was 'Iti'el. These are the worst of all. It is their desire and ambition to rule the Divine and destroy Him, chopping off the divine tree along with all its branches. Then there went forth a decree from the divine Will that their annihilation be similar to the first two. A decree was then proclaimed that no similar emanation would ever again come forth into the ether of the world, nor would it ever be mentioned again. And these are the worlds about which our Sages of blessed memory said: "He constructed worlds and then destroyed them . . ."[12]

After the destruction of these worlds it was the desire of the Will to bring forth the souls emanated from potentiality to actuality. Among them were the myriads of angels and their encampments, seven groups in all. The leader of each of these groups is known to those who are aware of this tradition. From their power the firmaments and planets—called the seven moving stars according to the scientists—were emanated. God willing, I will write about them.

There are many other names that should not be written out for I am not completely certain what the order is and until I see the order

171

of their spelling and their emergence and their rank, I will not write it, for I might make a mistake, either in thought or on paper. There is, however, a tradition to the effect that in a single moment and by a single expression seven other princes were emanated along with their retinues, and they are all known. Once in response to a question from a student from Avile I was compelled to search for their names and I put them in order, inspired by a certain idea.

But before I mention their names I would like to point out to the reader of this book that the seven groups of princes belonging to the above-mentioned angels were all arrayed with bows drawn for a pitched battle. This war of enmity and jealousy between them and the seven princes will never cease *(ta'abor)* in the heavens, for their objective is the Lord of all who created them from the root of emanation according to His Will and Desire, from the power of the emanation of Repentance. We will explain this great jealousy and will interpret its reason. It is of a divine source which created beings cannot grasp. The reasons derive from the manifestations of emanation. The "secret of intercalation" *(sod ha-'ibbur)* is a spiritual mystery that none can comprehend or understand. The secret is hidden from the angels—"How much more so those that dwell in houses of clay, whose foundation is in the dust" (Job 4:19). Even the allusions are too awesome for man, and the secret is one aspect of the statement "Silence! Such is the decree."[13]

6. I will now set down the names of the princes of jealousy and enmity. Yet since their essence and their service is true and pure, their mouths are free from mendacity and neither lies nor falsehoods pass between them.

The first prince and accuser, the commander of jealousy, is evil Samael, accompanied by his retinue. He is called "evil" not because of his nature but because he desires to unite and intimately mingle with an emanation not of his nature, as we shall explain.

The second prince is called his deputy, and his name is Za'afi'el, accompanied by his entourage.

The third prince is called third-in-command, and his name is Za'ami'el, accompanied by his staff.

The fourth prince is Qasfi'el, accompanied by his retinue.

The fifth prince is Ragzi'el, accompanied by his staff.

The sixth prince is 'Abri'el, accompanied by his staff.

The seventh is Meshulhi'el, accompanied by his staff. These latter comprise the delegation of evil angels.

Now I shall allude to you the reason for all the jealousy between these latter princes and the former princes of the seven groups of holy angels which are called "the guardians of the walls." A form destined for Samael stirs up enmity and jealousy between the heavenly delegation and the forces of the supernal army. This form is Lilith, and she is in the image of a feminine form. Samael takes on the form of Adam and Lilith the form of Eve. They were both born in a spiritual birth as one, as a parallel to the forms of Adam and Eve above and below: two twinlike forms. Both Samael and [Lilith, called] Eve the Matron—also known as the Northern One—are emanated from beneath the Throne of Glory. It was the Sin which brought about this calamity, in order to bring her shame and disgrace to destroy her celestial offspring. The calamity was caused by the Northern One, who was created beneath the Throne of Glory and it resulted in a partial collapse and weakening of the legs of the Throne. Then, by means of Gamali'el and the primeval snake Nahashi'el, the scents of each intermingled: the scent of man reached the female, and the scent of woman reached the male. Ever since then the snakes have increased and have taken on the form of biting snakes. Thus it is written, "The Lord sent fiery snakes among the people" (Numbers 21:6). This requires a full explanation in a separate treatise for it is very deep—no one can find it out.[14]

7. Now I shall make allusions according to the tradition passed from ancient Sages to possessors of this wisdom. We know for a certainty that Rabbi Sherira and Rabbi Hai were learned and steeped in this wisdom which came to them rabbi from rabbi, sage from sage, gaon from gaon. They all utilized the secret knowledge of the *Lesser Heikhalot*, which is the secret knowledge of demons, so that they could ascend the ladder of prophecy.

It is well established that all the philosophers agree that there are no corporeal entities above the spheres. However, we have seen and heard that the learned of Israel vary on this point, some agreeing and some disagreeing with the philosophers. But according to what we have received from Rabbi Sherira Gaon, and his son Rabbi Hai, and the venerable traditionist Rabbi Joseph Ibn Abitur the great Gaon, and Rabbi Issac Ibn Ghayyat of blessed memories[15]—they decided the issue according to what they had received from their ancestors, elder from elder, gaon and gaon, all the way back to a tradition of Tannaim and Amoraim. They thus decided the issue in accordance with what they received from the ancient elders: that neither in all the primordial emanations nor in the next set of emanations is there anything corporeal. There is only spiritual emanation. So too the created angels—they and their princes—and the princes of jealousy and their forces are like the form of man created in the image of the great fire. Even the forms of the fire-steeds are all spiritual forms, and their armor and their chariots are as a raging fire, though not of the essence of elemental fire. . . .

9. The four encampments of the divine Presence are nothing but spiritual emanations, in the image neither of bodies nor of bodily form. But not all the angels are this way; only those of the tenth degree are similar to the sons of Adam beheld by each prophet according to his stature. Everyone agrees that they have an appearance too awesome to apprehend.

The prophet and visionary sees all the various powers change from form to form until they take on the power of the form visible to him. Then it transforms like the form of an angel and this form changes before him and becomes able to receive the prophetic force. Then the engravings of spiritual channels are inscribed in his heart.

When he completes and fulfills his mission, the prophet then is divested of the power of the revealed form and is invested with the power of his first form. He sheds a form and dons a new form. Then everything is arrayed together, uniting and growing ever stronger. Then all his corporeal powers return to their first state. Then he speaks and functions like all other people. This, then, is the tradition of those pious men,[16] may they all be remembered for good. . . .

10. Another tradition: It has been transmitted by the masters of the divine Names that at various known times they used the demonic ethers to attain a few of the prophetic qualities. This is the utilization of the ether of the Holy One, blessed be He.

There are also those who can transport themselves magically by attaining the ether which includes the secret knowledge of demons. There is a great and wise traditionist whom we met in Narbonne who testified along with many others that Rabbi Eleazar of Worms of blessed memory could occasionally ride upon the form of a magic cloud to faraway places and then return, especially when a good deed needed to be performed far off. Sometimes, though, he would ride upon an animal for many days like all other men. Once he had to perform a circumcision in a far-off place and he flew off by means of his usual incantation. But he forgot something that is required by people who have mastered this wisdom and he fell from his low-flying cloud. He became lame in his hip and no worldly remedy cured him until the day of his death.[17]

11. The tradition we received has it that there are three ethers above. The first ether is ruled by the great and holy prince whose name is Qedoshi'el. He is the prince of the hosts, and from his power and might spring forth battalions of princely armies and all the heavenly soldiers, the angels of the heavenly armies and those of the heavens above the heavens. All these are emanated from them, and the emanation of their emanations has neither image nor substance nor corporeality. The second ether is the secret knowledge of prophecy. It is the ether donned by the prophets and the high priest and the other priests and the Levites and all who have a supreme soul and intelligence. This is the second ether. The third ether is the ether of the secret knowledge of demons. This is the text of the *Sefer ha-Malbush*.[18]

12. We shall now discuss the third ether. The scholars of tradition said that it is a received tradition from their fathers that this ether is divided into three parts: an upper part, a middle part, and a lower part. The upper part was given over to Asmodeus, the great king of the demons. He does not have permission to accuse or cause confusion except on Mondays. We will expand on this in the treatise as best we can.

Even though Asmodeus is called the great king, he is subservient to Samael. He is called the great prince with reference to the emanations above him and the king of kings with reference to the emanations underneath him. Asmodeus is governed by him and is subservient to him.

Samael, the great prince and great king over all the demons, cohabits with the great Matron Lilith. Asmodeus, the king of the demons, cohabits with the Lesser [Younger] Lilith. The scholars of this tradition admit to many horrendous details concerning the forms of Samael and Asmodeus and the images of Lilith the bride of Samael and Lilith the bride of Asmodeus. Happy is he who merits this knowledge.

The middle part was given over to the king who rules spirits. Qafqafoni is his name and his young mate is Sar'ita', with whom he cohabits for half the year. For the other half of the year he fornicates with another mate whose name is Sagrirta'. Their offspring take on different forms. They have bodies and seem to be two-headed, while the sons of Sar'ita' take on the image of lepers. Some scholars of tradition say that all lepers are the result of this despicable offspring. The sons of Sagrirta' have faces which are ulcerated and they wage a pitched battle among themselves. Evil spirits abound in the ether and all sorts of storms and horrors go forth from the power of these interminglings. Nevertheless, the rule and terror of Asmodeus is imposed on them. . . .

The third part of the ether is occupied by fiends created and clad in many varying forms. Some are in the form of dogs, created by human sins. And the dog formed from this evil issuance happens upon man and bites him, and to cure him is most difficult. Sometimes it changes form from a dog to a slightly different form. It barks and howls and bites again and again and finds no worldly cure until it dies and returns transfigured, mixed in this ether with the power of the form. This is its punishment and annihilation. Because of this secret there is the prayer "Deliver my soul from the sword, my precious life from the clutches of a dog" (Psalms 22:21).

Some take the form of he- and she-goats. From these are 'Aza' and 'Aza'el. Each separately has the form of the image of real men. When they fell from heaven—a part of the above-mentioned ether— they donned the power of this ether just above us and they took on the bodies of men. Then the upper power weakened and they received the lower power. But the progeny which issued from them was more towering and powerful than all mankind.

Some take other forms, like the form of man from birth. Some take the form of men and some the form of women. The only difference is the lies and falsehoods. They are jealous of men and they seek to cheat and foil them. They would have destroyed everything they saw were it not that the attribute of Kingdom summoned her own emanation, Yufi'el, the great prince of the countenance, who is beloved and near to the divine Presence. He rules over the king of that pernicious group. Were it not that the power of his emanation and his terror fills them, they would never leave creatures alone, nor would lowly creatures be able to stand up against them. The name of the king ruling over them is Qafsefoni and the name of his mate is Mehetabel, daughter of Metrad.[19] Their progeny jumps in one bound from one end of the ether to the other. Sometimes they are given permission to rectify the injuries that befall mankind and to inform mankind of its future when they appear as men. They have no rule over lies or falsehoods. He who asks of them will find his answer according to [Qafsefoni's] will, depending on whether the questioner merits an answer. If he does not merit an answer, they will appear to the questioner only by means of an incantation, but they will answer him that they do not have permission to answer his question. . . .

14. This ruling prince and all his warriors are subservient to Asmodeus the great king. Their rule and the force of their actions are commensurate to the power of emanation which reaches each of them. All that is below and above is subject to the rule of Samael, king of kings. His emanation and the emanation of his chariots will spread forth upon all the troops. All the princes will scurry about at his command until the coming of the word of the divine Will, which will reveal the time and day of revenge which is hidden in His heart and sealed in His treasury. He will then bring down the rule of this red one *(edom)*, as it is written: "I will destroy his fruit from above and his roots from beneath" (Amos 2:9). Amen. Hurriedly and in our days!

15. Now we will finish the matter that we started. Occasionally the prince whose name is Qafsefoni can, commensurate to the permission granted him, unite and cohabit with one creature whose name is Lilita. She is in the image of Hagar the Egyptian according to some of the men of this wisdom, though there is some disagreement over this point. . . .

17. Back to what I started regarding the array of heavenly evil armies and their layout from first warrior to last: they were all created from one emanation which came forth from the power of the emanation of Repentance. This is the opening words of the treatise.

But before I finish discussing this issue I will speak to you of something else you need to know. The first creations of the Hidden-from-all, the Cause of causes and the Reason of reasons, were powers which were crowns before Him. They are called "the special world" or "the secluded world," and it is a world which is entirely good. He chooses only good so that the good ones would merit a world which is entirely good. Then His incomprehensible Wisdom chose to create a world that was entirely evil in order to chastise the erring: Maybe they will return in a perfect repentance to achieve merit—if not, this would be their final obliteration. Regarding these two worlds it is said: "He makes peace and creates evil" (Isaiah 45:7). . . .

The world of peace comes first in the verse because it is before the entirely evil world. And even though it has no part in the entirely good world, His first emanation is not from the evil emanation. This is what we meant when we said that He chooses only the good. And though he formed evil from this good, we cannot understand the profundity of this hidden mystery for it is sealed.

Go and learn of this from the first man who was not the child of any woman but was created from a pure and pristine likeness [of God], lacking any evil inclination to sin. God commanded him and warned him to keep one commandment for his own benefit so that he could enjoy everlasting life. But he transgressed this first commandment.

We believe that the Creator did not want him to sin, nor did He decree that he should. He simply commanded the good. This is the case with other people and pious individuals. The patriarchs serve as an example—from them came Esau and Ishmael and Hezekiah and Manasseh and many other [sinners]. From the good came forth evil, and God neither commanded nor demanded it. All this falls under the category of silence: do not dwell on it—it is so awesome that you ought not inquire, so hidden that you ought not pursue it.

I have explained all this first in order to remove all doubts, and the enlightened will understand. Out of abundant love I have tried to hide part of the whole of which I revealed to you. At first I hinted and concealed when I laid out the order of the princes and their forces, saying that they were all created from a single emanation. I did not say that they were created from the power of a single emanation. Then I said that they were created from the power of the emanation of Repentance, but I did not write that they were from the emanation of Repentance. By this method it was my intention "to reveal a little and conceal much."[20] "Happy is the man who fears the Lord, who is greatly devoted to his commandments" (Psalms 112:1).

18. This is the order of all the armies, a circle within the circles of the *sefirot*. They are above everything, surrounding and influencing in a general way all that is spiritual by means of their emanations. From the emanation of Repentance come six powers and from the sixth emanation—called Keruzi'el—the emanation of the seventh prince called Masukhi'el is brought forth. All of them are holy and God is in them. From the seventh and onward, ten groups of opposing powers are emanated, parallel to the ten holy *sefirot*. The upper three had no existence and were obliterated. The seven remaining princes along with their forces constantly instigate war with the seven princes of the pure and perfect crowns and occasion-

ally with the seven princes mentioned above in the book we have already written.[21] "Happy is the man who fears the Lord, who is greatly devoted to His commandments" (Psalms 112:1). God is in them: Miṣvati'el, Ḥafṣi'el, Me'odi'el, the practical commandments are built in golden basis and they were emanated from these three princes who in turn were emanated from the middle pillar called *Tav*.[22] This is the meaning of "You shall not covet the wife of your neighbor" (Exodus 20:14)—it is a description of "the beauty of days," which corresponds to the middle pillar.[23] "The wife of a neighbor"— these are evil Samael and his mate Lilith. Ḥemdat'el, Ishti'el, Re'uvel: From these three princes the prohibitions were emanated. They radiate forth from the emanation "Beauty of Water." O Ḥemdat'el! Holy of Israel! Grant us the merit to perceive and grasp a perfect knowledge of the secrets of His Torah, as wonderful and dear as pure gold. Grant us life in the world to come. Amen.

19. In answer to your question concerning Lilith, I shall explain to you the essence of the matter. Concerning this point there is a received tradition from the ancient Sages who made use of the *Secret Knowledge of the Lesser Palaces*, which is the manipulation of demons and a ladder by which one ascends to the prophetic levels. In this tradition it is made clear that Samael and Lilith were born as one, similar to the form of Adam and Eve who were also born as one, reflecting what is above. This is the account of Lilith which was received by the Sages in the *Secret Knowledge of the Palaces*. The Matron Lilith is the mate of Samael. Both of them were born at the same hour in the image of Adam and Eve, intertwined in each other. Asmodeus the great king of the demons has as a mate the Lesser (younger) Lilith, daughter of the king whose name is Qafṣefoni. The name of his mate is Meheṭabel daughter of Maṭred, and their daughter is Lilith.

This is the exact text of what is written in *The Chapters of the Lesser Palaces* as we have received it, word for word and letter for letter. And the scholars of this wisdom possess a very profound tradition from the ancients. They found it stated in those *Chapters* that Samael, the great prince of them all, grew exceedingly jealous of Asmodeus the king of the demons because of this Lilith who is called Lilith the Maiden (the young). She is in the form of a beautiful woman from her head to her waist. But from the waist down she is burning fire—like mother like daughter. She is called Meheṭabel daughter of Maṭred, and the meaning is something immersed (*mahu*

179

tabal). The meaning here is that her intentions are never for the good. She only seeks to incite wars and various demons of war and the war between Daughter Lilith and Matron Lilith.

They say that from Asmodeus and his mate Lilith a great prince was born in heaven. He is the ruler of eighty thousand destructive demons and is called "the sword of king Asmodeus." His name is Alefpene'ash and his face burns like a raging fire *('esh)*. He is also called Gurigur, for he antagonizes and struggles with the prince of Judah, who is called Gur Aryeh Yehudah (Lion-cub of Judah). From the same form that gave birth to this war-demon another prince, a prince whose root is in Kingdom, was born in heaven. He is called "the sword of the Messiah." He too has two names: Meshihi'el and Kokhvi'el. When the time comes and when God wishes, this sword will leave its sheath and verses of prophecy will come true: "For My sword shall be drunk in the heavens; Lo, it shall come down upon Edom" (Isaiah 34:5). "A star rises from Jacob" (Numbers 24:17). Amen. Soon in our days may we merit to see the face of the Messiah our righteous one; we and all our people. . . .

22. I shall now teach you a wonderful innovation. You already know that evil Samael and wicked Lilith are like a sexual pair who, by means of an intermediary, receive an evil and wicked emanation from one and emanate to the other. I shall explain this relying on the esoteric meaning in the verse "In that day the Lord will punish with His great, cruel, mighty sword Leviathan the twisted serpent and Leviathan the tortuous serpent"—this is Lilith—"and He will slay the dragon of the sea" (Isaiah 27:1). As there is a pure Leviathan in the sea and it is called a serpent, so there is a great defiled serpent in the sea in the literal sense. The same holds true above in a hidden way. The heavenly serpent is a blind prince, the image of an inter-mediary between Samael and Lilith. Its name is Tanin'iver.[24] The masters of tradition said that just as this serpent slithers without eyes, so the supernal serpent has the image of a spiritual form with-out color—these are "the eyes." The traditionists call it an eyeless creature, therefore its name is Tanin'iver. He is the bond, the ac-companiment, and the union between Samael and Lilith. If he were created whole in the fullness of his emanation he would have de-stroyed the world in an instant. . . .

When the divine Will arrives and the emanation of Samael and Lilith weakens the emanation achieved by the blind prince, they will be completely annihilated by Gabriel prince of Strength, who instigates war against them with the aid of the prince of Lovingkindness. Then the verse which we have expounded according to its secret meaning will come true. . . .

24. I found written in the name of an ancient traditionist and in the name of the perfect Ḥasid of blessed memory[25] that Lilith is also Taninsam.[26] They said that this name is based on the serpent who is in the image of an intermediary between Lilith and her mate. He will eat deadly poison at the hands of the prince of Strength; it is an elixir of life for all whose inclination overcomes them. Then he participates with Michael, the prince of Lovingkindness, in defeating the rule of evil in heaven and on earth. Then the verse will come true: "For His Lovingkindness has overcome us; the truth of God endures forever. Hallelujah" (Psalms 117:2).

The secret of the covenant of salt *(melaḥ)*[27] is the kingdom of the accompaniment of beauty.[28] Therefore they hinted with secrets regarding the salted fish [Leviathan] to feed the righteous in future times. Happy is he who understands these things as they are.

Notes

1. A term for the Kabbalists.
2. *Sefer Yesirah* 1:4.
3. According to Psalms 44:19.
4. The *sefirah* Kingdom.
5. *SaGaSG'eL* equals 157 and "old man" *(ZaQeN)* has the same value.
6. Part of the Sabbath greeting ritual of Rabbi Yannai as recorded in BT Shabbat 119a.
7. See Psalms 113:9 and Canticles 8:5.
8. "One" *('-Ḥ-D)* equals 13.
9. Jacob, the symbol of Beauty, unites with Kingdom.
10. An expression referring to the uppermost *sefirah*.
11. For a discussion of this passage, see J. Dan, "Samael, Lilith, and the Concept of Evil in Early Kabbalah," *AJSreview* 5 (1980), p. 32.
12. *Genesis Rabbah* 9:2.
13. See BT Menahot 29b. The secret of intercalation refers to the leap month of the Jewish lunisolar calendar, and is thought to be a great secret.
14. According to Ecclesiastes 7:24. See Dan, "Samael," pp. 18f.
15. The latter two are eleventh-century Spanish rabbis. Ibn Abitur was a contemporary of Hai Gaon.
16. See beginning of chapter 5. On this and the following chapters, see Dan, "Samael," pp. 23–32.
17. See Isaiah 11:10.
18. Most of chapter 11 is in Aramaic and is the text of one version of the *Sefer ha-Malbush*, the title of several magical texts from Geonic times.

19. See Genesis 36:39.
20. Based on BT Nedarim 20b.
21. Scholem believes that chapter 18 was a later addition to the *Treatise* inserted by Rabbi Isaac. The list of princes varies from that in chapter 5; it refers to "the book we have already written"; it ends with a concluding formula. But in light of the admonition at the end of chapter 17, we tend to believe that chapter 18 is an integral part of the original *Treatise*.
22. The *sefirah* Beauty *(tif'eret)*.
23. The "beauty of days" is a term representing Kingdom, which along with Beauty is located along the middle pillar.
24. Literally: "blind serpent."
25. Rabbi Judah the Ḥasid?
26. Literally; "poisonous serpent," but also "blind" *(suma')*.
27. See Numbers 18:19.
28. *Malkhut Leviat Hen.*

Glossary

aggadah—homiletic expositions of the Rabbis.

amora—name for the Rabbis responsible for the *gemara*, the last literary layer of the Talmuds, between roughly 200 and 550 C.E.

Binah—"Understanding," the third *sefirah*. A primal female symbol, located at the top of the left column of the Kabbalistic tree.

devequt—"communion," usually with the divine realm.

Eyn Sof—literally, "No End," a Kabbalistic term for the hidden God who emanates forth the sefirotic tree.

gematria—numerology. Every Hebrew letter has a numerological value, and by adding the sum of letters in words the esotericist can weave and interrelate concepts and terms that at first glance have no relation.

Gevurah—"Strength," the fifth *sefirah*. Also called *Din* (Severity). Most often linked with the forces of evil, it is called "the raging inferno of the Lord."

golem—a homunculus.

ha'aṣalah—The Hebrew term for "emanation."

halakhah—literally, "the Way," the legal parameters of Judaism.

ḥasid (pl. *ḥasidim*)—literally "pious." Many Jewish groups have called themselves by this term. In this volume, *ḥasid* applies to the German pietists of the twelfth and thirteenth centuries.

GLOSSARY

heikhalot (sing. **heikhal**)—"Palaces." A central motif of early visionary mysticism during the Talmudic era centered around the ascent of the mystic through a series of palaces to a final
Throneroom, where the divine Glory and Its retinue are situated. See *merkavah*.

Ḥesed—"Lovingkindness," the fourth *sefirah*. Linked with the patriarch Abraham, the color white, and the element of water.

Hod—"Majesty," the eighth *sefirah*.

Ḥokhmah—"Wisdom," the second *sefirah*, situated at the top of the
right column of the sefirotic tree and linked to the male principle
of the structure.

Kavod—the divine Glory. See *Shekhinah*.

ha-keruv ha-meyuḥḥad—"the Special Cherub," a divine power and
intermediary in the theology of certain circles among the German Pietists.

Keter—"Crown," the first *sefirah* in the Kabbalistic tree. The precise
relationship of *keter* to Eyn Sof was often confused in early Kabbalah, with some authors stating that there is no substantial difference between the two, and others citing massive essential
differences between the source of emanation and the first emanated product.

ma'amarot (sing. *ma'amar*)—literally, "Utterances," specifically related to the rabbinic tradition of "the ten Utterances by which
the world was created." In Kabbalistic literature, often a synonym for *sefirot*.

Malkhut—"Kingdom," the tenth and last *sefirah* in the Kabbalistic
tree, also called the "unreflecting mirror." The realm of the immanent *shekhinah*.

merkavah—literally, "chariot." Jewish mystics of Talmudic time
conceived of the divine realm as a series of chambers and chariots, based on the visions of Ezekiel. See *heikhalot*.

mitzvah (pl. *mitzvot*)—literally "commandment," a divine ordinance
in the *halakhah* based on either biblical or Talmudic premises.

Neṣaḥ—"Victory," the seventh *sefirah*.

pardes—literally, "garden." According to rabbinic tradition, a small
circle of second-century C.E. Rabbis "entered *pardes*," a probable reference to some esoteric theological speculation. In the

184

medieval Jewish exegetical tradition after the thirteenth century, *PaRDeS* became an acronym for the fourfold levels of interpretation found in the biblical text: (1) *peshat*—the literal, or "simple" meaning; (2) *remez*—the homiletic "hint"; (3) *derash*—the legal "elucidation"; and (4) *sod*—the "secret" interpretation.

qiddush ha-Shem—"sanctification of the Divine Name," or martyrdom. A theme common in German pietism.

sefirah (pl. **sefirot**)—a term first coined in the *Sefer Yesirah* (*sefirot belimah;* "closed *sefirot*"), derived from "number." The Kabbalistic term for the ten divine powers, attributes, or emanations that constitute the revealed aspect of the Divine.

Shekhinah—the immanent divine Presence, a term first used during the rabbinic period. In the Kabbalah, a term for the feminine divine Presence, often linked with the tenth *sefirah*. See *Kavod.*

Shi'ur Qomah—literally, "Measurement of the Body," in this case the divine body. Fantastic descriptions of God's body were current in some *merkavah* mystical schools.

tanna—title for those Rabbis who are mentioned in the Mishnah, roughly between 400 B.C.E. and 200 C.E.

tefillin—the prayer amulets worn on the head and arm during weekday morning prayers, in which are contained handwritten parchments composed of verses from Numbers and Deuteronomy.

Tif'eret—"Beauty," the sixth *sefirah*, also known as the "reflecting mirror." This *sefirah* is linked to Jacob, and stands at the middle of the central column of the sefirotic tree.

Yesod—"Foundation," the ninth *sefirah*.

Select Bibliography of Early Kabbalah

ENCYCLOPEDIAS

Encyclopaedia Judaica. Jerusalem, 1972. 16 vols. & supplements.
The Jewish Encyclopedia. New York, 1907. 12 vols.
Scholem, G. *Kabbalah.* New York, 1974. (A collection of his articles from the *Encyclopaedia Judaica.*)

BIBLIOGRAPHY

Bibliography of the Writings of Gershom G. Scholem. Jerusalem, 1977.
Scholem, G. *Bibliographia Kabbalistica.* Leipzig, 1927.
Wijnhoven, J. "Medieval Jewish Mysticism," in *Bibliographical Essays in Medieval Jewish Studies.* New York, 1976.

TEXTS AND STUDIES

Altmann, A. "The Motif of the 'Shells' in Azriel of Gerona." *Journal of Jewish Studies* 9 (1959): 73–80.
Azriel of Gerona. *Perush ha-Aggadot le-Rabbi Azri'el.* Ed. Tishby. Jerusalem, 1943.
Barzillai, Judah ben. *Commentar zum Sepher Jezira.* Ed. Halberstam. Berlin, 1885.
Chaze, M. "Le sens ésotérique du voeu et du serment solon quelques

auteurs des xiiie et xive siécles en Espagne et en Italie." *REJ* 138 (1979): 219–254.

Chernus, I. *Mysticism in Rabbinic Judaism*. Berlin, 1982.

Cohen, M. *The Shi'ur Qomah: Liturgy and Theurgy in Pre-Kabbalistic Jewish Mysticism*. Lanham, 1983.

Dan, J. "The Concept of Knowledge in Shiur Komah." In *Studies in Jewish Mysticism and Intellectual History Presented to Alexander Altmann*. Birmingham, 1979, pp. 67–73.

———. *The Esoteric Theology of Ashkenazi Ḥasidism* (Hebrew). Jerusalem, 1968.

———. *Ethical and Homiletical Literature* (Hebrew). Jerusalem, 1975.

———. *The Hebrew Story in the Middle Ages* (Hebrew). Jerusalem, 1974.

———. *Hugey ha-Mequbbalim ha-Ri'shonim*. Jerusalem, 1972.

———. "Samael, Lillith and the Concept of Evil in the Early Kabbalah." *AJSreview* 5 (1980): 17–40.

———. "The 'Special Cherub' Circle in Ashkenazi Ḥasidism" (Hebrew). *Tarbiẓ* 35 (1966): 349–372.

———, ed. *Ashkenazi Ḥasidic Theological Texts* (Hebrew). Jerusalem, 1978.

———, ed. *The Kabbalah of Rabbi Asher ben David* (Hebrew). Jerusalem, 1979.

Dan, J., and Talmage, F., eds. *Studies in Jewish Mysticism*. Cambridge, 1982.

Ehrepnis, M. *Die Entwicklung der Emanationslehre in der Kabbala des XIII Jahrhunderts*. Frankfurt a. M., 1896.

Ezra of Gerona. *Le Commentaire d'Ezra de Gerone sur le Cantique des Cantiques*. Tr. and ed. Vajda. Paris, 1969.

Goitein, S. "Abraham Maimonides and his Pietist Circle." In *Jewish Medieval and Renaissance Studies*. Ed. Altmann. Cambridge, 1967: 145–164.

Gottlieb, E. *Meḥqarim be-Sifrut ha-Qabbalah*. Ed. Hacker. Tel Aviv, 1976.

Graetz, H. *Gnosticismus und Judenthum*. Krotoschin, 1846.

Grossman, A. "The Migration of the Kalonymus Family from Italy to Germany" (Hebrew). *Zion* 40 (1975): 154–186.

Gruenwald, I. *Apocalyptic and Merkavah Mysticism*. Leiden/Köln, 1980.

———. "Knowledge and Vision." *Israel Oriental Studies* 3 (1973): 88ff.

BIBLIOGRAPHY

Guberman, K. "The Language of Love in Spanish Kabbalah: An Examination of the *'Iggeret ha-Kodesh.*" In *Approaches to Judaism in Medieval Times*, ed. D. Blumenthal. Chico, 1984, pp. 53–105.

Habermann, A., ed. *Sefer Gezerot Ashkenaz ve-Ṣarfat.* Jerusalem, 1946.

Heschel, A. J. "The Mystical Element in Judaism." In *The Jews: Their Religion and Culture*, ed. L. Finkelstein. New York, 1971, pp. 155–176.

Idel, M. "Ereṣ Yisra'el ve-ha-Qabbalah be-Me'ah ha-Shalosh-'Esreh." *Shalem* 3 (1981): 119–126.

———. "ha-Sefirot she-me-'al ha-Sefirot." *Tarbiz* 51 (1982): 239–280.

———. "The World of Angels in Human Form" (Hebrew). *Jerusalem Studies in Jewish Thought* 3 (1983/84): 1–66.

Jacobs, L., tr. and ed. *Jewish Mystical Testimonies.* New York, 1977.

Katz, J. *Halakhah and Kabbalah* (Hebrew). Jerusalem, 1984.

Marcus, I. *Piety and Society: The Jewish Pietists of Medieval Germany.* Leiden, 1981.

Matt, D., tr. *Zohar: The Book of Enlightenment.* New York, 1983.

Nahmanides. *Kitvey Rabbenu Mosheh ben Naḥman.* Ed. Chavel. Jerusalem, 1964. 2 vols.

Neumark, D. *Geschichte der judischen Philosophie des Mittelalters.* Berlin, 1907. 2 vols.

Safran, B. "Rabbi Azriel and Nahmanides: Two Views of the Fall of Man." In *Rabbi Moses Nahmanides (Ramban): Explorations in His Religious and Literary Virtuosity.* Ed. Twersky. Cambridge, 1983, pp. 75–106.

Scholem, G., tr. *Das Buch Bahir.* Leipzig, 1923.

———. "Colours and Their Symbolism in Jewish Tradition and Mysticism." *Diogenes* 108 (1979): 84–111.

———. "The Concept of Kavvanah in the Early Kabbalah." In *Studies in Jewish Thought*, ed. A. Jospe. Detroit, 1981, pp. 162–180.

———. " 'Iqvotav shel Gabirol be-Qabbalah." In *Me'assef Sofrey Ereṣ Yisra'el.* Tel Aviv, 1940, pp. 160–178.

———. *Jewish Gnosticism, Merkabah Mysticism and Talmudic Tradition.* New York, 1960.

———. *Major Trends in Jewish Mysticism.* New York, 1954.

———. *The Messianic Idea in Judaism.* New York, 1971.

———. "The Name of God and the Linguistic Theory of the Kabbala." *Diogenes* 79 (1972): 59–80; 80 (1972): 164–194.

BIBLIOGRAPHY

——. "A New Document for the History of the Beginning of the Kabbalah" (Hebrew). In *Sefer Bialik*. Ed. Fichman. Tel Aviv, 1934, pp. 141–162.

——. *On the Kabbalah and Its Symbolism*. New York, 1965.

——. "Peraqim Hadashim me-'Inyaney Ashmoday ve-Lilit." *Tarbiz* 19 (1948): 160–175.

——. *ha-Qabbalah be-Geronah*. Ed. Ben-Shlomo. Jerusalem, 1964.

——. *ha-Qabbalah be-Provans*. Jerusalem, 1963.

——. "Qabbalot R. Ya'aqov ve-R. Yishaq." *Mada'ey ha-Yahadut* 1 (1926): 165–293.

——. "Seridim Hadashim mi-Kitvey R. 'Azri'el me-Geronah." In *Sefer Zikaron le-A. Gulaq u-le-Sh. Klein*. Jerusalem, 1942, pp. 201–222.

——. *Re'shit ha-Qabbalah*. Jerusalem, 1948.

——. *Ursprung und Anfänge der Kabbala*. Berlin, 1962.

Septimus, B. *Hispano-Jewish Culture in Transition*. Cambridge, 1981.

Shäfer, P. *Synopse zur Hekhalot Literatur*. Tübingen, 1981.

Shahar, S. "Catharism and the Beginnings of the Kabbalah in Languedoc" (Hebrew). *Tarbiz* 40 (1971): 483–507.

——. "The Relationship between Kabbalism and Catharism in the South of France." *Les Juifs dans l'histoire de France*. Leiden, 1980, pp. 55–62.

Singer, S. A., tr. *Medieval Jewish Mysticism: Book of the Pious*. Wheeling, 1971.

Stenring, K. *The Book of Formation*. London, 1923.

Tishby, I. "Gnostic Doctrines in Sixteenth-Century Jewish Mysticism." *Journal of Jewish Studies* 6 (1955): 146–152.

——. "Kitvey ha-Mequbbalim R. 'Ezra' ve-R. Azri'el me-Gerona." *Sinai* 16 (1945): 159–178.

——. *Studies in Kabbalah and Its Branches* (Hebrew). Jerusalem, 1982.

Twersky, I. *Rabad of Posquieres*. Cambridge, 1962.

——, ed. *Rabbi Moses Nahmanides (Ramban): Explorations in His Religious and Literary Virtuosity*. Cambridge, 1983.

Vajda, G. "An Analysis of the Ma'amar Yiqqawu ha-Mayim by Samuel b. Judah Ibn Tibbon." *Journal of Jewish Studies* 10 (1959): 137–149.

——. *Recherches sur la philosophie et la Kabbale dans la pensée juive du Moyen Age*. Paris, 1962.

BIBLIOGRAPHY

Verman, M. *Sifrei ha-Iyyun*. Ph.D. dissertation. Harvard, 1984.
Wirszubski, C. "Aqdamot le-Biqoret ha-Nusah shel Perush Sefer Yeṣirah le-R. Yiṣhaq Saggi Nehor." *Tarbiẓ* 27 (1958): 257–264.
The Zohar. Tr. H. Sperling and M. Simon. London, 1931–1934. 5 vols.

Index to Introduction

INDEX

INDEX

divine palaces, 2, 7, 18, 25, 27, 28
Heikhalot Rabbati, 2, 29
Heikhalot Zutartey, 2
Ḥiyya, Rabbi Abraham bar, 18, 28

Ibn Ezra, Rabbi Abraham, 18, 19, 25, 28
Idel, Moshe, 38*n*3
Interpretation of the Four-Lettered Holy Name, The, 27
Isaac the Blind, Rabbi, 31–35
Ishmael, Rabbi, 2
'Iyyun circle, 26–27, 37

Jeremiah, 24
Judah the Pious, Rabbi, 18, 19, 25
Judaism, Rabbinic, 2, 5

Kabbalah: and Albigensianism, 6; and Catharicism, 6; as a conservative force, 12; emergence of, 1–7; in Gerona, 34–36; and Gnosticism, 5–6; Lurianic, 6; nature of, 7–14; and Scripture, 10–12; and the *sefirot*, 8–9, 12–13; and symbolism, 7–10
Kavod (Divine Glory), 19, 28
Kohen brothers, 36–37
Kohen, Rabbi Isaac, 36–37
Kohen, Rabbi Jacob, 36

Light, 13
Lilith, 37
Luria, Isaac, 6

Ma'ayan ha-Ḥokhmah (Fountain of Wisdom), 27
Maimonideans, 17
Maimonides, Abraham, 17, 31
Maimonides, Moses, 15, 17
Martyrdom, 23, 38*n*8
Measurement of the Divine Height, The, 3
Merkavah, literature of, 2, 7, 18, 20, 24, 27, 28
Meshiv Devarim Nekhohim (The Response of Correct Answers), 33, 35
Messiah, 37
Midi, 17
Midrash, 11
Mishnah, 2
Mishneh Torah, 31
Mitzvot, 11, 13, 22
Mysticism, Jewish, 1–4, 7

Naḥmanides, 34–35
Names, the Holy Divine, 29
Neoplatonism, 8, 10, 12, 27
Neumark, David, 16
No End (*Eyn Sof*), 8
Numerology, 7–8, 20

Palaces, divine, 2
Palestine, 4
Parables, 29
Persecution, 23
Philosophy: Aristotelian, 8, 16–17; Gnostic, 5–7, 13, 16–17; Jewish, 8, 10, 12, 14–45; Neoplatonist, 8, 10, 12, 17; Platonic, 15
Pietism, German, 4, 18, 24–25, 29, 36
Pleasure, 22–23

INDEX

Pleroma, 30
Powers, divine, 27, 30
Prayer, 16, 18–21, 32
Provence, 4, 17, 26, 28, 31–32, 37
Providence, 21
Pseudepigraphy, 2, 24, 27–28

Qiddush ha-shem, 23

RaBaD, 31
Rationalism, 17, 25
Raza' Rabbah (The Great Secret), 28–29
Regensburg, 18
Response of Correct Answers, The (Meshiv devarim Nekhohim), 33, 35
Revelation, 18–19, 25

Saadianic Paraphrase, 19
Satan, 23, 37
Scholem, Gershom, 1, 5, 26, 28, 34, 36
Sefer ha-Bahir (The Book of Brilliance), 1, 6, 26, 28–29. *See also Bahir*
Sefer ha-Enunah ve-ha-Bittahon (Faith and Trust), 27, 35
Sefer ha-Hayyim (The Book of Life), 25–26, 39n36
Sefer ha-'Iyyun (The Book of Contemplation), 26, 27
Sefer ha-Zohar (The Book of Splendor), 1. *See also Zohar*

Sefer Hasidim (The Book of the Pious), 19
Sefer Yesirah (The Book of Creation), 4, 7, 14, 20, 24–28, 31–32
Sefirot, 7–9, 12–13, 26, 28–29, 32–33, 36–37
Sexual motif, 29–30
Shekhinah, 29
Shi'ur Qomah, 3, 11
Sin, 13–14, 22–23
Smaller Book of Celestial Palaces, The, 2
Song of Songs, 3, 34
Spain, 4, 15, 17
"Special cherub," 24
Sufism, 17
Symbols [and symbolism], 6, 7–9, 20, 26–32

Talmud, 11, 21
Tannaim, 2, 29
Tannaitic age, 3
Tishby, Isaac, 34, 38n3
Torah, 10, 5–16
Treatise on the Left Emanation, 37

Vajda, Georges, 38n3

Yohai, Rabbi Simeon bar, 4

Zohar, 1, 3, 6, 7, 36, 37

Index to Texts

INDEX

Ben ha-Qanah, Rabbi Nehunia, 46
Ben Harkinas, Rabbi Dosa, 123
Ben Naḥman, Rabbi Moses, 109
Ben Sheshet of Gerona, Rabbi Jacob, 109
Ben Tradiyon, Rabbi Hanina, 46, 137, 147
Ben Yoḥai, Rabbi Simeon, 115
Beziers, 170
Binah. See Understanding
Book of Creation, The (Sefer Yesirah), 47
Book of Faith and Reliance, The (Sefer ha-Emunah ve-ha-Biṭṭaḥon), 109
Book of Knowledge, The, 136
Book of Palaces, The, 46
Book of Reliance, The, 54
Book of Speculation, The (Sefer ha-'Iyyun), 45
Book of the Foundation of Wisdom, The, 55

Calculation (*ḥeshbon*), 46
Calneh, 146
Canticles, Book of, 127, 129, 130, 159, 167
"Chambers of Splendor, The," 47
Chapters According to Rabbi Eliezer, The, 100–01
Chapters of the Lesser Palaces, The, 179–80
Chariot, divine, 45, 154, 158–63
Chavel, H., 109
"Cherub," 47
1 Chronicles, 98, 147
Colors, 52, 74, 94
Combination (*ṣerruf*), 46

Commentary to Talmudic Legends, 87
Counsel ('*eṣah*), 101
Covenant of Salt, 181
Creation, 80
Crown, divine, 62, 80–82, 162–65, 169
"Curtain, the," 47

Dan, J., 71
Daniel, Book of, 101, 117, 128, 142, 154
Dashi'el, 74
David, 136, 161, 162
Day of Atonement, 166
Dead Sea, 107
Decalogue, 156
Demons, 173, 175
Deuteronomy, Book of: 4:6, 140, 144; 4:24, 66, 139; 4:26, 140; 4:36, 139; 6:4, 117, 158, 169; 7:16, 141; 10:20, 125, 143; 10:21, 125; 11:4, 115; 12:2, 141; 14:5, 143; 15:6, 151; 18:9, 55; 18:13, 68; 28:10, 168; 28:48, 115; 30:20, 143; 32:3, 99; 32:11, 81, 168; 33:2, 102, 119, 125; 33:27, 107
Diadem ('*atarah*), 80–85, 159, 163, 168–69
Din. See Severity
Dualism, 140

Earth, 80, 82, 83
Ecclesiastes, Book of: 1:7, 83; 3:11, 89; 5:7, 82; 7:12, 98, 100, 116; 7:16, 120; 7:18, 115; 8:1, 100; 8:17, 89;

INDEX

INDEX

Maṣliah, Rabbi, 169
Masukhi'el, 170–71, 178
Me-ayin (Nothing), 81
Megillah, 147
Mehetabel, 176, 179
Memeriron, 166
Me'odi'el, 179
Mercy, 75–76, 106, 118
Meshihi'el, 180
Meshulhi'el, 172
Messiah, 101, 130, 180
Metrad, 176, 179
Micah, Book of, 66, 135, 144
Michael, 84, 122, 129, 181
Mishael, 127–28
"Mist," 47
Miṣvati'el, 179
Moses, 50–51, 65–69, 76, 117–19, 127, 131, 160
Musajoff collection, the, 43
"Mystical Torah—Kabbalistic Creation, The," 71

Nahashi'el, 173
Nahmanides, 109
Name[s], 47, 54, 99, 102–03, 130, 133, 139, 174
Narbonne, 166, 174
Naṣhiriron, 167
Nashri'el, 168
Nebat, 120
Nesah, 75
Northern One, 173
Nothing, 81
Numbers, Book of, 59, 61, 97, 118, 123, 173, 180
Numerology, 59, 77, 101, 123

Outer Holy Place, 46

"Outer Palace of Holiness, The," 47
Ozar Midrashim, 43

Pahad (fear), 68, 85, 94–95
Pani'uri'el, 75
Passover, 114
Pazi, R. Yudah b., 107
Peace, 122
Pelatiah, Rabbi, 170
Pentateuch, 138
Perush ha-Aggadot le-Rav 'Azri'el, 87
Perush Shem shel Arba' Otiyyot, 43
Phineas, 123
Pietists, German, 56
Piety, 111
Powers, 45, 47, 74, 75, 95
Presence, 158–59, 168, 170, 174–75
Primeval light, 51
"Primeval wisdom," 47
"Process of Emanation, The," 71
Prophet, 174
Provence, 166
Proverbs, Book of: 1:6, 118; 3:10, 134; 3:19, 77, 100, 101; 3:19–20, 101; 3:35, 63; 6:23, 101, 102; 7:4, 99; 8:14, 101, 105; 8:24, 102; 8:30, 73, 99; 10:27, 157; 15:23, 100; 21:14, 161; 23:15, 148; 24:3, 126; 25:2, 84; 25:11, 46; 31:24, 134
Psalms, Book of: 6:6, 146; 10:16, 47; 11:4, 145; 18:12, 103, 117; 18:34, 160; 19:2, 60, 135; 19:8, 140; 19:15,

INDEX

INDEX

Other Volumes in this Series

Francis and Clare • THE COMPLETE WORKS
Gregory Palamas • THE TRIADS
Pietists • SELECTED WRITINGS
The Shakers • TWO CENTURIES OF SPIRITUAL REFLECTION
Zohar • THE BOOK OF ENLIGHTENMENT
Luis de León • THE NAMES OF CHRIST
Quaker Spirituality • SELECTED WRITINGS
Emanuel Swedenborg • THE UNIVERSAL HUMAN AND SOUL-BODY INTERACTION
Augustine of Hippo • SELECTED WRITINGS
Safed Spirituality • RULES OF MYSTICAL PIETY, THE BEGINNING OF WISDOM
Maximus Confessor • SELECTED WRITINGS
John Cassian • CONFERENCES
Johannes Tauler • SERMONS
John Ruusbroec • THE SPIRITUAL ESPOUSALS AND OTHER WORKS
Ibn 'Abbād of Ronda • LETTERS ON THE SŪFĪ PATH
Angelus Silesius • THE CHERUBINIC WANDERER